Living as an outsider may not seem to spark [...] Simon show us how we find joy when we fo[...] disorienting culture. Their message counters [...] and loathing perpetuated in politics and media. They offer practical hope for every Christian in this engaging, accessible book.

Collin Hansen, vice president for content/editor-in-chief, The Gospel Coalition; host, *Gospelbound* podcast

This is a needed book in our day. In a time when Christians are often unaware of our own gifts and callings or find it easy to chastise brothers and sisters with different gifts and callings, this book provides helpful handles—a broad overview of orientations and traits—that can help God's people *together* fulfill our mission. A resource full of wisdom and grace.

Trevin Wax, vice president of research and resources, North American Mission Board; visiting professor, Cedarville University; author, *The Thrill of Orthodoxy*

Patrick Miller and Keith Simon have written a timely and practical book for readers to embrace living in the unresolved tension of our present-day metaphorical Babylon. *Joyful Outsiders* offers a fantastic way to engage the culture around us—not by becoming "insiders" but by in fact becoming more like Jesus in his role as an outsider. I found myself excited to consider how I could move into the various outsider roles of the trainer, the advisor, the artist, the ambassador, the protester, or the builder while learning the pitfalls of each. This book will fortify your spirit and invite you to reframe cultural tension as beautifully ripe with possibility. As Miller and Simon tell us, "Babylon is everywhere, and Jesus has given you the responsibility of cultivating good within it." You'll love this book and will want to read it with others as you seek to cultivate good right where you are.

Heather Holleman, PhD, speaker; professor; author, *The Six Conversations: Pathways for Connecting in an Age of Isolation and Incivility*

Following and embodying the way of Jesus in our fractured world often feels like a futile, fruitless endeavor. But as Dietrich Bonhoeffer reminded us, "When Christ bids a man come, he bids him come and die." How do we do this? *Joyful Outsiders* offers us a prophetic and pragmatic way forward. Rather than providing a rigid set of to-dos, Miller and Simon remind us that "[Our] exile is creative tension. It is holy improvisation." This culturally astute and pastorally sensitive book is an important resource for all those who long to live the way of Jesus amid the idolatry of our modern Babylon.

Jay Y. Kim, pastor; author

This is a much-needed book! As Christians, we are living as exiles in Babylon, and there are many reasons why we should not feel at home in the world. Miller and Simon remind us that we are called to be good citizens, to love our neighbors and enemies, but we should never be shocked when our values are considered strange or even offensive to the world around us. *Joyful Outsiders* is soaked with biblical truth, and it's presented with much pastoral wisdom gained from lived experience. If you want help living in the tension of resisting worldly values while graciously reaching the world, then this book is a must-read.

Preston Sprinkle, host, *Theology in the Raw* podcast

I'm unusually excited about this book. We need this. Read it. Think about it. Share it. Discuss it. Above all: Let's *do* it. And thank you, Patrick and Keith. Now I don't have to write this book, and mine wouldn't have been this good.

Brant Hansen, radio/podcast host; bestselling author, *Unoffendable*

Christians in the West are asking themselves what faithfulness looks like in an increasingly hostile world. Patrick Miller and Keith Simon are two pastors who do not merely theorize about this tension but live it out as local church pastors. What you'll find in *Joyful Outsiders* is a road map for living as Christian exiles who love their community, city, and country. They advocate neither withdrawal nor rage for rage's sake. Instead, the reader is given helpful, scriptural tools for when to fight, when to build bridges, and, most importantly, how to represent Christ well in this moment to which we are called. Pastors and lay leaders will want this book both to better lead the people they serve and to give to those confused by life in America in the twenty-first century.

Daniel Darling, director, The Land Center for
Cultural Engagement; author, *Agents of Grace*

How should Christians navigate the uncertain waters of late modern culture? This is one of the most pressing questions facing the church today. Should we critique, or should we cultivate? Should we resist, or should we seek to serve? Enter Patrick Miller and Keith Simon's *Joyful Outsiders*: a practical, elegant handbook to help everyday Christians chart a course marked by faithfulness, discernment, and joy. Wisely rejecting a one-size-fits-all approach to cultural engagement, Miller and Simon present six complementary models, drawing profound lessons from figures like Esther, Daniel, Fannie Lou Hamer, and Dietrich Bonhoeffer. This book is a rich resource for Christians who want to live well in our complex cultural moment.

Christopher Watkin, associate professor of European languages,
Monash University, Australia; author, *Biblical Critical Theory*

Joyful Outsiders is the book the church needs right now. In a deeply divided society, many Christians feel torn. Should they retreat, relent, or rage against the culture? Patrick and Keith show why there are far better options on offer for Christ followers. Compelling biblical insights are matched by practical examples of how Christians can live faithfully for God in the midst of Babylon. I hope every pastor, leader, and congregant will read this book and put it into practice.

Justin Brierley, broadcaster; speaker; author,
The Surprising Rebirth of Belief in God

Joyful
Outsiders

Joyful Outsiders

Six Ways to Live Like Jesus in a Disorienting Culture

Patrick Miller & Keith Simon

ZONDERVAN
BOOKS

ZONDERVAN BOOKS

Joyful Outsiders
Copyright © 2025 by Patrick Keith Miller and Keith Simon

Published in Grand Rapids, Michigan, by Zondervan. Zondervan is a registered trademark of The Zondervan Corporation, L.L.C., a wholly owned subsidiary of HarperCollins Christian Publishing, Inc.

Requests for information should be addressed to customercare@harpercollins.com.

Zondervan titles may be purchased in bulk for educational, business, fundraising, or sales promotional use. For information, please email SpecialMarkets@Zondervan.com.

ISBN 978-0-310-36877-9 (audio)

Library of Congress Cataloging-in-Publication Data

Names: Miller, Patrick Keith, 1987– author. | Simon, Keith, author.
Title: Joyful outsiders : six ways to live like Jesus in a disorienting culture / Patrick Miller and Keith Simon.
Description: Grand Rapids, Michigan : Zondervan Books, [2025]
Identifiers: LCCN 2024033096 (print) | LCCN 2024033097 (ebook) | ISBN 9780310368748 (softcover) | ISBN 9780310368755 (ebook) | ISBN 9780310368779 (audio)
Subjects: LCSH: Outsiders in the Bible. | BISAC: RELIGION / Christian Living / Personal Growth | RELIGION / Christian Living / Inspirational
Classification: LCC BS579.O87 M55 2025 (print) | LCC BS579.O87 (ebook) | DDC 220.6—dc23/eng/20240909
LC record available at https://lccn.loc.gov/2024033096
LC ebook record available at https://lccn.loc.gov/2024033097

Unless otherwise noted, Scripture quotations are taken from the ESV® Bible (The Holy Bible, English Standard Version®). Copyright © 2001 by Crossway, a publishing ministry of Good News Publishers. Used by permission. All rights reserved.

Scripture quotations marked NIV are taken from The Holy Bible, New International Version®, NIV®. Copyright © 1973, 1978, 1984, 2011 by Biblica, Inc.® Used by permission of Zondervan. All rights reserved worldwide. www.Zondervan.com. The "NIV" and "New International Version" are trademarks registered in the United States Patent and Trademark Office by Biblica, Inc.®

Scripture quotations marked NIrV are taken from the Holy Bible, New International Reader's Version®, NIrV®. Copyright © 1995, 1996, 1998, 2014 by Biblica, Inc.® Used by permission of Zondervan. All rights reserved worldwide. www.zondervan.com. The "NIrV" and "New International Reader's Version" are trademarks registered in the United States Patent and Trademark Office by Biblica, Inc.®

Scripture quotations marked NKJV are taken from the New King James Version®. Copyright © 1982 by Thomas Nelson. Used by permission. All rights reserved.

Scripture quotations marked NLT are taken from the Holy Bible, New Living Translation. Copyright © 1996, 2004, 2015 by Tyndale House Foundation. Used by permission of Tyndale House Publishers, Inc., Carol Stream, Illinois 60188. All rights reserved.

Any internet addresses (websites, blogs, etc.) and telephone numbers in this book are offered as a resource. They are not intended in any way to be or imply an endorsement by Zondervan, nor does Zondervan vouch for the content of these sites and numbers for the life of this book.

Names and identifying characteristics of some individuals have been changed to preserve their privacy.

Published in association with Don Gates of the literary agency The Gates Group, www.the-gates-group.com.

Cover design: Micah Kandros
Cover illustration: Shutterstock
Interior design: Denise Froehlich

Printed in the United States of America

24 25 26 27 28 LBC 5 4 3 2 1

Contents

Foreword

It is difficult to find a good book on Christian cultural engagement. I think the reason for this is that you must zoom *out* of culture in order to speak *into* it well. You must take a wide and accurate view of your history to understand your moment. That's a hard task.

Because it is hard, most writers fail to do it, and many seem to resort to knee-jerk reactions to whatever the cultural zeitgeist is that year. Avoiding this tendency is one thing that makes the book you are holding unique.

Joyful Outsiders is a very good book because it lives up to its name. It steps well outside the confines of our moment to take a much wider view. We are offered a model of Christianity that has engaged with culture throughout history. By telling stories as old as Daniel and Hezekiah, or as different as Mother Teresa and Bill Bright, or as recent as Bonhoeffer and Martin Luther King Jr., *Joyful Outsiders* offers a close look at the diverse ways that Christians have faithfully wrestled with cultural influence, cultural protest, and cultural power. This view is both more global than Western and more historical than the twenty-first century, which makes it a great contribution to the Western church of the twenty-first century (which is where most of us reading it will find ourselves). This is the first reason I like this book.

The second reason I like it is that it doesn't pretend to provide a single answer. The wisdom of this should be obvious. Why would we assume the body of Christ is all thumbs when it comes to cultural engagement, or indeed all the *same*? Like classics that have preceded it, such as H. Richard

Niebuhr's *Christ and Culture*, this book provides varied, historic ways that faithful Christians have sought to engage and change culture. However, it doesn't stay in only in the land of theory. It gets practical quickly, giving habits, practices, virtues, and dangers for each different way of engagement. This practicality may be the greatest contribution of the book. One of the main problems facing the modern church is that by unconsciously adopting practices of cultural engagement that are far more American than Christian, we become malformed by those practices and become lost either through a failure to understand or a failure to do.

On this side of the kingdom of heaven, the church doesn't have another option. We will exist in relationship to culture, and that will *always* be hard. We are the exiles and outsiders. But after reading this book, I saw why that difficulty is also an opportunity for joy. The wilderness is the place of our mission. It is the place where Jesus meets us.

I joyfully commend this book to all my fellow outsiders who follow Jesus in our modern Babylons. May this book help us love him more and our neighbors better.

With great hope in Christ,

JUSTIN WHITMEL EARLEY
Richmond, Virginia

Preface

They wander this earth, but their life lies in heaven;
powerless though they be, their weakness protects
    the world.
While turmoil rages around them, they taste only
    peace;
poor though they be, they possess what gives them joy.
Suffer though they may, they remain joyful;
They seem to have died to the natural senses,
and instead live the internal life of faith.
When Christ, their life, will be revealed,
when someday he will show himself in glory,
then together with him as princes of the earth,
they will appear in glory while the world gazes
    in wonder.
Then shall they reign in triumph with him,
as glorious lights adorn the heavens.
Openly then shall joy burst forth.

—FROM "THE CHRISTIAN'S INWARD LIFE IS
SHINING" BY CHRISTIAN FRIEDRICH RICHTER,
A HYMN SUNG BY THE CHURCHES WHO
RESISTED HITLER'S RISE IN GERMANY

If you're reading this book, it's probably because you feel like an *outsider*. You feel it when you turn on the TV. You feel it at work. You feel it in disagreements with those you love. You feel it on the PTA, at the gym, at happy hour, and at the movies. You sense that you don't quite belong and that your way of life may not be welcome.

So you picked up this book looking for answers: How do I choose joy when it feels like the world is against me? How do I find peace when I feel trapped in contentious conversations? What role is Jesus calling me to play in culture? Am I to be for it? Against it? Or something altogether different?

You could fill the Grand Canyon with books explaining how Christians should engage the world. But most of them are written for pastors, professors, and thinkers. Few are written for everyday people. Few address everyday problems. As pastors, we've become painfully aware that the church lacks a necessary resource: a book about navigating culture for stay-at-home parents, business owners, nonprofit operators, finance executives, students, retirees, plumbers, and web developers. In other words, a book about cultural engagement for *ordinary* people.

We've spent almost six decades (between the two of us) helping people in our church cultivate and challenge their local culture in the name of Jesus. We've always said we want our church's presence to be such a blessing to our local culture that its absence would be felt for *good* reasons. We hope that the way we care for those in need, love our coworkers, support local arts, operate local businesses, and serve within civil institutions tastes of joy, goodness, truth, and beauty, not fear, acrimony, anger, and judgment.

By the grace and mercy of God, this has been largely (and imperfectly!) the case. Yet when people asked us for a resource to help them join

God's culture-changing cause locally, we never had a book to offer. *Joyful Outsiders* is that book. It is our humble attempt to share the lessons we've learned with other Christians seeking to love, challenge, and transform culture in ordinary, normal life.

Thus, our prayer is that by the time you turn the last page, you will have learned what many in our community know: God isn't confused or frightened by our culture. He's with people who feel like outsiders. So you have nothing to fear either. The deep truth at the center of this book is simple: Being an outsider isn't something to fear. It's something to embrace. This is because outsiders receive a joy from Christ that circumstances can't steal. Part 1 of this book will take you on the journey to becoming that sort of Christian—a joyful outsider.

We also hope that you will learn how to engage your culture *practically*. In God's wisdom, he didn't give the church one way to engage culture. Instead, he gave us countless ways, exemplified by Jesus and a whole cadre of biblical joyful outsiders. They cultivated and challenged the culture around them. In the pages of Scripture you will find *trainers* who changed culture by changing people's habits, *advisors* who changed culture by influencing leaders, *artists* who changed culture by making beauty, *ambassadors* who changed culture by winning hearts, *protesters* who changed culture by challenging injustice, and *builders* who changed culture by building institutions. We call these "the six ways." In part 2 you will learn which of the six ways God designed you to walk in. You will also deepen your appreciation for other ways—even those you've found frustrating or underwhelming in the past. On page 203 you can find a brief introduction to each way, as well as a personal inventory that will allow you to identify which of the six ways fits you best. We suggest taking that test with a friend or small group so you can help one another evaluate the accuracy of the results.

Above all else, we pray that this book will give you the unbreakable joy of Jesus. Though he made the world, the world rejected him. Though he loved his people, his people exiled him. Though he sought to heal his creation, his creation crucified him.

Jesus was an outsider like you and me. But he wasn't a combative outsider. Nor was he a conformist outsider. No, he was a *joyful* outsider. The author of Hebrews writes, "For the *joy* set before him he endured the cross."[1] Now he invites us to do likewise. As outsiders, we must fix "our eyes on Jesus," then "go to him outside the camp and bear the reproach he endured" for the joy set before us.[2] What is that joy? Hebrews explains, "We seek the city that is to come."[3] We live joyfully for the day when the heavenly city comes to earth and God's perfected people live in God's perfect presence. Until that day, we live as outsiders who joyfully seek to make our lives, towns, and cities a bit more like that future city.

So if you want to choose joy, keep reading. Your journey to becoming a joyful outsider starts today.[4]

PART 1

Outsiders

CHAPTER 1

Outsiders

*Here on earth, the church-community lives in a foreign
land. It is a colony of strangers far away from home.*
—DIETRICH BONHOEFFER

*The reason of my waking mind tells me that great evil
has befallen and we stand at the end of days. But my
heart says nay; and all my limbs are light, and a hope
and joy are come to me that no reason can deny.*
—FARAMIR IN *THE LORD OF THE RINGS*

Every January, our city celebrates the civil rights legacy
of Dr. Martin Luther King Jr. at a diversity breakfast. Civic and nonprofit
leaders from across the political spectrum attend annually. But in 2023,
the city ventured into new territory by including a drag show. As the drag
queens danced and lip-synced, most people in the crowd cheered. Some
gave the dancers cash tips. This would have drawn little public attention but for one problem, which turned a local diversity breakfast into a
national news story: Middle school students, bussed from local schools,
were in attendance, but the field trip permission slips said nothing about
a drag performance.

In an ideologically diverse city like ours, no one was shocked by the drag show. But most Christian parents expected they would be alerted before their kids attended one, so they hoped the school district would own its error and promise it wouldn't happen again. Instead, the opposite happened.

The superintendent wrote a public letter arguing they'd done nothing wrong and explaining that there would be no changes to their parental consent policies. He critiqued those who felt the drag show was an "adult" performance with a "sexual nature," arguing that such statements were "categorically false" and "harmful to our students, our staff, and our community."[1] The tone of the letter confused Christian parents who didn't think that requesting consent was controversial, much less *harmful*. But their concerns had made them outsiders.

What Would You Do?

One child who attended has severe autism. This was only his third field trip because the school district believed his disabilities were too severe. So his mother was ecstatic when he was invited. She hoped it would give him the opportunity to prove he could do well on field trips and go on more of them in the future. Then everything went sideways.

The afternoon after the drag show, she learned what happened, but because her son is nonverbal, he had no way to discuss it or express how it made him feel. He's highly attuned to entertainment, often miming the words and actions of movie characters, so his mom worried the show might have an outsized impact on him. But as an outsider, what could she do? What about you? How would you respond?

One Christian school leader who attended the event was surprised by the drag show. As an administrator, she knew it was a mistake to bring students without parental permission. Emails from concerned parents filled her inbox. She assured them that at her school, parents would be given sufficient information for consent in the future. But that wasn't enough for many parents. They wanted a change to the district's policy—a policy she was powerless to change. What would you do? How would you respond if you were an educator navigating emails from frustrated parents?

Christian public officials, from school board members to state representatives, faced different questions. Would they condemn what happened or condone it and move on? Would they issue public statements or work privately behind the scenes to change the policy? What would you do?

Christian parents whose children didn't attend the event responded in wildly divergent ways. One mom told me that kids already have smartphones, so they see drag shows online all the time. She might not approve of them, but this is the world we live in. Culture-warring over things we can't change just makes it harder for people to see the beauty and goodness of Christ. So it's better to stay quiet. A different mom agreed—there wasn't much hope for change—but argued that this meant it was time for Christians to abandon public schools and try homeschooling or private school instead.

Other parents disagreed with them both: schools *need* to change. One dad wrote charitable emails to teachers and principals requesting policy changes. But one of his friends took a different tack: This wasn't a time for gentleness. It was a time to defend children forcibly, lest schools harm children. He wrote scathing emails to principals and the district officials. In his view, outsiders must act with strength or they'll be pushed to the margins. So again: How would you respond? What do *you* do when you feel like an outsider?

Finding the Right Response

As pastors we wrestled with our own questions: How would we guide people through this conflict? Should we challenge the district prophetically in a sermon? Should we act as peacemakers reconciling warring parties? Should we quietly advise state officials to change laws? Should we avoid the conflict and focus on sharing the gospel? Maybe the answer seems obvious to you. It was anything but obvious to us. Every answer seemed right. Every answer seemed wrong. Only one thing was obvious: We felt like outsiders too.

After much prayer and reflection, we made the choice to speak publicly. This wasn't easy because it's not what we normally do. But we thought we could lower the temperature of the conflict by inviting everyone involved to find common ground. To that end, we wrote an article in *Newsweek* arguing that while our diverse community may never agree on the value of drag performances, most of us value parental consent.[2] It doesn't matter whether that's consent for a prayer rally or drag show. We hoped the article would challenge the superintendent to re-engage concerned parents, while also modeling the tact and thoughtfulness we want Christian parents to show educators.

The day after the article was published, we met with the superintendent and a school board member. Before the meeting, we wrote down a list of goals. Our first goal was to make a friend. But the meeting didn't go that way. The superintendent and school board member immediately made their position clear: They'd done nothing wrong, and we were the modern-day equivalent of Jim Crow segregationists, heightening levels of suicidality in trans children.

Afterward we wondered if the article was foolish. Yes, we'd spoken the truth with grace. But we hadn't changed hearts or minds. Yes, the school district eventually changed its policies. But broken bridges remained broken.

So did we do the right thing? We're still not certain. Today we wonder if a "right" response ever existed. After all, what would a "right" response be? Speaking the truth? Winning converts? Condemning wrongdoing? Building bridges? Protecting children? Defending parents? Supporting teachers? Remaining silent?

When we live in a chaotic, confusing culture, tension is the norm. Uncertainty is a state of existence. There aren't black-and-white answers to gray questions. Navigating a culture as an outsider requires wisdom. It demands a sober assessment of what's possible and what's not. It calls for the weighing of consequences. It invites improvisation. And even while we do our best to get it right, we all play wrong notes from time to time.

At the end of the entire debacle, we were certain about three things. First, Christians *are* outsiders. Second, Christians can rarely agree how to respond when they feel like outsiders. Third, how you and I respond is determined by *why* we think we're outsiders. Let me show you why that's the case.

Why "The Why" Matters

If you counsel enough marriages through conflict, you'll learn that the reason *why* someone thinks he's in conflict calibrates his response. I always ask both parties, "Why are you fighting?" And of course, both blame the other and defend themselves. So if a husband believes his wife's impatience is the cause of their quarreling, he will justify how he reacts: by disappearing for hours. If a wife thinks her husband's laziness is the cause of their daily squabbles, she will justify how she reacts: by lashing him with a daily barrage of critiques. As the pastor, I need to help both people nuance their perspective and realize that the answer to "why?" is far more complex than either realizes.

I apply a similar principle when I'm helping people navigate thorny cultural situations. I start by asking, "Why do you think you're an outsider?" How would you answer? One popular response is simple: because everything is changing! Sometimes people blame "those progressives" or "those conservatives." Sometimes they blame an activist agenda or a protest leader. But what most answers share is an underlying assumption: Our status as outsiders is *new* and *abnormal*. It's a problem created by culture. Therefore, it's a problem that can be fixed—should be fixed!

But what if our underlying assumption is wrong? What if the reason *why* has less to do with our culture, politics, and national leaders and more to do with our fundamental identity as followers of Jesus?

The anti-Nazi Christian dissident Dietrich Bonhoeffer wrote, "Here on earth, the church-community lives in a foreign land. It is a colony of strangers far away from home."[3] He's riffing on an idea present throughout the entire Bible: *God's people are outsiders.* Scripture isn't about cultural insiders who felt at home in the world. It's a minority report written by *outsiders.* Consider these examples:

- Jacob was a "wandering Aramean" whose nomadic family found themselves in regular conflict with the surrounding nations.[4] Jacob was an *outsider* in Canaan.
- The Egyptians saw the Hebrews as a national threat, so they enslaved them.[5] The Hebrew slaves were *outsiders* in Egypt.
- When the Israelites assimilated to the pagan cultures around them, God challenged their idolatry through prophets.[6] Those prophets were *outsiders* in Israel.
- In 586 BC, the Babylonians conquered Judah and forcibly relocated the population to urban centers across the empire.[7] The exiles were *outsiders* in Babylon.
- The early Jesus movement was so ostracized by their neighbors that Peter called them "exiles."[8] Christians were *outsiders* in Greco-Roman culture.

Jesus was also an outsider. His parents hailed not from the halls of power but from the backwaters of Galilee. They lived under military occupation and fled from a violent king.[9] Jesus died "outside the city" as a social and religious outcast.[10] Our king was cast outside his city, condemned as a criminal, forsaken by his Father, rejected by his people, abandoned by his friends, and exiled by his own creation.[11] But as painful as it all was, none of if it was an accident. Jesus *chose* to be an outsider. The author of Hebrews tells us why: "For the *joy* set before him he endured the cross, scorning its shame, and sat down at the right hand of the throne of God."[12] Jesus knew that death as an outsider was the only path to a joyful future. So he walked in the way of outsiders, through death unto life. He rose to life *outside* the city and called his followers—exiles, outcasts, and powerless pilgrims—to join him as outsiders.

This is why the early Christians shared willingly in Christ's death by taking up their own crosses and living as outsiders in the world. They willingly embraced the tension between the Roman Empire and the kingdom of God. Some were persecuted. Others were murdered. One was exiled to an isolated island. Most were treated like social pariahs. Yet this movement of outsiders grew and eventually turned the world upside down. They too became joyful outsiders.

So do you want to know *why* you're an outsider in this world? It's *not* because the world is changing or because of a political agenda or because of a leader. It's because you worship an outsider king who has invited you to glorify and enjoy him by becoming an outsider yourself. You are not an outsider by accident any more than Jesus was! You're an outsider because your Creator called you to be one. As the author of Hebrews wrote, "So Jesus also suffered *outside* the gate in order to sanctify the people through his own blood. Therefore let us go to him *outside* the camp and bear the reproach he endured."[13] This is calling you to embrace your role as an outsider. To bear the reproach. To wear the tension. To walk in the way. So perhaps it's no surprise that the apostle Peter viewed our outsiderness as a fundamental part of our identity. He identified people who spent their entire lives in the Roman Empire as "elect exiles."[14] I'm sure that identity was jarring for those who never expected that following Jesus would make them foreigners in their homeland. But Peter doesn't shy from the truth. The sovereign creator of the universe made you an outsider. That's *the divine why* behind the tension you feel between yourself and your culture. It's the divine calling you're being invited to accept.

Will You Accept Your Calling?

When the Bible calls you a "foreigner," "sojourner," "resident alien," or an "exile," it's not saying you left your homeland but that you no longer belong to it. Your passport remains unchanged. But internally (and eternally) your primary citizenship is now in heaven. Of course, this generates tension in the present. But the tension isn't a problem to be solved. It's a divine calling to be heeded.

When we forget this divine *why*, we respond to our culture in destructive ways. Some try to resolve the tension between themselves and the world because they don't see the tension as a normal part of the Christian life. Thus, they make poor choices to resolve tension, which leaves them *more* confused, fearful, and combative than when they started. In the process, they lose the very joy God means them to have as outsiders. They miss out on his beautiful calling for their lives.

Do you want to accept Jesus's invitation to be an outsider at his side? Do you want to learn how to make friends with tension rather than resolve it? If so, you must first unearth the ways you've tried to fix the tension you feel, the ways you've been the *wrong* kind of outsider.

CHAPTER 2

The Wrong Kind of Outsiders

The church exists to be a witness to the world, showing what it looks like to live in God's reign of justice and peace.

—STANLEY HAUERWAS

Blessed are you when people insult you, persecute you and falsely say all kinds of evil against you because of me. Rejoice and be glad, because great is your reward in heaven, for in the same way they persecuted the prophets who were before you.

—JESUS

Bill and Susan married right after college, and it wasn't long before they had three boys.[1] They raised them in the church and talked about God at the dinner table. They were good parents who tried their best to raise their children in the way of Jesus.

To someone looking from the outside in, everything was going well as their children became adults. When their oldest son got married, the wedding was a family celebration. Bill and Susan expected their middle son, who was in a serious relationship, to get engaged next. But that's not what happened. Instead, their youngest son announced that he was getting married to his best friend—a man.

The announcement knocked them off balance. They didn't want to hurt their son, but they couldn't support a gay marriage any more than they could support one of their boys sleeping with his girlfriend. They weren't prepared for this and didn't know how to respond. But before they could find an answer, Bill and Susan's other two sons called and said that if they refused to be as enthusiastic for their brother's same-sex wedding as they were for the oldest son's marriage, then they wouldn't lose just one son. They'd lose all three.

There are few worse choices I can imagine than choosing between my allegiance to Jesus and my relationship with my children. It's far easier to be an outsider in your culture than it is to be an outsider in your family. So I know that if I were Bill, I would want to resolve the tension at any cost.

The British pastor, missionary, and theologian Lesslie Newbigin described the way we feel in such moments as "unbearable tension."[2] Because Christians are outsiders in this life, their faith often comes into conflict with the world around them. We face terribly difficult choices without clear or easy answers. Thus, we're tempted to resolve the tension between ourselves and the world.

How do we do that? Put yourself in Bill and Susan's shoes. The easiest way to resolve the tension would be assimilation. If they changed their views on sex and sexuality, the tension would evaporate *and* they'd preserve their relationship with all three boys. Alternatively, Bill and Susan could have removed the tension by cutting off their sons. Although more painful than the first option, they wouldn't have to worry about relational tension in the future because there would be no relationship in the future. Or they could go on the offensive: self-righteously deride their youngest son's choice and mobilize guilt to cow the others. They could resolve the tension by *forcing* their children to change instead of changing themselves.

Of course, these aren't the only ways to resolve tension. But Bill and Susan's story illustrates the point: When we feel the unbearable tension created by our God-given status as outsiders, our default temptation is to resolve it. There's nothing new about this temptation. It's precisely what all humans do under stress. All humans but Jesus, that is.

In Jesus's day the Jewish people were outsiders in the wider Roman world. So it's no surprise that they, just like us, wanted to find ways to resolve the tension. Some Jews assimilated to Roman culture to resolve the tension. Others fled Roman culture to escape it. Still others fought Roman culture, hoping to destroy the empire causing the tension. Their temptations were the same as our own.

Jesus could've joined any one of their movements, but he refused them all. He understood that if he resolved the unbearable tension, he wouldn't cease to be an outsider. He'd simply become the *wrong* sort of outsider. A conformist outsider. A combative outsider. A cloistered outsider. *Not* a joyful outsider.

While the movements Jesus rejected scattered in the century after his resurrection, they live on in spirit and take shape in every generation. They're alive and well in the church today. So in this chapter we'll look at five ways Jewish movements in Jesus's time tried to resolve tension. Then we'll explore how we're tempted to do likewise and why doing so is destructive to our souls. We can become joyful outsiders only if we turn from these five temptations, just as Jesus did.

Conformist Outsiders

After the Romans conquered Judea in 63 BC, local leaders vied for power. In the end an Idumean named Herod won Caesar Augustus's favor and began a decades-long reign of terror over the Jewish people. A group of Jews called the Herodians sought to resolve the tension by assimilating to Herod's way of running things. They supported his violence, vanity, and sexual immorality. They are mentioned three times in the Gospels, and in every instance they conspire against Jesus in favor of Herod's dynasty. The

Herodians were *conformist* outsiders. By conforming to the Romanized culture around them, they became cultural elites, enjoying power, prestige, wealth—and had little tension with the powers at large.

The Herodians were not unique. Christians conformed to Nazism in Germany and slavery in the South for similar reasons. Doing so allowed them to resolve the tension between their faith and their culture *and* secure prosperity and influence.

In a similar way, we're often tempted to assimilate to the elites around us. We want to look identical to our most prestigious neighbors by indulging in consumerism, sexual immorality, militarism, the LGBTQ+ agenda, or whatever new fad has taken Hollywood and the academy by storm. Like chameleons, we blend in with the environment around us. Yes, we may still call ourselves Christians, but we're careful not to be *that* kind of Christian. The kind satirized with long skirts and self-righteous monologues in sitcoms. The kind who can't get with the times. The kind who can't have fun. The kind that don't fit in.

Conforming is tempting because it's quick and easy. You need only change yourself. Better yet, conformity makes us look savvy and enlightened. If you walk this path, you will feel less tension. But it will cost you your integrity. A chasm will open between you and God. After all, if you reject his wisdom and goodness in one area, it won't be long until you reject God himself.

Jesus refused to conform to Rome's cult of death, sexuality, selfishness, slavery, and destruction. The cross was Rome's punishment for not playing by its rules. But Jesus knew that his kingdom of love, justice, and mercy wasn't of this world. He was a different kind of king. If he aped Caesar, he would cease to be himself. He would have nothing to offer the world.

When we give in to the temptation to conform to the culture around us, we also have nothing to offer. We're like salt that has lost its saltiness. We lack the flavor of God's kingdom and taste no different from the broken world around us. Our uneasy consciences haunt us, and as a result we move away from Jesus.

Combative Outsiders

Simon "the Zealot," one of Jesus's twelve disciples, was given his nickname because he was a member of a political movement known as the Zealots. They were willing to use violence to overthrow the Roman government. The Sicarii, which means "dagger men," were a later offshoot of the Zealots. They hid knives up their sleeves and killed any Roman soldier they found alone. Their ultimate goal was to run the Romans out of Judea and establish a Jewish kingdom where Jews would experience no tension. The Zealots were *combative* outsiders. They rejected Jesus's call to love and instead became culture warriors whose violent means mirrored those of the Roman soldiers they sought to cast out.

In a similar way, we're often tempted to attack the world around us. Because of its immorality and injustice, our attacks look justified and righteous. Although we may not use physical force, we do weaponize words. We mock, demean, and belittle our opponents in private or online. Like the Zealots, we don't see our enemies as lost sinners in need of God's love but as existential threats to our way of life.

Combativeness is tempting because it promises power. Not just power over those you fear but also power to make the world in your own image. In such a world, we imagine there would be no tension. To take that power, we deploy righteous indignation. But the more you vent your anger, the angrier you become. Violence begets violence. In the process you end up becoming more like the very people you're fighting against: a dark reflection of the world's anger, vitriol, and hunger for power. If you walk down this path, you will lose the joy of Christ. You will abandon the Spirit's peace. Rather than cultivating the world around you, you'll leave behind nuclear waste.

The Zealots expected a Messiah who would overthrow Rome. But they were sent a Messiah who was crucified by Rome. Combatants often turn to strong men to fight their cause, but when they do, they turn away from the Prince of Peace. Jesus told Peter to put away his sword.[3] He refused to call legions of angels to defend himself and instead submitted to torture and crucifixion.[4] He forgave his enemies and died for their sins.

When we become combative outsiders, we act as though Jesus's self-sacrificial approach was naive. We know better: There are only winners and losers, and winners take the world by force. But in truth we've only given ourselves over to an awful master: anger. We've left the gentle King Jesus behind.

Cloistered Outsiders

The Essenes are one of the most mysterious first-century Jewish sects because their response to the corruption of the priesthood and the domination of Rome was to withdraw into cloistered communities cut off from the world. They escaped the tension by separating themselves from the environment that caused the tension. They lived isolated lives of study, ritual, and devotion, hoping that if they remained pure, God would send a rescuer to liberate them from the corrupt world around them. The Essenes were *cloistered* outsiders. They rejected Jesus's call to be in the world, self-righteously avoiding and judging all others as corrupt, immoral, and spiritually dangerous.

Christians face this same temptation today. We hope that if we keep our kids out of secular schools, attend the most serious churches, and avoid relationships with corrupting coworkers, then God will protect us from the dirty world around us. We resolve the tension by cutting off any relationships that cause it.

If you do this, you will feel a sense of self-righteous superiority. You'll think you're better than the people you cut off, because you're a serious Christian. But you will also live in constant fear of God's judgment. You will worry that he might withdraw his protection if you fail him in small matters. You'll also fear losing relationships with loved ones if they fail God, because you've trained yourself to cut off people rather than live in tension with them. Lastly, you'll fear the world itself: It is bigger than you are and always lurking around the corner to steal that which you hope to protect.

Jesus didn't start a holiness commune. Instead, he spent so much of his time with prostitutes, revelers, and tax collectors that people called him a drunkard and a glutton.[5] He said, "It is not the healthy who need a doctor, but the sick. I have not come to call the righteous, but sinners to repentance."[6] Rather than separating himself and protecting himself from others, he took responsibility for their sins. He laid down his life to rescue humanity from evil.

When we become cloistered outsiders instead of being lights on a hill, we become fearful shadows hiding under baskets. We can't follow Jesus because he steps straight into the corrupt world we fear most.

Nostalgic Outsiders

The Pharisees longed to return to the halcyon days of Israel's past, back when Jews honored God, obeyed the law, and served a Jewish king. They hoped that if Israel returned to its roots, and carefully observed the law of Moses, then God would bring the past into the present and launch a new golden age of tensionless life under a Jewish messiah. The Pharisees were *nostalgic* outsiders who tried to resolve the tension by turning the clock backward.

We feel the same temptation, though we may long for a different past, like the 1950s, when churches were full, kids prayed in school, divorces were less common, the nation respected leaders like Billy Graham, and presidents were baptized in office. Just as Pharisees policed the immorality of their culture, nostalgic outsiders police the present by checking in with Libs of TikTok, watching conservative cable news, and attending churches that celebrate God *and* country.

The preacher in Ecclesiastes warns, "Do not say, 'Why were the old days better than these?' For it is not wise to ask such questions."[7] He's right. If you give in to nostalgia, you'll be tempted by the same dead legalism the Pharisees practiced. You'll take comfort in your black-and-white fantasy of the past, rather than the true multichromatic dream of Jesus: his kingdom on earth by *his* means. You'll grow bitter and curmudgeonly and lose the creativity required to cultivate a better future.

Jesus didn't die to turn the clock back. He said you can't put new wine into old wineskins. After all, there was no golden era in Israel's history. In every generation men and women gave themselves over to idolatry and sin. Jesus didn't even die to take us back to Eden. Jesus died and rose again to carry us forward into a new garden city. Yes, he will incorporate all that was good from the past. But it's not a gaudy replica. It's a fresh reality. It's new wine. The old wineskins just won't work.

When we become nostalgic outsiders, instead of moving forward with Jesus, we keep our eyes fixed on the past. As a result, we miss out on the joy, love, and hope that Jesus's promised future gives us.

Conflict-Avoidant Outsiders

Cloistered outsiders have a close cousin: conflict-avoidant outsiders. But the conflict-avoidant don't seek to separate from culture. Instead, they live in the world but try to avoid conflict at all costs. They're simply too exhausted by the tension to care. No movements in Jesus's day represent this view, but that's because exhausted, conflict-avoidant people rarely build movements. They try to live their daily lives quietly, avoid eye contact with bullies, change the subject, stay silent, and pretend like nothing's wrong. Galilee was full of peasants and fishermen who did exactly that— and hoped they could eke out a meager living so long as no one noticed them. They were *conflict-avoidant* outsiders.

We face the same temptation today. Sometimes we make spiritual excuses for our ambivalence about the world: "Let's focus on discipleship, small groups, and prayer, and avoid all this controversial stuff. It just pushes people away from Jesus." But more often we simply hide, stay quiet, and avoid. We hope that if we pretend the tension doesn't exist, it will go away.

If you're tempted to avoid conflict, it's probably because you fear either broken relationships or personal embarrassment. You know that if you become embroiled in controversy, your reputation may take a hit or you may lose a friend. But conflict avoidance comes with a cost: You neglect those you love. Hard truths remain unspoken, and lives crumble as a result. When that happens, you're partially culpable. Just ask yourself, "If I had cancer, what would I say if I found out my doctor was hiding it from me to avoid tension?"

The irony is that while avoidance may resolve *external* tension with others, it only elevates *internal* tension. You will live with a low, thrumming fear that someone might make you share your thoughts. You'll anxiously worry that others might notice your silence. And you'll fear that God might hold you accountable for the ways you've neglected your responsibility to others.

Jesus did not avoid conflict. He said he didn't come to bring peace, but a sword. That's because he knew that true peacemaking is not ambivalent or avoidant. Yes, we should seek to live in harmony with all people. But sincere love doesn't remain silent in the face of evil. This is why Jesus confronted sin and called Herod a fox. Jesus's words could cut. Though he only cut to heal.

When we give in to the temptation to avoid conflict, we choose false peace for ourselves at the cost of love for others. We neglect our neighbors. And we live in fear that one day we won't be able to escape conflict. When that day comes, and it always does, we won't have the muscles we need to stand. They'll be atrophied and exhausted, and thus we may very well give in to the world and conform.

Know Yourself

As you read this chapter, you probably saw yourself in one or two of the temptations. But I'm sure you have questions and pushbacks. Aren't Christians called to combat injustice? Doesn't Jesus call us to be separate, different from the world? Isn't there value in looking to the past? Didn't Paul command us to live peaceful, quiet, harmonious lives? The answer to all these questions is yes, and we'll explore them more fully in the second part of the book.

But here's the key: If we do those things to relieve the tension between ourselves and the world, then we do them for the wrong reason and will inevitably do them in the wrong way. When we seek to soften our divine calling as outsiders by conforming to culture, attacking it, separating from it, avoiding conflict with it, or retreating into nostalgia, we deny the very calling God gave us: to be salt and light, to bless those who persecute us, to hope for God's future. Worse yet, our tension-relief strategies often backfire. The tension never disappears. We only grow angrier or more afraid.

Indeed, we end up becoming more like the world around us because we've embraced the world's ways. Lesslie Newbigin wrote, "When the Church tries to embody the rule of God in the forms of earthly power it may achieve that power, but it is no longer a sign of the kingdom."[8] When we try to resolve the tension, we become a reflection of the world. We mirror its anger and violence. Or we mirror its values. Or we mirror its fear. Or we mirror its nostalgia. Or we mirror its false peace.

How have you been tempted to relieve the tension caused by your calling as an outsider? Does the pressure cause you to conform? Does the tension make you combative? Does your longing for security make you cloister? Does your frustration with the present make you nostalgic? Does fear make you conflict avoidant?

If you're feeling disheartened, there's good news: We don't resist these temptations by a force of will. We resist them by turning back to God and receiving his forgiveness. It's never too late. Jesus showed this by calling Zealots, Herodians, and Pharisees into his kingdom. Jesus invites you, too, onto a better path, forgiven of your failures and empowered by his grace to do what would otherwise be impossible: living in the unbearable tension by means of *his* joy.

As Nehemiah said, "Do not grieve, for the joy of the LORD is your strength."[9] The tension *is* grievous if you face it alone. But you aren't alone. Your joyful king is with you. His joy is the only steel strong enough to withstand the tension, and he offers you that joy freely by grace. So set down your fear and anger, and take up his gift. Choose joy today.

To help you do that, we'll explore how outsiders choose joy in chapter 4. But before we're prepared to take up the gift of joy, we must take one last step into the unbearable tension in order to answer a burning question some of you have been asking since chapter 1: "Even if it's true that we're called to be outsiders, isn't it also true that our culture is becoming more antagonistic toward Christianity, and that's at least part of why the tension is heightening?" That is a fantastic question, and answering it will also help you to name the tension and live in less fear of it.

CHAPTER 3

Naming the Tension

The world as it now exists is not our true home.
—TIMOTHY KELLER

We must always, it seems to me, in every situation, be
wrestling with both sides of this reality: That the Church
is for the world against the world. [And] the Church is
against the world for the world.
—LESSLIE NEWBIGIN

A middle-aged woman on her company's diversity, equity, and inclusion (DEI) board proposed a solution to resolve internal disagreements over new LGBTQ+ initiatives: "We should just fire all the Christians who don't agree with us on this. *They* create a dangerous work environment for queer people, so *they* can go." Sitting quietly across from her was my friend Bryce, a young man in his twenties. Everyone at the table nodded in agreement except for him. He suspected that none of them realized the truth: He was a Christian. They were talking about him.

He found his way onto the DEI board quite by accident. A friend nominated him without his permission. He never campaigned or asked for anyone's vote. On election day he was offsite, assuming no one—including himself—would vote for him. But he was wrong. Bryce won a seat on the board. This was his first meeting, and the board was considering a proposal to fire him and all the other Christians working in the office.

As he debated how to respond, he realized he was caught between two competing interests. On the one hand, he wanted his coworkers to know Jesus. He knew fighting with them wouldn't make Jesus more attractive. But on the other hand, he wanted to protect fellow followers of Jesus from discriminatory policies. If he said nothing, people could lose their livelihoods.

What would you do? Stay silent and hope for the best? Or embroil yourself in a DEI debate? That meeting was a pressure cooker. It was a small dose of unbearable tension, and Bryce had only a few moments to make his decision.

But before he could say anything, the head of human resources stepped in: "I understand your concern, and it's totally reasonable. It's not a bad idea, but legally we can't do it. We'll need to find a different solution." Bryce felt an immediate wave of relief. They couldn't fire all the Christians. But the tension remained. Someone *wanted* to fire them, and the head of HR found the proposal *reasonable*. Perhaps their final solution would be less punitive than the original proposal, but Bryce doubted it would be good.

It's hard to imagine a story like this taking place in a small Midwestern town just ten years ago. But a lot has changed in ten years. Bryce's story illustrates that while unbearable tension is a fact that all joyful outsiders must face, it is a liquid fact. The tension changes over time. It takes many forms. And there's no doubt the tension is escalating in certain spaces, like corporate DEI boards. This is why entire books have been written suggesting that the real reason we feel like outsiders in twenty-first-century America isn't because of a divine calling to live as outsiders but because the once Christianized West is now post-Christian. As one author put it, Christians used to live in a "positive world" where our faith was respected and celebrated, but we now live in a "negative world" where our faith is despised and rejected.[1] If you've found yourself thinking this way, you aren't crazy. America has undeniably changed.

Everything's Changed

While some people reject the idea that Christians live in a "negative world"—they'd say things aren't bad and we ought to stop complaining—major sociological shifts suggest otherwise. Changing religious demographics, language, and moral norms all show that the way of Jesus *has* lost its luster stateside. Let's consider each in turn.

Shifting Demographics

A recent study revealed that the United States is undergoing one of the largest religious shifts in its history since the post–Civil War church attendance boom.[2] But the contemporary shift is different from those of the past because for the first time in American history, it is a movement *away* from Jesus. We aren't in a Great Awakening. Instead, we've begun the Great Slumbering. Over the last twenty-five years, forty million Christians have stopped attending church.[3] More people have left the church than joined it during the first two Great Awakenings and Billy Graham's crusades *combined*.[4] For the first time in the last century, a majority of American adults do *not* identify as Protestant or attend a church.[5] Between 1953 and 2022, self-identified Protestants dropped from 70 to 34 percent of the population.[6] The fastest-growing religious group in America is the "nones"—people who believe in God but hold to no particular faith or tradition.

Most nones are what Tara Isabella Burton calls "religiously remixed."[7] They combine spiritual ideas from pop culture, self-care gurus, and various religious traditions into a bespoke, personalized religious identity. Nones currently comprise almost a quarter of the US population, and within a few years, they will eclipse Protestants.[8]

These massive demographic shifts mean that fewer Christians are running companies, researching in universities, working in news media, serving in politics, and making decisions in Hollywood. Ordinary followers of Jesus no longer feel that "people like me" are in power or adjacent to power. Despair over cultural decay is a vibe for a reason: There's less salt and less light in America.

Shifting Language

Language is a shared social space through which we communicate ideas. To work, language requires some level of mutual understanding and shared meaning. In previous generations, Christianity functioned as the common religious tongue of the people. Average Americans understood how words like *sin*, *heaven*, *hell*, *God*, and *salvation* fit together. In the mid-twentieth century, evangelists like Billy Graham didn't need to define these words. They simply called people to action: Repent of your sins. Receive salvation from God. Go to heaven.

But today *sinful* is as likely to refer to a decadent dessert as it is to moral deviation from God's law. Words like *harm*, *toxic*, and *repression* have become the new lexicon of wrongdoing. And they're not applied when people act immorally. You're "toxic" if you pressure others to act in *any* way that violates their sense of authenticity or autonomy. You're "harmful" if you tell someone to resist their internal desires. You're "repressed" if you don't embrace sexual self-expression. For modern people, it's a sin to violate the law of self, not the law of God.

Salvation has slipped almost entirely out of our lexicon, as has *hell*—unless you're cussing. *Heaven* fares little better. It's no longer God's throne room or the place Christians go to be with Jesus as they await the resurrection. Heaven is where everyone goes! Most Americans who believe in heaven assume that people from all religions are there.[9] Heaven is a McMansion in the sky, and everyone is welcome under those golden arches. That said, you're not likely to hear younger generations talk about heaven at all. Reincarnation is the fastest-growing view of the afterlife among young people. And why not? If you worship in the temple of self-expression, what better hereafter could there be than a second shot at being myself? Christianity no longer defines our shared linguistic space. We've lost a common religious tongue and replaced it with the parlance of authenticity, self-care, and self-expression.

Shifting Moral Norms around Sex and Sexuality

American views of sex and sexuality are also changing rapidly. In the latter half of the twentieth century, Christians could assume their neighbors agreed that same-sex relationships were immoral, as was premarital sex. That's not to say they acted on that shared vision or that there weren't large pockets of the population dissenting. But it is to say that once upon a time, even Miley Cyrus, Selena Gomez, and Nick Jonas had to wear purity rings to win a wide audience. Culture at least gave lip service to abstinence.[10] In 2004, Oregon voted to put John Kerry in the presidential office *and* ban gay marriage. This shows that just two decades ago, a majority of Americans—including former president Barack Obama—held quite traditional views of sex, gender, and marriage *uncontroversially*.[11]

At worst, America's *stated* moral vision of sex and sexuality ran diagonal to Jesus's sex ethic but not entirely against it. But the cultural consensus has broken down. Today 71 percent of Americans affirm same-sex relationships as morally acceptable.[12] And 69 percent of Americans believe that premarital sex is morally acceptable.[13] The vast majority of Americans (85 percent) reject abstinence-only education.[14] In a period of two decades, Christians went from being mainstream to countercultural. We're the deviants now.

Shifting Prominence and Acceptance

Christianity's place in public life is increasingly marginal. For example, after the 9/11 terrorist attacks, Billy Graham preached at the memorial service in Washington, DC. But just a decade later, in 2011, the ten-year memorial service at Yankee Stadium excluded *all* clergy and prayers. This should shock no one. Trust in religious leaders is at a historic low.[15]

But Christian leaders aren't the only ones who've lost prominence and trust. It's not uncommon to hear broadsides against everyday Christians on cable news or social media. Alexandria Ocasio-Cortez may have best articulated the feelings of many during a House Oversight Committee meeting: "The only time religious freedom is invoked is in the name of bigotry and discrimination."[16] To her, Christianity isn't just outmoded. It's *dangerous*.

When you put all the pieces together, the total amount of change is jarring. Demographically, America is increasingly irreligious. We no longer share a common religious tongue. The moral consensus about sex and sexuality opposes Jesus's teachings. Christians are not only absent in public life—they're often derided.

So who can deny the truth? We *do* live in a "negative world." We *are* outsiders. The question is whether we ever lived in a "positive world." Was there ever a time, however brief, when Christians weren't outsiders?

There was a time in my life when I would've said yes. Nostalgia tempted me and I took the bait. But God was gracious. I met a wise man and came to realize that Christians have always been outsiders. The unbearable tension we experience today isn't new. It's been there from the beginning.

Unbearable Tension Is Nothing New

I sat in my seminary's student center on a dreary December day and spoke with Mike for over an hour. Our life experiences could not have been more different: I'm a millennial, he's a baby boomer; I'm white, he's Black; I was childless, he was a father; I grew up in an affluent, suburban, middle-class household, he grew up in an urban home with limited resources; I am a civilian, he is a former army colonel.

But during this conversation, one difference mattered most: He was a wise man. He understood the past. I was a young man who only saw the present.

I began that conversation by complaining about the tension I felt doing college ministry on a secular campus. In the past, I explained to Mike, ministry was simpler and easier because Christianity was the norm. But now we're outsiders. Now there's division over every conceivable political, moral, and cultural matter—and that makes the claims of Jesus implausible to an intractably irreligious generation. In a fit of nostalgia, I asked, "Don't you wish you could go back in time?"

Mike smiled and asked a question that changed how I understood the history of Christian tension in the US. "Do you really think that if either one of us went back to Mississippi in 1960 and spoke biblical truth about race, intermarriage, and segregation, it would be simpler or easier for us than it is today?"

"No," I said sheepishly, immediately seeing how silly my question was. Mike went on to point out that Black Christians, abolitionists, and civil rights activists in America have *always* felt like outsiders because of their faith. They've always lived in the unbearable tension. He gave me a few examples.

After Olaudah Equiano won his freedom from slavery in 1765, he wrote his life story, detailing his conversion to Christianity and using the words of Scripture to castigate Americans for participating in the transatlantic slave trade. Equiano experienced terrible tension between the abolitionist ethics of his faith and a culture besotted by slavery. He was an outsider. He lived in unbearable tension.

In the nineteenth century, Frederick Douglass quoted the Bible throughout his abolitionist speeches. In his jeremiad "What to the Slave Is the Fourth of July?" he compares the American slave's experience to the Jewish exile's experience in Babylon. He quotes Psalm 137, in which the exiles lament the tension they feel as outsiders in a foreign empire. They long for Jerusalem. But they live in Babylon. They wander cities awash in brazen injustice, idolatry, and immorality. So they weep:

> By the rivers of Babylon we sat and wept
>> when we remembered Zion.
> There on the poplars
>> we hung our harps,
> for there our captors asked us for songs,
>> our tormentors demanded songs of joy;
>> they said, "Sing us one of the songs of Zion!"
>
> How can we sing the songs of the LORD
>> while in a foreign land? (Psalm 137:1–4 NIV)

For Douglass, America was a modern *Babylon*. When he considered American indifference toward slavery and the awful torture, rape, and trading of slaves, he felt terrible tension between his faith and culture. Douglass was an outsider. He lived in unbearable tension.

In the twentieth century, segregationist police officers shoved forks up the nose and down the throat of John M. Perkins, a Christian civil rights activist. They nearly beat him to death in prison for protesting. He wrote, "I can't forget their faces, so twisted with hate. It was like looking at white-faced demons. Hate did that to them. But you know, I couldn't hate back. When I saw what hate had done to them, I couldn't hate back. I could only pity them. I didn't ever want hate to do to me what it had already done to those men."[17]

Perkins explained that he almost became like them. He *almost* became like Babylon. But the grace, mercy, and forgiveness of Jesus won out. So he spent most of his life in terrible tension between a faith that called him to love his enemies and a culture that wanted to disfigure him with hatred. He was an outsider. He lived in unbearable tension.

Mike didn't condemn me with these stories. Instead, he used them to open my eyes to a profound reality: *Orthodox Christians have always felt like outsiders in America. They've always lived in the unbearable tension between the kingdom of God and the kingdoms of the world.* Yes, they felt the tension in different ways, in different places, and to different degrees. But the fundamental truth remained the same: To follow Jesus is to be an outsider living in tension.

He taught me that although there have always been Christians who mistook America for a new Jerusalem, history reveals that faithful followers of Jesus—even those who love their country—have seen America in a different way. *It's a type of Babylon.*[18]

Naming the Tension: You Live in Babylon

Thus, while it's true that Christians live in a "negative world" today, it's a nostalgic misrepresentation of the past to suggest that there ever was a "positive world." No, we've *always* lived in a negative world. In more biblical terms, we've always lived in Babylon. And Babylon has always been (and will always be) in need of fresh missionary encounters with Jesus's kingdom.[19] From a vertical perspective, the tension is ever with us because God called us to live as outsiders. From a horizontal perspective, the tension is with us because we reside in Babylon as outsiders.

In the Bible, "Babylon" is sometimes used as a metonymy. If you're not a language nerd, a metonymy is a figure of speech that uses part of something to describe the whole. For example, we commonly use "the White House" to refer to the executive branch of the United States government. We use a *part* of the executive branch to refer to the *whole*. In the Bible, "Babylon" is a metonymy for human systems and structures that inculcate hatred, normalize idolatry, and reinforce injustice.

Babylon debuts in Genesis 11, when Nimrod gathered humans to use a brand-new technology—the mud-brick—to construct a towering temple.[20] Today we would call it a ziggurat. In ancient Mesopotamia, ziggurats were symbolic mountains, the peaks of which functioned as a gateways between heaven and earth.[21] Nimrod's followers believed that if they built it high enough, they could invade heaven or, at the very least, usurp God's throne.[22] It was a vain effort to crown human pride, autonomy, and technological mastery as the chief power in the universe.

The Tower of Babel, as we know it today, should probably be translated as "The Tower of Babylon" because "Babel" is the Hebrew word for Babylon.[23] However we translate it, the point is clear: The tower-temple of Babylon is a dark reflection of Eden. It promises much of what Eden offered—security, purpose, meaning, knowledge, beauty, social order, and creativity—but with a human-centered spin.

If J. Richard Middleton is correct, the earliest Israelite readers of Genesis 11 would've seen through the farce immediately because details in the Tower of Babylon story recalled their own enslavement in Egypt.[24] Just like Egypt, the original Babel/Babylon coerced humans into participating in an imperial monoculture. One language. One worldview. One nation. One power.[25] Additionally, the story implies that the tower was built with slave labor. When ancient Israelites read that it was constructed with mud-bricks, they would've mentally hyperlinked to the story of the Exodus when their enslaved ancestors constructed monumental structures for the Egyptians out of mud-bricks.

The point of Genesis 11 is clear: Outside of Eden, humans use technique and technology to build their own Babylons. Mark Sayers wrote,

Safe in the walls of [Babylon], the human finds respite from their fears. . . . When we are anxious, we seek out [Babylons]. When we cannot find a [Babylon], we build one. . . . Once a [Babylon] is established, it will become attractive to those who find themselves in uncertain, in-between spaces. A [Babylon] becomes magnetic, a vision of hope and home for the worried and lost. [Babylons] that appear adequate and sturdy will become beacons to those who find themselves filled with the anxiety of living in the in-between spaces. They grow in size and power, taking on lives of their own.[26]

Throughout the course of history, these Babylons have been monocultural social orders: city-kingdoms, empires, and nations. But Babylon can take many forms: ideological movements, religious movements, economic systems, and political parties. In a world of globalized commerce and communication like our own, many Babylons can coexist in the same place. Though they rarely do so peacefully.

While Babylon comes in many shapes, sizes, and varieties, the core is always the same: *a rejection of God's image in every human, a denial of God's vision of good and evil, and the oppression and exploitation of God's creation. Babylon is thus any pervasive, totalizing system through which the powers and principalities of darkness habituate humans to practices and modes of thinking that militate against the kingdom of God.*

This explains why later biblical authors call non-Babylonian empires Babylon. For example, Peter described the church in Rome as the church "in *Babylon*."[27] Rome was a type of Babylon because it embodied the Babylonian way: death, oppression, sameness, cruelty, violence, and soulless trade and industry.

We live in Babylon, but none of us belong to Babylon. We were born in Babylon, but we've been reborn as citizens of God's kingdom. We live under Babylon's hegemony but serve the true king, Jesus. Followers of Jesus feel like outsiders because they *are* outsiders in Babylon. We feel tension on a horizontal, sociological level because our operating system is fundamentally different from the operating system of the world around us.

That reality creates a constant missionary conflict between two worlds: the city of God and the city of man, the kingdom of God and the kingdom of Babylon, the way of Jesus and the way of the world.

Thus, if you want to understand the unbearable tension you're feeling alongside every Christian in history, you must understand the conflict between Babylon's operating system and the kingdom of God's operating system.

The This-Is-Thatness of Babylon

In my office is a spinning object that rolls on casters attached to a single post holding a plush cushion attached perpendicularly to a metal frame covered with fabric mesh. If you asked an adult what the object was, they would declare: *That's a desk chair.* But if you asked my son, you'd get a different answer: *That's a merry-go-round.* Try as I might, I can't convince him simply to sit in the chair, because his internal "this-is-that" operating system is in conflict with my own. My operating system says *this* rolling object is *that*: a chair. My son's operating system says *this* rolling object is *that*: a carnival ride. If he's on the ride, the ride must spin.

We all have a this-is-that operating system running below our conscious awareness.[28] Mostly, you'll find that your this-is-that operating system aligns well with your neighbor's. For example, if you hear someone use a racial slur, your this-is-that operating system identifies it as barbaric, immoral racism. My this-is-that operating system would do the same thing. But what about a neo-Nazi? His this-is-that operating system might see a racial slur as an act of courage.

Christopher Watkin has suggested that when wide parts of a population disagree about the this-is-thatness of an issue, belief, or behavior, you end up getting culture wars.[29] In a culture war, tribes with competing this-is-that systems battle over who has the right to definitively say *this* is *that* for all people.

Consider the following examples: A same-sex wedding between two partners. Is this a beautiful expression of love, or is it a reversal of God's moral order? A drag-queen story hour for children. Is this a powerful expression of inclusivity, or is it grooming children for sexual deviance? An athlesiure advertisement. Is this a harmless ad for comfortable sweats, or is it an idolatrous declaration that buying more stuff will make you happy?

In a country as large and diverse as the US, multiple this-is-that operating systems run concurrently, which explains why news media driven by different operating systems can interpret the same event in wildly different ways.

Here's the point: Every Babylon has a this-is-that operating system. It may change, fractalize, and develop over time, but it never stops operating. This is part of how Babylon exercises its power over human life: by demanding that individuals and communities conform to its way of seeing the world. Whether it's the this-is-that system of the Right or Left, consumerism or minimalism, or individualism or collectivism, every iteration of Babylon wants your allegiance.

The kingdom of God has its own this-is-that operating system. Jesus's kingdom makes its own claims on your daily reality. Where Babylon sees a merry-go-round, the kingdom of God sees a chair. Where Babylon sees foolishness, the kingdom of God sees wisdom. Where Babylon sees weakness, the kingdom of God sees power. This inevitably makes Christians feel like outsiders in Babylon. Look at how the apostle Paul engaged the this-is-thatness of three opposing operating systems in his day, the kingdom of God, Greco-Roman culture, and Jewish culture:

> Jews demand signs and Greeks look for wisdom, but we preach Christ crucified: a stumbling block to Jews and foolishness to Gentiles, but to those whom God has called, both Jews and Greeks, Christ the power of God and the wisdom of God. For the foolishness of God is wiser than human wisdom, and the weakness of God is stronger than human strength.
>
> Brothers and sisters, think of what you were when you were called. Not many of you were wise by human standards; not many were influential; not many were of noble birth. But God chose the foolish things of the world to shame the wise; God chose the weak things of the world

to shame the strong. God chose the lowly things of this world and the despised things—and the things that are not—to nullify the things that are, so that no one may boast before him.[30]

Paul was an outsider with his fellow Jews because their Jewish operating system saw weakness where Paul's kingdom operating system saw power. Where his Greco-Roman neighbors saw foolishness, Paul's kingdom operating system saw wisdom. These competing systems have real-world consequences. According to Paul, our understanding of the cross as wisdom and power should lead us to care for the weak, poor, and uneducated differently than both Jews and Greeks.

The same tension exists today. Where you see beauty, Babylon sees ugliness. Where you see dignity, Babylon sees dishonor. Where you see invaluablity, Babylon sees disposability. *That* is why you feel tension on a horizontal, sociological level. You see the world differently, and that leads you to live differently in the world.

Explaining the Unbearable Tension

The competition between operating systems explains the unbearable tension you experience every day. You are a de facto dissident. You live out of step with the world around you. That is precisely why the tension is something you can't resolve. To do so, you would need to become like Babylon, destroy Babylon, or leave it altogether. You live in two worlds at the same time: the world that is and the world to come. Michael Goheen wrote, "This unbearable tension is the result of being members of two communities anchored in two different stories. On the one hand, the believer is a member of the cultural community that shares and is shaped by the cultural story. On the other hand, that same believer is a member of the Christian community, a citizen in the kingdom of God, a people formed by the story of the Bible."[31]

You live in unbearable tension because you live in the story God is writing, not the story Babylon is scribbling. God's story begins in a garden called Delight.[32] But everything went sideways when humanity refused to enjoy God's goodness. Instead, we chose idolatry, selfishness, and injustice, creating one Babylon after another to normalize our destructive choices. Yet God refused to give up on his world; he worked through Abraham's family—a family of outsiders, sojourners, and exiles—to replant the delightful garden humanity vandalized. Jesus came as a child of that family to inaugurate his kingdom of love, justice, and mercy. And he now invites anyone who wishes to follow him to become an outsider alongside him and receive the very joy he promises will one day cover the earth as the waters cover the sea. Until that future comes, we live in unbearable tension. A tension made bearable by *his* joy and his joy alone.

Because you have a kingdom operating system, you must not conform to Babylon and become complicit in its evil. If you do so, you will relieve the tension, but you will also cease to be Christian in any meaningful sense.

Because you have a kingdom operating system, you must not become a combatant seeking to overthrow Babylon. Revelation 19 is clear: Babylon will fall, but not at your hands. When Jesus returns, he will strike the final blow. When you become a combatant, you usurp Jesus's kingly timing, authority, and justice.

Because you have a kingdom operating system, you must not avoid or separate from Babylon. Babylon is everywhere, and Jesus has given you the responsibility of cultivating good within it.

Because you have a kingdom operating system, you must not seek the solution in a nostalgic past but in God's future. Only then can you celebrate what he's given you in the present even as you seek to play a role in his future.

How would your life change if you stopped trying to resolve the tension you can't resolve? What if you embraced the kingdom's operating system and sought to cultivate *and* challenge Babylon using God's upside-down ways?

Instead of seeking to resolve the tension, you must learn to wear it. As the Dutch missionary Hendrik Kraemer once observed, Christians are at their healthiest when they have a deep consciousness of the tension *and* a deep willingness to take that yoke upon themselves. He wrote, "The more oblivious of this tension the Church is [and] the more well established and at home in this world it feels, the more it is in deadly danger of being the salt that has lost its savor."[33]

He's right. The tension you feel is not a sign that something is amiss but a sign that something beautiful is growing in your soul. Don't resolve the tension and give up on the future God promises to outsiders. Instead, learn to see the beauty in the tension you can't escape. Because when you're in the tension, you're in it with the beautiful one whose presence promises steadfast joy. You're with the joyful outsider king: Jesus.

CHAPTER 4

Joyful Outsiders

Joy is the infallible sign of the presence of God.
—PIERRE TEILHARD DE CHARDIN

Consider it pure joy, my brothers and sisters, whenever you face trials of many kinds.
—JAMES

We live in one of the most consumeristic cultures in human history. Babylon promises that happiness comes in an abundance of possessions. But Jesus taught the opposite: "Life does not consist in an abundance of possessions."[1] And he warned that "no one can serve two masters. . . . You will hate the one and love the other. . . . You cannot serve both God and money."[2]

Jesus's teachings put joyful outsiders in constant tension with the massive marketing machine churning around us on smartphones, billboards, and TV ads. When we look at a car, house, or outfit we want, we must ask whether we see those things as Babylon does or as Jesus does. If we let our kingdom operating system take the lead, we will seem strange to "normal" people. They'll say, "Why wouldn't you treat yourself? You deserve it. Just imagine how happy you'd be if you bought it!"

In the early years of our church, we met in the auditorium of a local high school. We used classrooms for children's programming and student ministries. It was a fantastic setup. But it didn't last. The school let us know we needed to move on, so we searched for other space but found nothing that could fit our congregation. We realized that if we didn't build a building, our church would need to shut down. But to do that we needed to raise funds from our congregation. They gave with incredible, humbling generosity.

I will never forget opening one pledge in particular. It came from a couple named John and Tanya. When I saw the number on the pledge, I did a double take. It didn't sit well with me. They'd promised too much. I feared they couldn't afford it. But I wasn't sure what to do next. When you're desperate to raise enough money to keep a church alive, it's counterintuitive to call people and encourage them to give less. But that's exactly what I did.

John said I was wrong: It wasn't too much. They'd spent years saving for a boat so they could take their family to the lake on the weekends. But he explained, "We decided we'd rather invest the money in changing lives than in something that will sit in the driveway and need to be waxed." When they saw the need of the church, they decided there was greater joy in giving their money away. Happiness is *not* found in an abundance of possessions.

Of course, plenty of people would find their decision incomprehensible. How could giving make you happier than weekends on the lake? But to this day, John and Tanya don't regret their decision. They tell me that when they see the building full of people worshiping Jesus, and hear the stories of changed lives, they know they made the better choice. They didn't miss out when they gave generously. They chose joy that day. Or, more accurately, Jesus gave them joy, by giving them the strength to live as outsiders in a consumeristic culture.

John and Tanya's story shows that you can't resist the influence of Babylon if you don't love something more than Babylon. You can't say no to Babylon's false promises if you don't know the promises of God. You can't say no to Babylon's false joy if you don't know the true joy Jesus alone offers. In Peter's second letter to the "elect exiles" living in Asia Minor, he makes this point quite clearly: "His divine power has given us everything we need for a godly life through our knowledge of him who called us by his own glory and goodness. Through these he has given us his *very great and precious promises, so that through them you may participate in the divine nature,* having escaped the corruption in the world caused by evil desires."[3]

Peter is saying to those elected to the office of outsider that they will resist the corruption of Babylon *only if* they know God's "precious promises." John and Tanya knew that "it is more blessed to give than to receive."[4] And because they saw the promise of *future* blessing and joy, they were free to resist Babylon's influence in the *present.* Likewise, Jesus endured the cross not by gritting his teeth but by setting his eyes on "the joy set before him."[5] He knew that on the other side of death was resurrection, and after that the throne of heaven. So, scorning the shame that Babylon cast on him for his crucifixion, he obeyed his father in Gethsemane and laid down his life for the world.[6] Thus, when he chose to take up his cross, he chose to take up joy.

To become a *joyful* outsider yourself, you must know the "very great and precious promises" God offers to those who live faithfully as exiles, sojourners, and resident aliens. To help you see those promises in all their glorious goodness, I want to introduce you to an ancient outsider named Ezekiel. He didn't initially experience his exile as a joy. But God showed him his promises, and that changed everything.

Happy Birthday, Ezekiel!

When Ezekiel awoke on his thirtieth birthday, he probably *wanted* to be happy. Many of his friends never made it to their third decade. Instead, Babylonians had slaughtered and burned them in Jerusalem. Ezekiel was one of the lucky few. He survived.

But was *this* life a life worth living? The Babylonians forced Ezekiel to relocate nine hundred miles to the east, where he was expected to conform to their culture, learn their language, and worship their gods. He labored for his conquerors. His captors forced him to cheer, "Long live the king!" to the man who destroyed his hometown.

Before Ezekiel's exile, he'd trained to be a priest in the temple—the dwelling place of Yahweh's presence on earth. So today, his thirtieth birthday, should have been the happiest day of his life. It was supposed to be the day he was admitted into temple service. Instead, he was an exile in Babylon.

Yes, it was his birthday. But there was nothing happy about it. So he walked along a riverbank and wept. He wept for himself. He wept for Jerusalem. He wept for his lost friends. He wept because he would never see the temple again. He wept because his God seemed impossibly distant.

On the horizon a windstorm was blowing in. Lightning illuminated dark clouds. It would almost be a relief for the storm to sweep over him, for a single lightning strike to turn him into cinder and ash like the friends he'd left in the conflagration of Jerusalem. He would never forget the sight of their incinerated bodies, left in a valley just outside Jerusalem. Only their dried bones remained.

But as the storm overtook him, something strange happened. The clouds broke open. A celestial throne emerged on spinning wheels, lifted up by angels, shining like shook foil. A cosmic human figure sat on the throne. His skin glowed like heated bronze. Light danced around him. He was so bright Ezekiel could hardly keep his eyes on him. And with a rush, Ezekiel realized what he was seeing: *this is the glory of Yahweh*. He fell on his face. This was what he'd always wanted but never dreamed possible. Even if he entered the temple, he could never presume to see God's glory. But here was God's glory *in Babylon*.

A voice from the heavens spoke. "Son of man, stand up on your feet and I will speak to you."[7] But Ezekiel couldn't move. A supernatural wind blew over him, carrying him upward like a small boat on a great wave. In many ways this was *not* a happy birthday. And yet it was the best of all birthdays because on it Ezekiel received a joy he'd never imagined possible in exile, a joy he never would've received had he stayed in Jerusalem: the joy of the living presence of God.

God's Promise to Outsiders: Presence

After this experience, Ezekiel's oracles were not always happy ones. I don't think he was a happy, clappy guy in general. But the last third of his writings are chock-full of promises *he* needed to hear as an outsider and that *we* need to hear as well. His prophetic book begins with a beatific vision, not just because that was the moment God called him. It's also because God's presence is the most precious promise outsiders need to know if they want to choose joy.

The promise of God's presence is where we must start because the most common way Babylon gets its hooks into us is by means of *intimidation* and *exclusion*, both of which create a fear that can't be dispelled apart from God's presence.

In chapter 3 we read the story of Bryce, whose DEI board members wanted to fire all the Christians. That's an example of *intimidation*, or hard pressure. But Babylon can be much more subtle. It often uses soft pressure to coerce outsiders to conform. It gently suggests that if you don't get with the program, you might miss out on opportunities like promotions, wealth, and relationships. It quietly warns that if you don't get in line, your reputation may take a hit. It silently threatens embarrassment and shame.

In chapter 2 we read the story of Bill and Susan, whose sons threatened to cut them off if they didn't enthusiastically support the same-sex marriage of their youngest son. This is an example of *exclusion*: the threat that you will lose relationships if you don't conform to Babylon.

Ezekiel was familiar with both tactics and experienced them in far more traumatic ways than the average Christian in the West. Intimidation and exclusion had their intended effect: They made him fearful for his life and livelihood. And there's no escaping the fear, because the fear *is* rational. But it's precisely *in* fear that God offers you a precious promise: *I am with you.* God gave this exact promise to exiles through the prophet Isaiah:

> Fear not, for I am with you;
> Be not dismayed, for I am your God.

I will strengthen you,

Yes, I will help you,

I will uphold you with My righteous right hand.[8]

When I (Patrick) read this, I think of the time I took my daughter Iris bouldering for the first time. After ascending two feet, she broke into a full-blown panic. The entire gym echoed with her cries: "Get me down. *Get me down. GET ME DOWN!*"

I could've calmly replied with the truth: "You're barely off the ground." But that wouldn't have helped. When panic takes over, logic rarely calms us. So instead, I got close to her. I placed my hands firmly on her shoulders. Then I made a promise: "I'm with you. I won't let you fall. Do you trust me?" She nodded, slowed her breathing, extended her arm upward, and climbed on. When she got back down, I showed her the place where she panicked. She laughed and said, "That's not high at all!" I agreed. She gave me a hug and said, "Thanks for being with me, Dad."

My presence chased away her fear. It gave her the courage to climb. And in the end, she experienced immense joy. In the same way, God promises to be with you as an outsider. Sometimes he'll call you to little more than a two-foot climb. But other times he'll call you to the utmost heights of courage. On your own you can't do either. Fear will take over. But that's precisely when you need to take hold of his promise: *He is with you. He will help you. He will uphold you with his righteous right hand.* When you grip his promised presence like a rock on a climbing wall, you will find both bravery and joy because there's no greater happiness than being with him. So choose joy. Resist Babylon's threats by means of God's promised presence.

God's Promise to Outsiders: An Eternal Future Restoration

The exiles in Babylon knew far more loss than you or me. They lost family, friends, possessions, and homes. They had little, and what little they had left them hopeless about their future. But God gave Ezekiel a vision of future restoration: "They say, 'Our bones are dried up and our hope is gone; we are cut off.' Therefore prophesy and say to them: 'This is what the Sovereign LORD says: My people, I am going to open your graves and bring you up from them; I will bring you back to the land of Israel.'"[9]

God promised that the dry bones of the long dead would one day come back to life. He would draw his people back to himself, end their exile, and restore all that was lost. Because God was with them in the *present*, they could rest assured that he would carry them into his promised *future*.

God makes the same promise to you: He has secured your future. He promises to restore all things, resurrect you, and live with you forever. Whatever Babylon takes from you in the present is paltry compared with what Jesus has secured for you in the age to come. This is a promise outsiders need to hear, especially when Babylon threatens to take the things we *think* we need to survive.

Consider the joyful outsiders living in China. Jesus followers there are faced with a terrible choice: either worship in heretical state-sanctioned churches or join an underground house church and risk losing everything.[10] The outsiders who choose to trust God know they'll experience police raids. The question is how they will respond. The answer? They take hold of God's promise to give them a restored future.

When the police threaten to confiscate their homes, they respond, "Then we will be free to trust God for shelter as well as for our daily bread."[11] When the police threaten to beat them, they respond, "Then we will be free to trust Jesus for healing."[12] When the police threaten to throw them in prison, they respond, "Then we will be free to preach the good news of Jesus to the captives, to set them free."[13] When the police finally threaten to kill them unless they stop worshiping Jesus, they respond, "Then we will be free to go to heaven and be with Jesus forever."[14]

None of these Christians want terrible things to happen to them. They don't want their houses confiscated. They don't want to be beaten, thrown in prison, or killed. Yet they're free to respond with joy and *without* fear because they understand God's promise to outsiders: *I will give you a future. I will gather together my people. I will resurrect the dead. I will restore what was lost. I will set wrongs to right.*

We, too, can suffer with joy today. Not because it's pleasant. But because we know it's temporary. We know that "this light momentary affliction is preparing for us an eternal weight of glory beyond all comparison."[15] So we look beyond the suffering everyone else sees and set our eyes on "things that are unseen."[16] We fix our gaze on God's promised future. We take hold of this eternal truth: Outsiders will not only know God's presence in the present but will also enjoy his presence into eternity. We choose to suffer *because* we choose joy.

What do you fear losing because you're an outsider? A job? Jesus has an eternal vocation for you! Your comfort? Jesus will eternally wipe away your every tear! Your security? Jesus will keep you safe forever! A friend? Jesus will be the dearest friend you've ever known. Your life? Jesus will resurrect you into eternal joy!

God promised ancient outsiders, "They will live in safety, and no one will make them afraid. . . . You are my sheep, the sheep of my pasture, and I am your God."[17] The same promise holds for you. Your shepherd is with you in exile. He promises to restore all you've lost and all you fear losing. Let that promise free you to live as a *joyful* outsider.

Tightroping across the Niagara

The greatest joy of outsiders is the nearness of God. But I hope you now understand that his nearness is reserved for those who let go of their fear and take hold of Jesus in Babylon. It's a joy you can't fully experience if you relieve the unbearable tension, because it's a joy that lives *within* tension. When I think on this, I think of the terrifying choice made by Harry Colcord in 1859. Two weeks before Colcord's courageous decision, a tightrope walker named Charles Blondin stretched a tightrope across Niagara Falls. Twenty-five thousand people came to watch, with more than a few hoping to see him perish.

"There were hundreds of people examining the rope," reported one witness, "and, with scarcely an exception, they all declared the inability of M. Blondin to perform the feat, the incapacity of the rope to sustain him, and that he deserved to be dashed to atoms for his desperate fool-hardiness."[18]

Blondin stepped out, and the crowd fell silent. Seventy-three-mile-per-hour winds buffeted him from every side. About halfway across, he sat on the tightrope and dropped a rope to a ship anchored 190 feet below him. Perhaps he was too tired or dizzy to continue? No. To the crowd's horror, he wanted some wine. Crew members tied a bottle to the rope, which Blondin pulled upward, uncorked, and enjoyed from his perch. Once finished, he completed the trek easily. The crowd erupted with applause.

But Blondin wasn't finished. During the ensuing weeks, he proceeded to accomplish more stunning feats. He carried a massive camera halfway across the rope and took a photo of the crowd. He tightroped backward. He tightroped without a balance beam. He tightroped with a bag over his head.

The crowds began to believe he could do anything. After two weeks of stunts, he tested their faith: *Would any man be willing to climb on his back and let Blondin carry him across?*

Only one man had the courage. Blondin's manager, Harry Colcord, raised his hand. The pair set out together, but their weight was more than the guy wires holding the tightrope steady could take. The wires began to snap. The rope swayed dangerously left and then right. Colcord's heart raced. His adrenaline pumped. Fear took hold.

Then Blondin said to him, "Look up, Harry. You are no longer Colcord. You are Blondin. Until I clear this place, be a part of me, mind, body, and soul. If I sway, sway with me. Do not attempt to do any balancing yourself. If you do, we will both go to our death."[19]

Colcord took Blondin's words to heart. He remembered what Blondin had already accomplished and allowed Blondin's confident, nonanxious presence to calm his nerves. For a brief moment Colcord became one with Blondin. Miraculously, they made it to the other side alive.

When you accept God's call to be a joyful outsider, you accept Jesus's invitation to crawl on his back and allow him to carry you to a better future. The journey is fraught with danger. Fear *is* a rational response. But if you refuse his invitation, you will be left behind in the crowd watching Jesus. Cheering for him, yes, but distant from him. Only those who receive his calling to be outsiders and take hold of his promises know the profound joy of clinging to his presence and becoming one with him on the tightrope. You don't climb on his shoulders because you're the most courageous, intelligent, or wise person. You don't take this journey because you're confident you know how to balance. No, you do it because you trust him. You do it because you know what he's already done. Jesus *already* passed through death once and came out the other side alive. He knows what he's doing. You take this journey because you *want* joy and you know there is no greater joy than being one with him on the tightrope.

The only reason you can climb on his shoulders is because you've already received one of his most precious promises. It's a promise Ezekiel saw in a vision. It's a promise Jesus fulfilled by dying on a cross: God promised to forgive us, cleanse us, indwell us, and transform us: "I will sprinkle clean water on you, and you will be clean; I will cleanse you from all your impurities and from all your idols. I will give you a new heart and put a new spirit in you; I will remove from you your heart of stone and give you a heart of flesh. And I will put my Spirit in you and move you to follow my decrees and be careful to keep my laws."[20]

You are forgiven and transformed and indwelled by God's Spirit. *That's* why you can raise your hand and clamber onto Jesus's back. God's promises are for outsiders. God's presence is with outsiders. God's future is for outsiders. God's mercy is showered upon outsiders. Take hold of these promises whether you're afraid, angry, or confused. If you do, you will come to know an unshakable joy that can only be experienced in the tension, on the tightrope with Jesus.

The Next Step on Your Journey

In the second part of this book, you'll discover practical ways to live as a joyful outsider. We'll learn six ways to live like Jesus in the unbearable tension. My hope is that you will closely identify with one or two ways and begin to actively practice them in your local community.

But as we close part 1 of this book, I pray that you more clearly understand the nature of your calling. God called you to be an outsider. He placed you in the tension. He elected you for this. Your outsiderness will not change, because it can't change until Jesus returns, renews the earth, and finally transforms it into the home we've always longed for. Until then I hope you resist the temptation to relieve the tension. I hope you choose joy by taking hold of God's precious promises. And I pray that you do all this by the Father's grace, the Spirit's power, and the Son's atoning blood. Fear not, friends. *He* is with you.

PART 2

Six Ways to Be Joyful Outsiders

CHAPTER 5

Finding Your Way

[Life] is like a play in which the scene and the general outline of the story is fixed by the author, but certain minor details are left for the actors to improvise.

—C. S. LEWIS

The church is not called to play the same scene over and over but to take the gospel into new situations. To be faithful in its witness, the church must constantly be different. Indeed, at times it must even improvise.

—KEVIN J. VANHOOZER

After the Bremerton High School football game ended, coach Joe Kennedy did exactly what he'd done after games for the last five years: He walked to the center of the field, took a knee on the fifty-yard line, and thanked Jesus.

Normally, these prayers lasted only thirty seconds. But this one was longer. Students, coaches, and fans from both teams joined him. But most of the spectators watched with dismay. *This prayer was grossly inappropriate for a public event.* Disgruntled fans bowled over the marching band, shouting curses at Kennedy, racing onto the field to hurl insults at everyone praying. It became so intense that one coach later told reporters he feared he might be shot.[1]

Why all the fervor? Because this prayer wasn't just a prayer. It was an act of protest. A week earlier the school district's superintendent, Aaron Leavell, ordered Kennedy to cease and desist his end-of-game prayers. In a letter to Kennedy, Leavell explained that although Kennedy didn't invite or encourage students to join him, his actions could be misconstrued as endorsing in-school prayer, "exposing the District to significant risk of liability."[2]

Kennedy refused to stop. A week after his first protest, he prayed again. Then again the week after that. Finally, the district had enough. Kennedy was placed on paid administrative leave. He wouldn't return to the field for another eight years, during which he was embroiled in a legal battle that made its way to the Supreme Court.[3]

But one part of this story is rarely told: The superintendent was *also* a devout Christian. In fact, Leavell and Kennedy attended the *same* church. Both were outsiders living in a city that, like much of the greater Seattle area, is largely nonreligious. Only a quarter of Bremerton's population identifies as Christian.[4] This means that Kennedy and Leavell were both navigating the same question: *How do I live as an outsider in Babylon?* But they came to radically different answers.

Leavell's position was in alignment with many historic Christian traditions. For example, the Southern Baptist Convention celebrated the Supreme Court's decision to ban school prayer.[5] Indeed, he may have believed that his approach followed Jesus's teachings about public prayer: "When you pray, do not be like the hypocrites, for they love to pray standing in the synagogues and on the street corners to be seen by others.... But when you pray, go into your room, close the door and pray to your Father, who is unseen."[6]

But Kennedy might demur. His position was also in alignment with a different teaching. Jesus told us not to hide our light and warned, "Whoever is ashamed of me and my words, the Son of Man will be ashamed of them."[7]

What do you think? Who was right? What's the best thing for an outsider to do? Anyone who's lived through a moment of intense cultural strife knows that Kennedy and Leavell aren't alone. Followers of Jesus in America rarely agree on the best approach to our post-Christian society. These disagreements easily flare into heated debates, church splits, or (as was the case with Coach Kennedy) people leaving the church.[8]

But when I consider such difficult questions, I find myself wondering if we're asking the wrong questions. What if searching for one "right" response distracts us from the possibility that there may be *many* right responses? What if there isn't a one-size-fits-all approach to our culture? What if we need protesters like Kennedy *and* leaders like Leavell? What if Jesus is inviting us into a complex song with many voices? A mosaic with many colors? A body with many parts?

Is There One Right Way to Live in Babylon?

To test my hypothesis, I want you to create a list of three Christians who have lived as outsiders and yet made a significant impact on Babylon. You can write them in the following space:

1.

2.

3.

My room would include three luminaries from three countries:

1. Dietrich Bonhoeffer, who lived during the rise of Nazism in Germany and founded an underground seminary. He joined a failed assassination plot against Hitler and later died in a concentration camp.
2. Martin Luther King Jr., who led the Civil Rights Movement in the US from 1955 until his assassination in 1968. He emphasized nonviolence as the core of effective *and* ethical Christian protest.

3. Saint Teresa of Calcutta, who founded hundreds of orphanages, hospices, and leper houses across India to care for those oppressed by India's caste system. She emphasized care for the poor and unborn.

Once you have your list, imagine bringing all three people into one room and asking them to explain their approach to culture. Do they all agree? Do they share the same emphases? Now imagine asking them, "How should outsiders faithfully represent Jesus in a hostile culture?"

Bonhoeffer might justify his assassination plot, saying, "We are not to simply bandage the wounds of victims beneath the wheels of injustice. We are to drive a spoke into the wheel itself."[9] But King might demur and say, "We adopt the means of nonviolence because our end is a community at peace with itself."[10] Finally, Saint Teresa might step in and say, "If you want to bring peace to the whole world, go home and love your family, your neighbor, the poor, and the unborn."[11]

So who is right? Who is wrong? The question becomes even more complex when we consider the biblical outsiders. Daniel might say, "I did not fight my enemies but allowed them to throw me into a lions' den so they could feast on my body," only to hear Esther retort, "I threw a feast to destroy my enemies!" Nehemiah might say, "I built a wall to keep the people of Samaria out," only to hear Jesus respond, "I spilled my blood to tear down the wall between Jews and Samaritans."

In the two millennia after Jesus, Christians have argued for a dizzying array of approaches. Some argue that Christians should seek to take power and become Christian magistrates who impose Christian laws. Others assert that Christians should embrace the concurrent reality of two kingdoms: (1) a worldly kingdom with temporary authority that orders common life and the state and (2) a heavenly kingdom with eternal authority that orders the church and salvation. Others say that the church should withdraw from the world and become a counterculture so it can witness to the truth and beauty of Jesus by collectively living true and beautiful lives, not taking worldly power. Still others have suggested that followers of Jesus should seek to transform the spheres in which they work by being a faithful presence.

Christ *over* culture. Christ *against* culture. Christ *transforming* culture. Feel dizzy yet? The debates rage on. The contours change with time. After all, what it means to be a joyful outsider in the era of Roman emperors is different than what it means to be a joyful outsider in the era of Christian monarchies or post-Christian prime ministers or anti-Christian totalitarians.

The simple truth is that a single view has never achieved widespread acceptance. And everyday Christians, who are already exhausted trying to navigate their everyday life as outsiders, find little help in highly theoretical debates. That's not to say these debates aren't of value. I rather enjoy highly theoretical disputations. I have opinions on all these things, which you can read in a very long endnote.[12] But here's the short version: I've come to believe that the value of each of these positions is found *not* by picking one and sticking with it but instead by learning from each of them and using all of them to *improvise* our part in a grand performance with many voices.

We need Daniel *and* Esther, Jesus *and* Nehemiah, MLK *and* Bonhoeffer. When they sing together, they sound not like a discordant muddle but a *harmonious whole*. As with an old fugue, each take the same melody— sung best and brightest by Christ—and sing it in fresh ways, harmonizing above and below one another in a polyphony so rich you would weep if you heard it.

We can join this song as well, but to do so we must learn to hold a second tension in ourselves: the tension between resisting and cultivating Babylon.

Holding a Second Tension: Resist or Cultivate?

If you've ever been in a situation like the Bremerton High School football prayers, you've probably found yourself debating with friends. By the end of the debate, you probably divide into two camps: those who think our calling is to *resist* Babylon and those who think our calling is to *cultivate*

Babylon. Kennedy and Leavell were a microcosm of this debate. The coach publicly resisted the non-Christian culture around him, while the superintendent sought to cultivate it.

But what if the key to singing in harmony *isn't* picking one side? What if we must do both at the same time? This is precisely what the prophet Jeremiah called the Jewish outsiders in Babylon to do. He told them to hold cultivation and resistance *in tension*.

To understand what I mean, imagine holding a short rope between your hands. If you want the rope to be taut, what do you do? You pull to the left and the right simultaneously. You *create* tension with opposing forces. If you let go of one side, the rope will fall limp. There will be no tension. If you try to move both hands to the middle, the rope will droop. There will be little tension. In a similar way, joyful outsiders can't choose one side (resistance *or* cultivation) and leave the other hanging. There would be no tension. Nor should we seek the middle position (resist halfway and cultivate halfway) and leave the rope drooping. Instead, the Bible calls use to pull hard in both directions: to resist Babylon courageously *and* cultivate Babylon self-sacrificially. No place is this clearer than in the words of Jeremiah, a prophet who wrote to the earliest exiles living in Babylon. Let's explore how he encouraged them to pull hard in both directions.

Resisting Babylon's Idolatry

Jeremiah warned the exiles that Babylon was a spiritually dangerous and temporary residence. They would be tempted to conform to its culture, but they needed to resist. Why? Because God's justice would fall on Babylon for its idolatry and injustice, and if the exiles conformed, they would be swept up in the currents of his just wrath:

> Announce and proclaim among the nations,
>> lift up a banner and proclaim it;
>> keep nothing back, but say,
> "Babylon will be captured;
>> Bel will be put to shame,

> Marduk filled with terror.
>> Her images will be put to shame
>> and her idols filled with terror."[13]

Bel (a favored god of Babylon) is destined to burn, and it would be better *not* to be caught in the conflagration. Instead, Jeremiah called the exiles to repent of the ways they conformed to Babylon, to "go in tears to seek the LORD their God" and bind themselves to him in an "everlasting covenant that will not be forgotten."[14] To do that they would need to develop loose ties to Babylon, knowing that one day they would need to flee. Jeremiah wrote,

> Flee from Babylon!
>> Run for your lives!
>> Do not be destroyed because of her sins.
> It is time for the LORD's vengeance;
>> he will repay her what she deserves.[15]

Jeremiah is telling the exiles that Babylon is something like a spiritual airport. It's an in-between place. Jerusalem was behind them, and their ultimate destination was before them. But in the present, they were wandering a glossy, soul-numbingly hollow airport, waiting for their plane to dock in the terminal and take them home. So Jeremiah's advice was straightforward. Keep your bags close. Don't fall in love with the airport's cruddy pizza, mediocre coffee, or lame magazines. This airport is not your home. You're only passing through. When the boarding call comes, be ready to run. After all, you can't resist something you love, so resist it by loving something better: the beautiful, eternal, gracious, loving king of the universe.

Cultivating Babylon

Paradoxically, Jeremiah *also* told the exiles to do the apparent opposite. He warned that they wouldn't be leaving any time soon and thus needed to cultivate their new residence. We see this message most clearly in a letter Jeremiah wrote to the exiled community. In it he warns them that false prophets would call them to become combative outsiders and revolt.[16] But Jeremiah explained that this wasn't what God wanted. Instead, he wanted the outsiders *to work for the welfare of Babylon*. Echoing the creation story in Genesis 1–2, Jeremiah's letter called the exiles to be fruitful and multiply and cultivate Babylon like a new Eden:

> This is what the LORD Almighty, the God of Israel, says to all those I carried into exile from Jerusalem to Babylon: "Build houses and settle down; plant gardens and eat what they produce. Marry and have sons and daughters; find wives for your sons and give your daughters in marriage, so that they too may have sons and daughters. Increase in number there; do not decrease. Also, seek the peace and prosperity of the city to which I have carried you into exile. Pray to the LORD for it, because if it prospers, you too will prosper."[17]

Joyful outsiders were not to become Babylonians, and yet they were to serve Babylon better than Babylonians. Their businesses, charities, and life together were never to become insular affairs. Instead, they were to become such good neighbors to their Babylonian captors that no one would want them to leave.

In conclusion, it is clear that Jeremiah wanted the exiles to hold cultivation and resistance together. Why? Because that tension generated the creativity they needed to live faithfully as joyful outsiders. Jeremiah would want the same thing for you! Your exile is creative tension. It is holy improvisation. It is living loosely to the powers of the world even as you serve them with excellence. It is building houses but never making a home. It is planting vineyards while waiting for the wine of God's kingdom. It is living like a foreigner and loving like a native. If you want to join the ancient, harmonious chorus, you must learn to hold this tension in yourself.

Improvising inside the Tension

Of course, a single individual can't hold *all* the tension of resistance and cultivation. The tension is too big, and the problems too complex. But thankfully God doesn't call you to hold it alone. He calls you to hold it with others.

If we could lower the volume on our fights about how best to react to Babylon, we would be able to hear that God ordered his church such that it can sing his song in many voices. That song is incomplete if any of the harmonies drop out. The greatest offering we can give our king is a song in which cultivation and resistance resonate and become one melody.

The apostle Paul said something similar by means of a different metaphor. He described the church as one body with many parts.[18] He was speaking about spiritual gifts, but I believe the same principle applies to how we outsiders flee from Babylon *and* make it flourish. Unity is not the same thing as uniformity. True unity occurs when diverse people with diverse temperaments and talents, hailing from diverse backgrounds, and living in diverse contexts, all merge into a single mosaic telling a single story.

The ancient outsiders whose stories fill the Old Testament were not cut from the same cloth. They responded to their moments with remarkable adaptability. Daniel advised King Nebuchadnezzar. But Shadrach, Meshach, and Abednego resisted him. Esther protested Xerxes's decree. But Ezra fulfilled the decree of Xerxes's son. Nehemiah rebuilt Jerusalem. But Malachi confronted its failures. The Bible is not a book of contradictions. It's a book that embraces improvisation and harmony. The question you must answer is which role God is calling *you* to play.

Finding Your Role in the Story

We all narrate our lives. We imagine ourselves to live in some sort of story, and the story we choose shapes our future more than few other things. Babylon is a master storyteller. It may be a grand story of an imperial destiny—which was the history founding of Babylon's mythology. Or it could be a bespoke story of personal discovery and self-actualization—the West's current favored tale. Either way, we must see ourselves in some drama, and once chosen we have little choice but to play our role.

Few lives illustrate the importance of story as well as Hiroo Onoda's. In December 1944, Onoda—a Japanese Imperial Army intelligence officer—landed on Lubang Island in the Philippines. After only a few weeks on duty, an Allied attack forced him to flee into Lubang's thick jungles. Hiroo dug in with a few friends, using their training in guerrilla warfare to continue their fight on behalf of the Japanese emperor.

Nine months later, World War II ended, but Hiroo had no idea. Using a hand-crank radio, he tuned in to broadcasts from Tokyo claiming the war had ended. But Hiroo believed they were Allied propaganda designed to fool guerrilla fighters into abandoning their positions.

Hiroo held his jungle post for thirty years. He never stopped believing the story he'd told himself: *The emperor still reigns over Japan. The war is not over.* As the years passed, his friends disappeared. Did they leave? Were they killed? Hiroo didn't know. In 1972 Hiroo witnessed his last friend die in a firefight with the Philippine military. Two years later, the local military begged Hiroo's former commanding officer to travel to Lubang to convince Hiroo to live in the true story: The war was long over. It was time to come home.

The officer came. He found Hiroo and convinced him of the truth. They emerged from the jungle together, Hiroo in well-kept fatigues. When Hiroo stepped out, he wept uncontrollably. He'd lost three decades living a lie. Now he could finally make sense of his life in light of the truth: *He was no longer a soldier. He was free.*

I fear that when it comes to culture, many followers of Jesus are living in the *wrong* story—thus, they become complicit, combative, cloistered, conflict-avoidant, or nostalgic. The goal of part 1 of this book was to set you free from those narratives and give you a better story: You are a joyful outsider.

But now, as we leave the jungle behind, we are much like Hiroo. Free from the past, we must now decide how to live *into* the future. That is what the remainder of *Joyful Outsiders* seeks to offer you: six ways to live like Jesus in Babylon. To do that I will share stories of our forefathers and foremothers in the faith, hoping that one or two of them might help you to play your future role with excellence. Perhaps it's to this the end that the author of Hebrews wrote, "Therefore, since we are surrounded by such a great cloud of witnesses, let us throw off everything that hinders and the sin that so easily entangles. And let us run with perseverance the race marked out for us, fixing our eyes on Jesus, the pioneer and perfecter of faith."[19]

Hebrews is saying you're part of an ancient story that lives on through you. So take joy in the drama of it all. Play your part with gusto! The following six chapters are designed to give you models based on the lives of people in that "great cloud of witnesses." As you read through the six ways, imagine yourself as an understudy, learning from the masters how to play your part well.

As you learn to play your part, you'll be challenged not merely to ape the deeds of the past but to improvise a new story in harmony with the greater story of Jesus. When you live out the gospel story in new contexts, you'll find that God calls forth fresh words, new actions, and new songs.[20] But we don't improvise for the sake of newness. We improvise for the sake of God's glory. So endeavor to know God's story so well that you won't botch your lines and will instead offer your king a faithful performance that delights him. His Spirit is with you in the acting. He will strengthen you to improvise with wisdom.

I also hope that as you read about the six ways, you'll remember that we've been *collectively* called to hold together the tension of resistance and cultivation. We must learn to appreciate each other and remember that this is not a drama with one character but many. Some of the six ways lean more heavily into resistance and others into cultivation, but the beauty is that *together* we hold the tension as one body. So I hope that as you learn about the ways that do not suit your temperament, interests, or talents, you will learn to appreciate them nonetheless as necessary parts of Jesus's story in Babylon.

Lastly, I hope you remember that even though you're an *ordinary* person, that doesn't mean you're too small, too weak, or too insignificant to be used by God. Quite the opposite. Lesslie Newbigin wrote, "It has been in situations where faithfulness to the gospel placed the church in a position of total weakness and rejection that the advocate has himself risen up and, often through the words and deeds of very 'insignificant' people, spoken the word that confronted and shamed the wisdom and power of the world."[21]

The weaker you are, the more God's strength shines through you. The smaller you are, the greater his greatness. It is when the world most rejects you that you come to know the magnitude of God's acceptance in Christ Jesus, your Lord.

What's Next

Before you move on, I recommend jumping to page 203, where I've supplied a short diagnostic that will help you determine which of the six ways you are most closely aligned with: the trainer, the advisor, the artist, the ambassador, the protester, and the builder. There are short descriptions of each way after the test. I recommend taking the test with friends who can help you evaluate your results.

Each of the following chapters follows a similar pattern: (1) How that particular way seeks to change Babylon. (2) Guiding principles for how to walk in that way, drawn from biblical characters. (3) A short biographical story of a Christian who walked in that way. (4) The temptations, or "shadow side," of those who walk in that way.

If you want to go further in practicing your way, then make sure to check out the section on key practices for each way at the back of the book. If you implement those practices, you will discover that you not only *know* your role but also can *live* it.

Finally, remember: I don't present these six ways as a means of earning God's favor or impressing your Christian friends. No, I offer them because you *already* have God's favor in Jesus. Thus, I trust that his Spirit is at work in you to shape you and guide you into the role he's set apart for you.[22]

So now it's time to begin the second leg of your journey and explore *how* to live as a joyful outsider.

Overview of the Six Ways

In the following sections, I briefly describe each of the six ways to follow Jesus in a confusing culture. These are also provided at the end of every chapter and after the six ways personal inventory on page 203. We provide them here so you can easily refer to them as you're reading through the remainder of the book.

It is worth noting that while we explore only six ways in *Joyful Outsiders*, that should not imply that there are *only* six ways. Likewise, there are certain aspects of each way that God calls every Christian to follow, so it's incredibly important that, although you may most identify with one or two ways, you do not neglect the breadth of God's call on your life. It won't do to say, "I'm not a trainer, so I don't need to have a regular practice of Bible reading" or "I'm not a protester, so I don't need to speak up when someone's being oppressed." God has called all of us to read his Word and speak up for the oppressed.

Thus, our hope is that the six ways will offer you a place to *start* on your journey toward becoming a joyful outsider and that in the course of your life you will learn to lean into all six.

The Trainer

Trainers are people who take deep joy in spiritual disciplines. They help others do likewise through one-to-one discipleship, small groups, teaching, or prayer. They have a passion for personal holiness and understand that spiritual practices are a key means by which God conforms us to the image of Christ. They earnestly want to help the church become a holy counterculture that attracts those whom Babylon discards and shows Babylon a better, more beautiful way to be human.

Key Insight: Trainers see that *all* humans share an internal readiness to do evil. But Jesus forgives us and promises to transform us. Thus, his Spirit can cultivate a readiness to do good in each of us when we structure our lives around the spiritual disciplines he practiced.

Orientation toward Culture: Trainers see that the church can change the world only if it is a holy counterculture, exemplifying life, goodness, kindness, justice, and generosity where Babylon does the opposite. To help the church become that sort of counterculture, trainers commit themselves to spiritual disciplines, which are the means by which God graciously transforms us.

Guiding Principles: Trainers understand that if we want to resist Babylon when the stakes are high, we must practice saying no when the stakes are low. Thus, they commit themselves to disciplines of abstinence like fasting, solitude, silence, and sabbath-keeping. They have a passion for renewal and revival but understand that it comes only by God's power. Thus, they embrace trusting prayer and personal sacrifice, waiting on him to act. Additionally, they're committed to the rigorous study, application, and teaching of God's Word, seeing it as the ethical and theological cornerstone of the church's countercultural witness. Lastly, they seek to help the church become a holy counterculture, understanding that the church changes the world by being a beautiful church.

Shadow Side: Trainers are often tempted by pride, believing that their superior discipline makes them superior followers of Jesus. If left unchecked, that pride bubbles into legalism. The trainer begins to create rules that others must follow to be serious themselves. Eventually legalism leads to judgmentalism. At this point trainers often become cloistered Christians, judging other followers of Jesus as half-hearted and uncommitted. They search for a more serious church with more serious Christians, rather than serving churches in need.

The Advisor

Advisors recognize that elite institutions have the power to shape culture. They pursue professional excellence and personal character, hoping to be invited into important discussions within those institutions where they can exert influence to resist evil and cultivate good within Babylon.

Key Insight: On both a national and local scale, certain individuals have an outsized influence. Their decisions affect more people than the average person's. Thus, advisors understand that access to the rooms where big decisions are made is necessary if you want to work for the common good.

Orientation toward Culture: Advisors recognize that they are outsiders in Babylon but can still influence outcomes if they are in the right room with the right people at the right time. Advisors seek to influence the influential, not for the sake of gaining power but for the sake of God's kingdom. They use their influence to encourage leaders to make choices that positively influence people's lives and resist choices that lead to injustice or harm.

Guiding Principles: Advisors know that only people who do their jobs with excellence, respect those in authority, and display character in their personal and professional lives get invited into the rooms where important decisions are made. Although they are personally above reproach, they know that Babylon doesn't share their values, so they develop the requisite wisdom to navigate morally ambiguous situations. When possible, they try to nudge Babylon toward the good, knowing that while perfection is never possible, *proximate* goodness is better than evil.

Shadow Side: The same competitive spirit that drives the advisor to pursue vocational excellence can lead them to put their personal priorities over the king's priorities. Seduced by power, many advisors become nothing more than court prophets who celebrate a leader's wrongheaded ideas and desires rather than courageously challenging them.

The Artist

Artists are those who see light in darkness, beauty in ugliness, hope in despair. They walk the border of heaven and earth, life and death, health and sickness. Through rigorous training and practice, they hone their artistic skills to create beauty. Not the cheap beauty of sentimentalism but the rich beauty of imaginative hope rooted in an equally rich empathy for Babylon's castaways. Artists make beauty both to confront the world's ugliness and to cultivate the good within it.

> **Key Insight:** Artists understand that God designed the human soul with a hunger for beauty. But evil and injustice have marred God's beautiful world and made much of it ugly. Thus, true beauty has the power not only to challenge the ugliness but also to paint a picture of our shared dream: God's kingdom on earth as in heaven.
>
> **Orientation toward Culture:** Artists do not join forces with culture warriors who value art only if it is useful for their particular interests: commercial, political, or ideological. Instead of culture-warring, artists practice culture care, intentionally giving away the gift of beauty, just as God gave us the gift of beauty in his creation. They understand that when humans feed on beauty, it not only nourishes them but also confronts Babylon's ugliness and points all people toward the lovely kingdom of Christ.
>
> **Guiding Principles:** Artists labor to practice and hone their craft, understanding that beauty can't be created without profound skill. They endeavor to live as "border walkers," those who live between heaven and earth, healing and pain. This allows them to empathize with the pain in the world (the opposite of sentimentalism) *and* project new possibilities for the world (the opposite of cynicism). To that end, they intentionally cultivate a hopeful imagination, which resists our modern penchant for irony and despair.
>
> **Shadow Side:** Artists are often misunderstood in the church, which

sometimes leads them to abandon the church. In their isolation, artists sometimes give themselves to their emotions, especially despair. If they do, they actively isolate themselves from others, giving in to the lies of self-loathing. In such a condition, they become easy prey for Babylon's artists, whose skill and influence sometimes persuade artists to leave behind not only the church but Jesus as well.

The Ambassador

Ambassadors find great joy in sharing the gospel with people and seeing them come to faith in Jesus. They know they represent Jesus to the people in their lives, so they are careful to live in a way that makes the gospel attractive and does not hinder their neighbor's faith journey. By leading people to Jesus, ambassadors hope to bring fundamental change to Babylon one heart at a time.

> **Key Insight:** Ambassadors believe that apart from Jesus, every human has a hole in their heart. So rather than fixating on all the secondary issues that plague humanity, they address the fundamental problem by sharing the gospel. This requires them to build bridges, make friendships, and practice hospitality.
>
> **Orientation toward Culture:** Ambassadors know that until we address the hole in every human heart, all our attempts to solve social problems will fall short. Genuine cultural change can't just be legislated. Therefore, ambassadors believe the best way to change Babylon is to help people develop a relationship with God.
>
> **Guiding Principles:** Ambassadors don't measure success by their personal comfort and reputation but by the gospel's progress in the world. They fervently pray for the lost, asking God to give them opportunities to talk to their neighbor about Jesus. They keep careful watch over their lives to ensure that they attract people to Jesus rather than repelling them with immorality or self-righteousness.

Shadow Side: An ambassador's enthusiasm to see people become Christians can lead them to treat people like projects. Likewise, it can cause them to water down the gospel message, emphasizing decisions for Christ over discipleship. They sometimes over-emphasize the importance of the individual and minimize the ways in which legal and cultural systems harm others.

The Protester

Protesters know God opposes injustice and invites his people to join their voices with his. They have sensitive consciences and deeply feel the plight of those in need. Thus, they speak courageously on behalf of the powerless, knowing they will often suffer as a result. They protest with words and actions, both public and private, knowing that the only way to cultivate justice in Babylon is by first resisting injustice.

Key Insight: God wants his creation to flourish, but corruption and oppression jeopardize his good plans. Protesters are strengthened by God's beautiful vision, knowing that the moral arc of the universe bends toward justice. They participate in God's mission by bending history toward God's ends with both words and actions that show the evil of injustice.

Orientation toward Culture: Protesters change Babylon by challenging injustice. They understand that those in power rarely change without external pressure. But exerting pressure requires a critical mass—people must be rallied. Once enough people join a cause, it's possible to generate legal and cultural change.

Guiding Principles: Protesters have a strong sense of moral clarity, rooted in biblical ethics, which allows them to discern when it is right to actively resist those in power. Doing so comes with great risk, which means protesters must be courageous. But they don't need just *any* kind of courage. They need the kind of courage that comes from confidence in God's promises. They commit themselves to Jesus's ethic of nonviolence, not only because it's effective but also because they seek to create communities that love their neighbor and their enemy. Above all else, they are hopeful: The world *can* change, and that means their work is not in vain.

Shadow Side: Protesters are tempted by easy, costless ways to protest online. When this happens, their protest becomes a performance. It's more about their reputation than the cause itself. Sometimes they go one step further, using the cause for personal gain: fame or fortune. In such scenarios, they have to gin up more grievances, and demonize their opponents, just to keep their protest running. God's cause fades into the background, and the protest is all that matters.

The Builder

Builders are individuals whom God has gifted to lead and preserve institutions like businesses, charities, schools, hospitals, churches, and governmental offices. Rather than chasing the American dream, they build institutions that seek Jesus's vision of the common good. This entails *wholistic* human flourishing, not just *material* human flourishing. Builders try to construct social structures that are durable and communal, not short-term and individualistic.

Key Insight: Builders understand that God designed humans to share a common life inside institutions. When that common life is aimed toward the common good, those institutions become catalysts for human flourishing.

Orientation toward Culture: Most institutions in America direct themselves toward the American dream: an individualistic life accompanied by material wealth and material consumption. But such institutions lead to loneliness, disconnection, and ugliness. Thus, builders construct their institutions both as an act of resistance (they reject the American dream) and as an act of cultivation (they build toward Jesus's dream).

Guiding Principles: Builders construct durable institutions designed to provide long-term wholeness, healing, and prosperity not only for those inside the institutions but also for those outside. They ensure that their institutions are communal. They value the good of the community over the builder's personal interests or the interests of a small group inside the institution. Builders use the space, schedule, and norms of their institution to inculcate virtue. They carefully and prayerfully define the purpose of their institution to ensure it's directed toward God-glorifying ends.

Shadow Side: Builders face the temptation to bully people inside and outside the institution in service of the institution's goals. They take an "ends justify the means" approach to leadership that turns them into narcissists and manipulators. If their behavior goes unchecked, they direct the institution toward their personal interests, using it as a platform for personal gain or celebrity.

CHAPTER 6

The Trainer

CHANGING BABYLON BY CHANGING HABITS

The restoration of the church must surely depend on a new kind of monasticism, which has nothing in common with its former self but proposes a life of uncompromising discipleship, following Christ according to the Sermon on the Mount.

—DIETRICH BONHOEFFER

Train yourself to be godly. For physical training is of some value, but godliness has value for all things, holding promise for both the present life and the life to come.

—PAUL

It was supposed to be a celebration of life. It became a massacre. On a cool January evening in Wilmington, California, a longshoreman and his wife rented out the local veterans' hall to host a baptism.[1] One hundred people gathered for the event and celebrated until midnight. Then everything fell apart. A local gang arrived and opened fire on the crowd. They unsheathed knives and stabbed screaming onlookers. When paramedics arrived, gang members rushed to their cars and ran them over to stop them from helping. A dozen people were seriously injured. Two people died.

A young woman at the shooting asked the question we all ask after incomprehensible violence: "Why? That's what everybody wants to know. Why did something like this happen?"[2] Psychologists, sociologists, and self-help gurus all offer different answers to the question, but most tend to agree: The problem is that our environment makes us maladjusted. It may be toxic relationships, systemic injustice, or toxins in our food, but with some therapy, legal reforms, dietary changes, and a self-actualization pilgrimage, we can solve the problem. Adjust your circumstances, and you can unfetter your innate goodness. Because they all agree: *Deep down, humans are good.* The problem is *out there,* not in every human heart.

Dallas Willard, a former philosopher of spirituality at the University of Southern California, disagreed with the experts. He argued that you can't explain (or fix) what's wrong with the world by retreating into naive fantasies about the goodness of every human heart. Instead, when we encounter real evil, we must dare to stare straight into its awful maw. If we do, we'll discover that every human this side of Eden shares *not* a pervasive readiness to do good (if only circumstances were right!). No, in truth we *all* share an internal readiness to do evil. According to Willard, "[our] ever-present readiness [to do evil] fills common humanity and lies about us like a highly flammable material ready to explode at the slightest provocation."[3] In other words, sometimes culture curtails our inner evil by normalizing good. For example, modern Americans rarely resort to physical violence to resolve feuds because our culture sees such violence as barbaric. But just as often, our culture normalizes our readiness to do evil and sets us free to do wrong. This is why revolution-era Americans *did* use violence to resolve feuds (just ask Alexander Hamilton). They saw it as honorable and manly. Willard warned, "There is a 'real presence' of evil scarcely beneath the surface of every human action and transaction."[4]

Babylon may justify our evil desires, but it is *not* the root cause of them. The root cause is our sinful nature—the long, awful, cascading consequence of Adam's decision (on behalf of the human race) to eat the forbidden fruit, and our decision to join him with sick glee.[5]

Trainers are joyful outsiders who seek to change the world by getting to the root of the problem: the human heart. Trainers see that even if Babylon were perfectly pure, the underlying problem would not change. To change the world, we must somehow reform our internal readiness to do evil. We must develop an internal readiness to do good so strong it can resist temptations both from within and without.

Of course, we can't do this on our own. But God can! Remember the promise God gave to Ezekiel: to forgive our sins and regenerate our hearts. Jesus has *already* forgiven you and given you a new heart. By receiving this undeserved gift, you developed the ability to resist evil and cultivate a readiness to do good in its place. How does God transform us? Through our daily habits: Bible reading, prayer, fasting, sabbath, and the like. Jesus uses these ordinary disciplines to change us from the inside out.

Trainers are the joyful outsiders who practice these disciplines habitually and *train* others to do likewise. As the apostle Paul told his protégé Timothy, "Train yourself to be godly. For physical training is of some value, but godliness has value for all things, holding promise for both the present life and the life to come."[6] Trainers want to change Babylon by reforming human hearts, and they understand that the only way to do that is by reforming human habits. Only through daily training can we develop a readiness to do good and resist evil. A readiness to cultivate Babylon *and* resist its wrongdoing.

How Trainers Change the World: The Spiritual Gymnasium

Imagine your car breaking down on a rural highway, miles from the nearest gas station. You don't have cell reception. It's blazing hot outside, and your infant daughter is in her car seat screaming. Your spouse turns to you and desperately pleads, "We need help. It's too hot for her."

So you get out and run. What happens next is largely dependent on your daily habits *before* the car stalled out. If you jogged regularly before the breakdown, then you will find help quickly. But if you never exercised, you will take much longer. By the time you find help, you will likely be injured and exhausted.

Every joyful outsider faces large and small crises in which our spiritual fitness is tested. Babylon may slap you on the cheek, but whether you turn to it the other is largely dependent on what habits you practiced *before* the first blow. Just as the body needs consistent exercise to rise to extraordinary occasions, so the soul needs consistent exercise to rise to the heights of costly obedience.

Jesus is the finest example of this truth. Unlike us, he had no internal readiness to do evil. Nonetheless, he disciplined himself with ultramarathon-grade solitude, silence, fasting, prayer, study, service, worship, chastity, sacrifice, fellowship, confession, and submission.[7] Despite lacking a sinful nature, Jesus still needed spiritual practices to strengthen his ability to do good. His daily habits were the means by which his heavenly Father strengthened him to resist the devil, take up his cross, and redirect the course of history. If *he* needed spiritual disciplines, how much more so do we?

Jesus also illustrates why we should embrace the disciplines. He *always* had his Father's favor. So we know he didn't train to *earn* the Father's love but to *enjoy* it. Jesus won God's favor for us on the cross. Our spiritual disciplines add nothing to his accomplishment. Instead, the disciplines are the means by which we *enjoy* God's favor and how God strengthens our readiness to do good.

In conclusion, it's hard to imagine Jesus changing the world *without* the disciplines. He withstood the devil by fasting in the desert. He took up his cross by praying in a garden. His habits empowered his mission, even as our habits empower our own mission to resist and cultivate Babylon. Only a holy, good, and loving church can be a living, breathing, countercultural witness to the darkness around it—and trainers know we can only become that kind of Babylon-changing church if we first change our habits.

Four Guiding Principles for Trainers from the Life of Ezra

Four hundred years before the time of Jesus, Ezra was born as an exile in Persia. He was a descendant of Israel's trainers—priests who once served in Jerusalem's temple and were responsible for preserving Israel's ancient traditions, the very practices God graciously used to develop a readiness to do good in his people. Ezra grew into an exceptional trainer. "For Ezra had devoted himself to the study and observance of the Law of the LORD, and to teaching its decrees and laws in Israel."[8]

The Persian king Artaxerxes was so impressed that he commanded Ezra to "to teach [God's laws to] any who do not know them."[9] To that end, he sent Ezra back to Israel with a small contingent of exiles. This was their chance to change their habits, embrace the old traditions, develop a readiness to do good, and see if they could change their small corner of Persia in the process. Here are four principles trainers can learn from the life of Ezra.

1. Practice Abstinence to Learn Resistance

Before Ezra left Persia, he called a collective fast "so that we might humble ourselves before our God and ask him for a safe journey."[10] He knew their nine-hundred-mile-long journey would be attended by hunger. There would be days when they *couldn't* eat. On those days they'd be tempted to grumble, turn back, or do wrong to take what they wanted. By fasting in the present, Ezra trained himself to suffer *obediently* and *joyfully* in the future. Thomas à Kempis wrote, "He who knows best how to suffer will enjoy the greater peace, because he is the conqueror of himself, the master of the world, a friend of Christ, and an heir of heaven."[11]

Have you conquered yourself? Have you mastered temptation? Have you prepared yourself to suffer with joy? Ezra shows us that *disciplines of abstinence* develop godly self-control. These practices involve temporary abstention from good things: sleep, food, drink, work, speech, and companionship. You abstain *not* because they're bad but because they're the very places through which sin often builds a stronghold.[12] Thus, we practice saying no to eating for a short time so we can say no to overindulgence (in any form) in the future. We practice saying no to speech for a time so we can say no to ungodly speech in the future. We practice saying no to work for a time so we can say no to workaholism and overstimulation in the future.

2. Embrace Trusting Prayer and Personal Sacrifice for Renewal

Normally, a caravan like Ezra's would need armed guards to travel safely along roads populated by robbers. But Ezra refused to ask for protection. Instead, he prayerfully trusted God to protect them.[13] He understood that he was leading a renewal movement and that apart from God's provision it was hopeless. So why not start the journey in total dependence?

Trainers, too, often forsake "the security of meeting our needs with what is in our hands" and instead abandon themselves to God in prayer, "stepping into the darkened abyss in the faith and hope that God will bear us up."[14] They do this both when they can't provide for themselves and when they can, in the hope that by trusting God to provide the small things in their lives they will prepare themselves to trust him for greater things. And the greatest thing they pray for is widespread renewal—something *only* his Spirit can accomplish.

The modern church relies heavily on strategies, plans, and programs to gin up the renewal the church requires to be a shining counterculture to Babylon's darkness. But the truth is that revival is in God's hands alone. Thus, like Ezra, trainers prayerfully set aside planning and scheming. They turn to God in praise and worship. They pray for him to do what they can't. Throughout history, the practice of the daily office, twenty-four-hour prayer movements, and worship services have all played a role in large-scale renewal. Trainers both participate in and lead such practices, not as a strategy to force God's hand but as an act of trust in God's power.

3. Practice Rigorous Study

Rigorous study of God's Word was at the core of Ezra's spiritual fitness regimen: "For Ezra had devoted himself to the *study* and *observance* of the Law of the LORD, and to *teaching* its decrees and laws in Israel."[15] Trainers must not ignore the order of this passage. First, Ezra *studied*. Then he *obeyed*. Lastly, he *taught*.

Today studying is easier than ever. Trainers are blessed with a surplus of Bible translations, commentaries, and theological books designed to help them learn. For many trainers—whether or not they wish to enter vocational ministry—seminary is an important step in their journey.

But Ezra's rigor wasn't revealed primarily by the hours he spent studying. It was made evident by his *practice* of God's Word. Likewise, trainers must submit themselves to Scripture in practice. If you're a trainer, you must *do* what you learn. If you do so, you will discover that a feedback loop exists between study and action. The more you obey God, the more you understand him. The more you understand him, the better you obey his Word.

Only after *study* and *obedience* did Ezra *teach*. For the church to become a counterculture that both resists and cultivates Babylon, we need more teachers. Unfortunately, seminary matriculation is decreasing, Christians are reading the Bible less, and Christian education is declining in churches.[16] We need more trainers to step into this gap, to work hard to become excellent teachers with excellent communication skills so they excellently exposit the excellencies of God's Word.

4. Develop Countercultural Holiness

When Ezra returned to Jerusalem, he found a people swamped in a morass of idolatry. Rather than resisting Babylon, his Jewish comrades had become like it. This grieved Ezra so deeply that he spent days mourning in silence. Unfortunately, what he did next was morally ambiguous: He forced Jewish men to divorce their pagan wives. We will return to this later when we discuss the shadow side of trainers.

For now, focus on what Ezra got right: He understood that the *collective* holiness of God's people matters tremendously. If we aren't collectively countercultural in our holiness, love, and mercy, then we won't be able to cultivate holiness, love, and mercy in Babylon.

New Testament scholar Preston Sprinkle argues that the church changes the world by being the church.[17] In other words, *if* the church embodies Jesus's own self-sacrificial readiness to do good, it will be like a shining city on a hill. Its upside-down, countercultural life together will draw those whom Babylon discards and oppresses. By its own beauty, love, and justice, it will show the ugliness of Babylon's injustice, hatred, and immorality. Theologians Stanley Hauerwas and William Willimon wrote that the church "seeks to influence the world by being the church, that is, by being something the world is not and can never be, lacking the gift of faith and vision, which is ours in Christ."[18]

They're right. God has given trainers to the church to help us develop the habits we need to say no to evil, trust God for renewal, and grow in our readiness to do good by his grace. If you are a trainer, or want to be a trainer, your journey begins by personally embracing those habits and then training others to follow suit.

Few lives in the last century illustrate the power of trainers better than that of Dietrich Bonhoeffer, a trainer who resisted the rise of Nazis in Germany by embracing and teaching spiritual disciplines.

Resisting Nazis by Means of Spiritual Training

Wilhelm Niesel and Dietrich Bonhoeffer agreed on a fundamental truth: The German church's capitulation to Hitler, nationalism, and Nazism was nothing short of heresy. In response, Bonhoeffer began an experimental underground seminary in the German town of Finkenwalde. Students would live like monks there, training their bodies and minds to resist the Nazis. He hoped they would become the sort of pastors who could cultivate an anti-Nazi counterculture in the German church. If he changed their habits, maybe they could change the country?

While Niesel agreed with Bonhoeffer's goals, he found Bonhoeffer's approach too austere and Catholic. He later said he was "suspicious of so much spiritualism."[19] So Bonhoeffer invited Niesel to come and see his underground seminary at Finkenwalde.

Three years before Niesel's visit, in 1933, Adolf Hitler's Nazi party outmaneuvered Germany's president, taking control of the legislature. Hitler won German Christians with nostalgic promises: Germany would return to its former glory. Germans would be as powerful as they were before World War I.

Under Hitler's leadership, a new national church, the German Evangelical Church, claimed authority over all churches in the country. He put forth his own religious advisor, Ludwig Müller, for election as bishop over the church, knowing Müller would use his influence to spread pro-Nazi propaganda through German pulpits. After his election, Müller added an Aryan paragraph to the national church's constitution. It banned Jews and people of Slavic descent from acting as pastors or being members of churches. A few months later, pro-Nazi churchmen advocated for even stricter restrictions: removing the Old Testament from German Bibles, defrocking pastors who resisted Hitler, and adopting exclusively Aryan depictions of Jesus in the church.

Christian dissidents like Niesel and Bonhoeffer formed a resistance movement called the Confessing Church. Together, they issued a declaration arguing that the church's doctrine and organization couldn't be controlled by the state. By the time Niesel visited Bonhoeffer's illegal seminary in 1937, Hitler had already arrested hundreds of dissident pastors, assassinated leaders of the Confessing Church, confiscated its funds, and banned it from taking offerings. By God's providence the Nazis ignored Bonhoeffer's boarding school. But that didn't mean it was safe. It was dangerous to associate with anything that smelled of dissidence.

When Niesel arrived at Bonhoeffer's dissident seminary, he took little encouragement. It was exactly what he'd expected. It wasn't quite a monastery, but Bonhoeffer's pupils *did* participate in monsatic cycles of prayer, shared meals, worship, confession, readings from the Psalms, solitude, and scriptural meditation. These practices shaped their common life. But in Niesel's view, they accomplished little. How could the daily confessions and prayers of a few men stop Germany's slide into fascism?

Creating a New Kind of Monasticism

For Bonhoeffer, discipleship was cross-shaped. The question was *how* to develop the strength required to live a cross-shaped life. Clearly the nazified German church lacked this level of spiritual fitness, so Bonhoeffer traveled Europe and North America in search of something different. On those journeys he encountered Catholics, Anglicans, Quakers, and the historic Black church. From their collective witness, he pieced together a vision of costly discipleship empowered by spiritual disciplines.

Bonhoeffer knew that gathering people to share such a life would raise eyebrows. He wrote his atheist, anti-Nazi elder brother, "Perhaps I seem to you rather fanatical."[20] But Bonhoeffer explained that despite some embarrassment, practicing the disciplines had not only made him deeply happy but also strengthened him for the storm to come. He believed that "the restoration of the church must surely depend on a new kind of monasticism, which has nothing in common with its former self but proposes a life of uncompromising discipleship, following Christ according to the Sermon on the Mount. I believe the time has come to gather the people together and do."[21]

So gather Bonhoeffer did. He launched an underground seminary, with a new form of monasticism at its center. His ragtag gang of dissident students shared a common life rooted in the belief that cheap grace—the idea that God's forgiveness is blithely offered to those who give mere intellectual assent to abstract theological truths—was no grace at all. There was only costly grace. God gave his *Son* to rescue sinners. Jesus died a horrific death on the cross. There was nothing cheap about God's grace. Thus, to receive Jesus's costly grace was to receive a costly call. He wrote in *The Cost of Discipleship*, "The cross is laid on every Christian. The first Christ-suffering which every man must experience is the call to abandon the attachments of this world. It is that dying of the old man which is the result of his encounter with Christ. As we embark upon discipleship we surrender ourselves to Christ in union with his death—we give over our lives to death.... *When Christ calls a man, he bids him come and die.*"[22] The seminary embraced the cost of discipleship in both word and deed. They died to themselves through rigorous disciplines so they'd be prepared to die for Christ when the Nazis came for them.

Becoming Stronger than Your Tormentors

When Wilhelm Niesel arrived at Finkenwalde, Bonhoeffer set out to prove the merits of his approach. He invited Niesel to row on the Oder Sound with him. When they reached the far shore, Bonhoeffer led Niesel over a hill into a clearing where they could see a Nazi airfield. Warplanes took off and landed. Soldiers marched in regimented patterns. Turning to Niesel, Bonhoeffer explained that the discipline these soldiers embodied was "for a kingdom . . . of hardness and cruelty."[23] If the Nazis were to be defeated by Christian love, then followers of Jesus would need to exhibit a higher discipline. Bonhoeffer later wrote, "You have to be stronger than these tormentors you find everywhere today."[24]

Niesel was deeply moved. He finally understood that it was only by embracing disciplines of abstinence that Christians could find the strength to say no to Hitler. He saw that it was only through prayer and sacrifice that the German church had any hope of renewal. Niesel paid a high price for his support of Finkenwalde. The secret police arrested him a year later.

Bonhoeffer, for his part, was afforded an opportunity to escape Nazi Germany two years later. Union Theological Seminary in New York City invited him to move abroad, and Bonhoeffer accepted. But just two weeks after his arrival, he felt he'd made the wrong choice and returned to Germany. He explained his reasoning to Union professor Reinhold Niebuhr:

> I have come to the conclusion that I made a mistake in coming to America this time. I must live through this difficult period in our national history along with the people of Germany. I will have no right to participate in the reconstruction of Christian life in Germany after the war if I do not share the trials of this time with my people. . . . Christians in Germany will have to face the terrible alternative of either

willing the defeat of their nation in order that a future Christian civilization may survive, or else willing the victory of their nation and thereby destroying our civilization and any true Christianity. I know which of these alternatives I must choose but I cannot make that choice from a place of security.[25]

Upon his return, Bonhoeffer continued to resist the Nazis by practicing the disciplines. Four years later, he was arrested for his participation in an assassination plot against Hitler and was subsequently transferred to Flossenbürg concentration camp. While Niesel survived his imprisonment, Bonhoeffer did not. He was executed by hanging just two weeks before American troops liberated the camp. During his imprisonment the disciplines continued to pattern his life. God strengthened him through them. So that even in a concentration camp he could find joy. He wrote,

[Christians] are patient and cheerful in suffering, and they glory in tribulation. They live their own life under alien rulers and alien laws. Above all, they pray for all in authority, for that is their greatest service. But they are only passing through the country. At any moment they may receive the signal to move on. Then they will strike tents, leaving behind them all their worldly friends and connections, and following only the voice of their Lord who calls. They leave the land of their exile, and start their homeward trek to heaven.[26]

There have been many Babylons throughout history, few worse than Nazi Germany. But Bonhoeffer's training for costly Christlike love was what empowered his extraordinary courage in the face of unfathomable evil. Without that training, he might have remained in America and returned after the war alive. But with it, he was empowered to embody the sacrificial love of Jesus, resisting the evils of Nazi Germany in word and deed, and bearing up the sins of his own nation in a death that continues to challenge Christians nearly a century later.

The Shadow Side of the Trainer

On your journey as a trainer, you must not imagine yourself becoming a saint overnight. You will face the same temptations Ezra and Bonhoeffer faced: the temptation to become proud, legalistic, and judgmental.

In my college years, I visited a small chapel on campus multiple times a day. Between classes I would go there to confess my sins, study my Bible, and pray fervently for spiritual renewal on our campus. I read the stories of people like Jeremiah Lanphier, a pastor of a dying church in New York City in 1857. He hoped for a renewal and thus began a midweek meeting at noon, where participants sang hymns, confessed sins, and prayed for God to work in the city. At first only a few people attended. But over time the meeting grew to one hundred participants. Moved by what God was doing, they decided to make the weekly meeting into a daily one, and over the next few months the movement spread to other churches, gathering thousands of people every day. Eventually news spread outside of New York, and similar meetings appeared in large cities across the country. Within a few years, a half million people joined churches as a result of those daily prayer gatherings.[27]

So I prayed every day in the chapel, asking God to do something similar on my campus. I felt certain he would answer my prayer. Soon that chapel would overflow with students. It would be a seedbed of revival. But I was wrong. Revival never happened. After a year, I grew irritated that none of my friends could match my discipline or commitment. They said they would show up to prayer meetings, only to forget or make other plans. My irritation soon metastasized into pride. I was better than them. I was more committed than them. Then my pride metastasized into legalism. I began guilting people into joining me, telling them that if they didn't follow my pattern of life, then they weren't serious about their faith. Finally, legalism metastasized into judgmentalism. They wouldn't show up because they weren't the real deal. I'd find more serious Christians who didn't mind the labor.

But I never found those Christians. My unrealistic expectations folded in on themselves. Reflecting on my immaturity, I suspect some of those friends took my critiques to heart. I said they weren't serious Christians, and some took me seriously. They considered leaving Christianity behind. Some stopped following Jesus altogether, and I wonder today whether my pride, legalism, and judgmentalism played a role. Ironically, there is currently something of a revival happening at the university I attended—almost twenty years after my daily prayers. I can't help but praise God for hearing my (and many others') petitions. I simply wish I had been patient—that I hadn't sullied my hope with pride, legalism, and judgmentalism.

Ezra experienced something similar. Most commentators agree that he believed he was leading a second exodus. Ezra, of course, played the role of Moses. But where Moses failed (much of his generation fell prey to idolatry) Ezra believed he would succeed. Perhaps his pride became legalism, because soon afterward he demanded that Jewish men discard their pagan wives—something the Bible never condones. While it certainly *does* call God's people not to marry unbelievers, it never requires divorce to unbelievers. But Ezra did. He justified himself by misreading and misapplying Deuteronomy. In the end, the results of Ezra's ministry as a trainer were mixed. After renewing God's covenant, the people returned to their old ways. They married pagan women once again and neglected God's Word.

All trainers face the same temptation. Their unrealistic expectations for renewal can create pride. When those expectations go unmet, legalism and judgmentalism are swift to follow. When they take root, people get hurt. And as a result, some abandon their walk with Jesus altogether.

Thus, if you want to practice the way of the trainer, you must do so with the meekness, humility, and gentleness of Jesus. You must never forget that you, too, were once a spiritual couch potato and that your current fitness is only the result of Jesus's gracious work in your life. The minute you start creating rules and judging others, you should know you're already in danger.

The best place for a trainer to train others isn't in a gym full of bodybuilders. Don't fall into the trap of becoming a cloistered Christian, seeking out the perfect church where everyone has perfect spiritual bods. Go where you're needed. Rely on God to do the work, not yourself. Take joy as you patiently await fruit. And know that even if it doesn't come in your life-time, it may blossom in the next generation. I've seen this firsthand, and I praise God.

Training for the Counterculture

If followers of Jesus want to resist and cultivate Babylon, they must begin by cultivating a readiness to do good in themselves. God gives us everything we need to start the germination process. He cleanses us and renews our hearts. And he's given us a pattern of practices, exemplified in the life of his Son, through which we can continue the journey toward Christlikeness.

If you feel called to be a trainer, I want you to know that the church desperately needs more people like you. But you must start with yourself, as Ezra did. Study Scripture. Embrace abstinence. Confess your sins. Grow in humility. Learn to trust God through prayer and sacrifice. And then a day may come when you have the chance to help a few others on the same journey, and maybe collectively you all can become the sort of loving, gracious, generous, good, and holy counterculture Jesus envisioned.

Indeed, the "most credible form of witness [to] the world," wrote Stanley Hauerwas and Will Willimon, "is the actual creation of a living, breathing, visible community of faith."[28] Without the trainers in our midst, encouraging us to develop the strength we need to answer the call to costly discipleship, there is little hope of this happening. So embrace this path for the glory of God and for the good of his world. By changing your habits, you may just see Babylon begin to change as well.

If you want to learn more about how to grow as a trainer, you can find additional practices and suggested reading at the end of the book.

Trainer Overview

Trainers are people who take deep joy in spiritual disciplines. They help others do likewise through one-to-one discipleship, small groups, teaching, or prayer. They have a passion for personal holiness and understand that spiritual practices are a key means by which God conforms us to the image of Christ. They earnestly want to help the church become a holy counterculture that attracts those whom Babylon discards and shows Babylon a better, more beautiful way to be human.

Key Insight: Trainers see that *all* humans share an internal readiness to do evil. But Jesus forgives us and promises to transform us. Thus, his Spirit can cultivate a readiness to do good in each of us when we structure our lives around the spiritual disciplines he practiced.

Orientation toward Culture: Trainers see that the church can change the world only if it is a holy counterculture, exemplifying life, goodness, kindness, justice, and generosity where Babylon does the opposite. To help the church become that sort of counterculture, trainers commit themselves to spiritual disciplines, which are the means by which God graciously transforms us.

Guiding Principles: Trainers understand that if we want to resist Babylon when the stakes are high, we must practice saying no when the stakes are low. Thus, they commit themselves to disciplines of abstinence like fasting, solitude, silence, and sabbath-keeping. They have a passion for renewal and revival but understand that it comes only by God's power. Thus, they embrace trusting prayer and personal sacrifice, waiting on him to act. Additionally, they're committed to the rigorous study, application, and teaching of God's Word, seeing it as the ethical and theological cornerstone of the church's countercultural witness. Lastly, they seek to help the church become a holy counterculture, understanding that the church changes the world by being a beautiful church.

Shadow Side: Trainers are often tempted by pride, believing that their superior discipline makes them superior followers of Jesus. If left unchecked, that pride bubbles into legalism. The trainer begins to create rules that others must follow to be serious themselves. Eventually legalism leads to judgmentalism. At this point trainers often become cloistered Christians, judging other followers of Jesus as half-hearted and uncommitted. They search for a more serious church with more serious Christians, rather than serving churches in need.

CHAPTER 7

The Advisor

CHANGING BABYLON BY INFLUENCING LEADERS

———————

You are not only a Representative for Yorkshire. You have the far greater honour of being a Representative for the Lord, in a place where many know him not, and an opportunity of showing them what are the genuine fruits of that religion which you are known to profess.

—REVEREND JOHN NEWTON TO WILLIAM WILBERFORCE, ABOLITIONIST AND MEMBER OF PARLIAMENT

Lin-Manuel Miranda said his song "The Room Where It Happens," from the musical *Hamilton*, is the best he ever wrote.[1] That's saying something, considering he's won five Grammys, three Tonys, two Golden Globes, and been nominated for two Academy Awards. The room to which the song refers was at Monticello, Thomas Jefferson's residence. Inside that room, Alexander Hamilton agreed to place the nation's capital on the Potomac River instead of in New York City or Philadelphia. In exchange, Jefferson and James Madison gave Hamilton's federal government the right to tax states.

The decision to embrace federalism wasn't put to popular vote or made by the people's representatives in Congress. It was decided by a small group of men hidden from the public eye. If someone wanted to influence *that* decision, he'd have to be in the room where it happened.

Advisors understand that this is how the world works. If you're an advisor and you want to change Babylon, then you need to find your way into the room. Even though you may not have the final word on important decisions, that doesn't mean you're without influence. Thus, to cultivate God's kingdom in Babylon, you must seek to be in the right room with the right people at the right time.

How Advisors Change the World

Advisors change Babylon by developing relationships with influential people operating inside powerful institutions. They want to be in the room where decisions are made because they know that cultural power, just like beauty or intelligence, isn't evenly distributed. Changing individual hearts and minds matters, but it may not have much impact if those hearts and minds aren't in the room where it happens.

Most important decisions—whether they're about federalism or gun control, COVID policy or school curriculum, the arts or journalism, AI or social media—aren't determined by popular vote. They're made by Babylon's cultural elites. James Davison Hunter has argued that the quality of one's influence matters more than quantity when it comes to culture-shaping. For better or worse, status trumps raw numbers. He wrote,

> *USA Today* may sell more copies of newspapers than the *New York Times*, but it is the *New York Times* that is the newspaper of record in America because it is at the center of cultural production, not the periphery, and its symbolic capital is much higher. Likewise, one can sell a hundred thousand copies of a book published by Loyola, Orbis, Zondervan, IVP, or Baker, and only 5,000 copies of a book published by Knopf, but it is the book by Knopf that is more likely to be reviewed in the *New York Review of Books* or the *New Republic*, or the *Washington Post* Book World

because Knopf is at the center and Loyola, Orbis, Zondervan, IVP, and Baker are at the periphery. Influence follows accordingly.[2]

Outsized influence belongs to the gatekeepers of industries, government, academia, entertainment, and media. They control what gets made, discussed, and taken to market. Here's Hunter again:

> The deepest and most enduring forms of cultural change nearly always occur from the "top down." In other words, the work of world-making and world-changing are, by and large, the work of elites: gatekeepers who provide creative direction and management within spheres of social life. Even where the impetus for change draws from popular agitation, it does not gain traction until it is embraced and propagated by elites.[3]

One YouTube executive has more cultural influence than thousands of streamers. One well-published professor has more influence over culture than thousands of students. A small team of algorithm developers at Meta has more influence than millions of Instagram users.

Advisors intuitively understand that if Christians want to change Babylon, greater numbers alone won't do the trick. Instead, we need Christians in the room where it happens, influencing our elite cultural institutions. When advisors are in the right room and have relationships with the right people, they can influence important decisions that make for a better community. They can resist decisions that undermine shalom. This doesn't happen only at a national level. Advisors often pursue the same in schools, city governments, and local businesses.

I saw the advisor's power when I planted The Crossing with my friend Dave Cover. Our first challenge was finding a place to worship. Churches have specific needs that are often hard to find in one affordable location. Besides a room outfitted with audiovisual hookups, a church needs space for kids' classes and plenty of parking. Initially, we rented rooms at the University of Missouri, but the space was small, the parking was abysmal, and by God's grace, we quickly outgrew it. While growth was good news, it was also bad because we suddenly needed a new meeting place. A local high school was our best option, but the teacher in charge of its auditorium had no interest in sharing her space with us. I didn't blame her. We'd only complicate her life and create extra work.

Enter the advisor. The school's principal had attended The Crossing several times. He told us that the teacher owned the final decision about who could use the auditorium but offered to set up lunch so we could meet her. At our meeting she changed her mind and graciously agreed to share her space with us.

In the story of God's work in our church's history, it's easy to praise the pastors and church staff and overlook that principal. But The Crossing wouldn't exist without him. God used him as the advisor who was in the right place at the right time and had the right relationships. He used his influence and credibility to help a seedling church take root and do good in our community.

But of course, he didn't simply wake up with influence. No advisor does. He spent years working with excellence, building relationships, and rising through the education system *before* he could influence that teacher. This is the normal path of advisors, a path Daniel exemplified.

Five Guiding Principles for Advisors from the Life of Daniel

King Nebuchadnezzar ruled over Babylon from 605 to 562 BC. During his reign, Babylon developed into an intellectual and cultural powerhouse. Religiously, it was polytheistic. The government was multiethnic, drawn from the peoples Nebuchadnezzar had conquered. But it worked exceedingly well. Its bureaucratic efficiency became the envy of the world.

If you recognize Nebuchadnezzar's name, it's not for those achievements. It's because of the Bible. He's also the king who sacked Jerusalem three times, taking waves of Israel's elite back to Babylon to assimilate them into the empire. Daniel was among their number. He was an outsider in Babylon. He spoke a different language, worshiped a different

God, ate different food. Yet Nebuchadnezzar and his successors turned to Daniel when they needed wisdom, counsel, and advice. Daniel interpreted their dreams, called them to repentance, managed their bureaucracies, warned them of impending judgment, and influenced national policy. Daniel was in the room where it happened. Daniel was an advisor.

His story, recorded in the book of Daniel, reveals how he gained such tremendous influence *without* conforming to Babylon. He found ways to cultivate and resist the empire by *pursuing excellence, showing respect, showing wisdom in gray areas, acting with character, and embracing proximate goods*. Let's look at each in turn.

1. Pursuing Excellence

Daniel's captors enrolled him in the Babylonian equivalent of a leadership academy. It was designed to teach captives the language, literature, and governmental systems of Babylon so they could usefully serve the king. Students endured rigorous examinations, and those who excelled were presented to the king, who determined which students would be invited to join his administration.

Nebuchadnezzar found Daniel and his friends to be the best students in their class and even better than his current advisors. They immediately entered the king's service. This pattern continued throughout Daniel's life and resulted in multiple promotions. Later, the Persian king Darius set Daniel "over the whole kingdom" because of his "exceptional qualities."[4]

An outsider can become an insider when they earn the trust and respect of the people in charge. They do this not by capitulating or conforming. That's a great way to gain short-term influence, not long-term. Advisors gain influence by working with excellence and waiting for leaders to notice the quality of their work, just as Daniel did. This often takes years of study, decades of hard work, and significant sacrifice to achieve. But there's no substitute for excellence. Because we're de facto outsiders, it's the *only* way to open doors without compromise.

2. Showing Respect

The most impressive miracle in the book of Daniel is easy to overlook. Some might not even call it a miracle. But I do. It's the manner in which Daniel spoke to the Babylonian authorities. Ask yourself: How would I speak to the king who took my family captive? To the king who demanded that I worship him or lose my life?

Daniel and his friends weren't combatants. They didn't give in to anger. They didn't go on the attack. Instead, they were always respectful. When Daniel decided he couldn't eat food from the king's table, he didn't demand a different diet but instead "asked the chief official for permission" to abstain.[5] When Nebuchadnezzar threatened to throw Shadrach, Meshach, and Abednego into a furnace, they remained calm and respectfully acknowledged the king's authority over them.[6] When the commander of the king's guard came to put Daniel to death, Daniel spoke not with anger and fear but with "wisdom and tact."[7] When Daniel delivered bad news to Nebuchadnezzar, he said he wished it applied to the king's enemies and not the king himself.[8]

In the fall of 2021, a video circulated of people in a San Antonio church chanting, "Let's go Brandon," a covert way of cursing President Joe Biden. While the pastor later issued an apology, the damage was already done. Advisors understand that using vulgarities to disrespect leaders rarely accomplishes whatever goals someone has in mind. They've learned that if you want to resist Babylon, you must do so with the utmost respect. Refuse to worship Babylon's gods, even as you refuse to curse its leaders—men and women made in God's image.

3. Showing Wisdom in Gray Areas

Babylon didn't just relocate and re-educate Daniel and his friends. They also renamed them. Their Jewish names celebrated Yahweh: Mishael (Who is like God?), Hananiah (God is gracious), Azariah (God is my helper), and Daniel (God is my judge). But their new names honored the Babylonian gods Bel (Belteshazzar), Aku (Shadrach and Meshach), and Nego (Abednego). Their captors weren't subtle. The new names told them they had a new king, a new identity, and new gods. Strangely, while Daniel and his friends resisted Babylonian food, there is no record of them objecting to their idol-laden names. Discerning what is right and what is wrong requires wisdom.

That said, I'm sure some of their fellow captives accused them of conforming to Babylon, of currying favor with powerful people. In fact, this is the most common critique of advisors: They capitulate on their values to gain influence. But that's not true. They've actually developed the wisdom necessary to navigate moral ambiguity. They fear the Lord, which doesn't make them think only in black and white but also in shades of gray. Thus, Daniel and his friends kept their Sharpies in their pockets when others would've drawn a big thick "Do not cross" line. Wisdom stilled their hands. Powerful pagan rulers weren't opening their meetings with prayers to Yahweh. They weren't consulting God's law before constructing their political programs. And in every instance, Daniel used wisdom to discern which plans he *needed* to reject on moral grounds and which he could support *even though* he disagreed with them.

Advisors understand that much of life is *not* black and white. It's not always clear where to draw lines. They're comfortable navigating moral ambiguity because they fear God and know that his Spirit is with them. This allows them to build relational bridges with people holding very different values and to wisely redirect those relationships toward the greater good. While advisors must refuse to compromise their integrity (more on this later), they must also refuse to play it safe and live inside a holy huddle. If they cloister, they lose influence.

4. Acting with Character

Daniel's character set him apart from corrupt Persian bureaucrats. While they engaged in court intrigue and politics, Daniel sought to act with integrity. This was one reason that "the king planned to set him over the whole kingdom."[9] In a fit of envy, his peers "tried to find grounds for charges against Daniel in his conduct of government affairs, but they were unable to do so. They could find no corruption in him, because he was trustworthy and neither corrupt nor negligent."[10] Exasperated, they weaponized worship, convincing the king to issue an edict condemning anyone who worshiped a god other than the king himself to be thrown into a lions' den. They used Daniel's character—he would worship none but Yahweh—against him.

It's not uncommon to hear influential Christians suggest that if Christians want to influence culture, they must chuck Christ's teaching. Of course, they never put it so bluntly. Instead, they encourage people to conform or engage in combat. Daniel shows advisors a better way. Yes, in the short term, standing by your values rather than conforming might land you in the lions' den. But in the long term, your integrity will make you valuable and reliable to those in charge. In the short term, becoming a combatant in the culture wars might win you a following. But in the long term, you'll never be taken seriously. Your antics will make you look clownish, not reliable.

The faithful advisor does God's work God's way. Even corrupt leaders value honesty, discipline, and integrity. At the very least, they know you won't lie and turn on them. If you prove yourself reliable and trustworthy, you'll be given more opportunities. Influence flows through relationships, and relationships are built on character.

5. Embracing Proximate Goods

Imagine you are a part of the exilic community living in Babylon. You strongly disagree with Babylon's immoral decisions. Would you judge Daniel negatively because you know he was in the room where it happened? Would you call him a pushover? Or would you be grateful that Daniel was there to resist evil and cultivate good, even in small ways? Daniel must have diverged regularly from his Babylonian peers. They undoubtedly overruled him on plenty of issues. But it's undeniable that Daniel shaped policy and did so in a way that improved people's lives. That's not enough for some people, but it's enough for advisors.

That's because advisors are realistic about how much change can happen inside Babylon. They've learned to embrace what Steven Garber calls "the proximate."[11] Proximate justice may not be *perfect* justice. But it is better than injustice. Advisors are not idealists. Babylon will never be the new Jerusalem. But there is *real* goodness in nudging a culture's trajectory away from darkness toward light. Even if you don't see the moment when the day fully dawns!

Daniel's example shows that excellence, character, respect, and wisdom in morally ambiguous circumstances are necessary aspects of advising. If an advisor follows these principles, they may have the opportunity to influence those in power and steer them in a God-honoring direction, as proximate to perfection as they can muster.

Advising the President

Starting with Harry S. Truman, Billy Graham advised twelve presidents while they were in office. He was in more important rooms for a more extended period than anyone in modern American history. Known as "America's Pastor," he became the consummate joyful outsider functioning as an insider—even though he was never elected or appointed to any government position.

Graham persuaded Eisenhower to run for office. He reassured Protestants about the first Catholic president by golfing with JFK. He advised Johnson on Vietnam and the Great Society. He became Nixon's personal confidant. He endorsed Ford's decision to pardon Nixon. He supported Carter on the nuclear disarmament treaty with the Soviets. He operated as Reagan's emissary to pro-Israel evangelicals, persuading them to sell AWACS (airborne warning and control systems) to Saudi Arabia. He prayed with George H. W. Bush before the first Gulf War. He counseled Bill and Hillary Clinton on forgiveness after Bill's affair. He led George W. Bush to Christ and helped him overcome a drinking problem.[12]

Graham did the unthinkable. His influence transcended partisan politics. He advised Democrats *and* Republicans. He stayed at the White House the last night of Democrat Lyndon Johnson's presidency and the first night of Republican Richard Nixon's. It sounds like a make-believe story out of a political fairytale. But it's true. And it begs the question: How did he do it? By building trust, rooting for the leader, and acting with character.

Building Trust

In 1934 Graham became a Christian at a tent revival led by Mordecai Ham in Charlotte, North Carolina. Fifteen years later he was preaching his first crusade in Los Angeles. As the weeks-long event was winding down, media mogul William Randolph Hearst told his magazines to "puff Graham."[13] Hearst agreed with Graham's anti-communist message and wanted more of it. The ensuing articles brought thousands to the "canvas cathedral," extending the crusade an additional five weeks and putting Billy Graham at the center of the nation's attention.

The threat of communism was a regular part of Graham's preaching. Long before advising presidents to resist its influence, he proclaimed in Los Angeles, "Communism has decided against God, against Christ, against the Bible, and against all religion. Communism is not only an economic interpretation of life—communism is a religion that is inspired, directed, and motivated by the Devil himself who has declared war against Almighty God."[14]

Having already bucked the tradition of keeping religion out of politics, Graham eagerly sought a meeting with President Truman. Wary of itinerant preachers, Truman reluctantly acquiesced, inviting Graham and three members of his team to the Oval Office. Graham spent most of the short meeting discussing the Korean War before hurriedly asking about the president's faith and offering to pray for him. Speaking with White House reporters afterward, Graham divulged his private conversation with the President, complete with a reenactment of their prayer. That was a painful mistake. He revealed secrets and used Truman to bolster his platform. It cost him a relationship.

But Graham learned from it. "After our gaffe, I vowed to myself it would never happen again if I ever was given access to a person of rank or influence."[15] The two didn't meet again until 1967, long after Truman had left the White House. Graham apologized, and Truman forgave. "Don't worry about it. I realized you hadn't been properly briefed."[16]

Graham kept his vow never to break trust with future presidents. Friendships are among the most important things that the presidency strips from those who hold the office. Whom does the president share intimate details of their life with? Whom can he be vulnerable with? Where does he turn when he has personal fears, marital strife, or guilt from bad decisions in office?

Presidents opened up to Graham because they knew that what they shared with him was safe. Biographers discovered that Eisenhower asked how he could be sure he'd go to heaven. He later became the first (and only) president baptized in office. JFK asked Graham whether he believed in the second coming of Christ. According to Hillary Clinton, Graham helped her forgive her husband's infidelity. Powerful people rarely have friends they can be so vulnerable with. Even rarer is that a series of presidents would have those conversations with one man. But this is the power of an effective advisor: They can bless, serve, and influence leaders no matter their background.

Rooting for the Leader

A pivotal moment in Graham's ministry came in the days leading up to the 1960 election between Richard Nixon and John F. Kennedy. Graham had known Nixon since he'd been elected a senator from California, the two men bonding over their love of golf and disdain for communism. So it was only natural for Graham to support his friend over JFK.

While officially maintaining his neutrality in the election, Graham quietly served as both spiritual and political advisor to Nixon during the campaign. In the closing days of the election, magazine magnate Henry Luce asked Graham to make his support public and write an article for *Life* extolling the virtues of Nixon without endorsing him.[17] Graham hesitantly agreed and submitted a piece for publication. News about the forthcoming article spread throughout the political class, and several of Graham's friends warned that this was getting him into partisan politics in a way he'd previously avoided. Meanwhile, the Kennedy campaign pressured Luce to extend the same offer to his campaign and publish an article by a religious leader on his behalf. At the last second, Luce pulled the article from the magazine. Graham was deeply relieved. It would've been a mistake.

In hindsight, Graham saw that the article would've cost him his pastoral voice and spiritual credibility with future presidents and most Americans. Years later Graham told Nancy Gibbs and Michael Duffy that he was glad to take a photo with president-elect Kennedy after they golfed in Palm Beach a few days before the inauguration. When the picture hit the newspapers, they both got what they wanted. The president got the pastor's tacit endorsement, and the pastor maintained his political neutrality.

Throughout his ministry, Graham struggled not to let his political convictions and partisan leanings rob him of his ability to serve leaders from both parties. He largely succeeded by rooting for the success of whomever God appointed. And he "would never, whatever his political bent, turn down any president who needed his help or asked him to dinner."[18] In his own imperfect way, Billy Graham put partisan politics in its proper place to be an advisor to leaders in need. He also showed what can happen when outsiders in Babylon find a way to build trust and operate as insiders. They don't have formal power, but they can, as advisors, influence leaders for the common good.

Acting with Character

Like Daniel, Billy Graham's best asset was his strong character. Daniel's character allowed him to advise kings from different empires. Graham's character allowed him to advise leaders from different parties. It's remarkable that after a long, very public ministry, no one leveled serious ethical accusations against Graham or his ministry. He finished in the top ten of Gallup's Most Admired Man list a record sixty-one times.[19]

Living above reproach was the agenda of a 1948 meeting in Modesto, California. A few months before his first evangelistic crusade in Los Angeles, Graham and his closest friends met to discuss how to avoid the traps other Christian ministers had fallen into, disgracing the church and dishonoring Jesus. The Modesto Manifesto committed the signatories to financial integrity, boundaries with women who weren't their wives, accuracy in publicizing crusade results, and commitment to healthy relationships with local churches.

In our highly polarized age, it's hard to imagine there will ever be another Billy Graham. But it's not impossible. When advisors build trust, root for leaders, and act with high character, they not only receive invitations to the room where it happens, they also influence the few who have the ability to influence the many.

The Shadow Side of the Advisor

In a fascinating interview, Sarah Pulliam Bailey asked the ninety-two-year-old Billy Graham, "If you could, would you go back and do anything differently?" After saying he'd have been more protective of his time with his family, Graham said, "I also would have steered clear of politics. I'm grateful for the opportunities God gave me to minister to people in high places; people in power have spiritual and personal needs like everyone else, and often they have no one to talk to. But looking back I know I sometimes crossed the line, and I wouldn't do that now."[20]

Vulnerability and transparency are reasons Graham has been so widely respected. Politics can bring out people's worst impulses, and Graham was no exception.[21] All advisors face the temptation to compromise values and jockey for power in unhealthy competition.

Compromising Values

Several years ago *Christianity Today* released an article titled "Should Christians Keep Advising a President They Disagree With?" It's not an easy question to answer. If you answer, "No, they shouldn't advise a president they disagree with," then you'd also have to argue that Daniel, Joseph, Esther, and Nehemiah should've resigned or refused to work for the unbelieving leaders they served. But if you answer, "Yes, they should," you may be encouraging others to risk their moral and spiritual credibility by associating with corrupt and dangerous leaders. While advisors must be comfortable living in the gray, they must also know when to draw lines and refuse to compromise their sincerely held convictions.

Reverend Johnnie Moore justified remaining on President Trump's evangelical advisory board after Charlottesville—where a white supremacist killed a counterprotester and Trump claimed there were good people on both sides—by saying, "You only make a difference if you have a seat at the table."[22] And that's true. But what's the point of being at the table if you're unwilling to challenge the president? You're not an advisor if you can't (or won't) do that. You're a court prophet.

When Israel's King Ahab and Judah's King Jehoshaphat discussed whether to go to war against the king of Aram, Jehoshaphat insisted they first seek God's counsel. Instead, Ahab called in four hundred *court prophets* and asked if they should go to war. The court prophets knew their job: tell the king what he wants to hear. So they did: "The Lord will give it into the king's hand."[23]

Jehoshaphat wasn't sold. He requested to hear from the prophet Micaiah. When Micaiah arrived, one of Ahab's messengers warned him, "Look, the other prophets without exception are predicting success for the king. Let your word agree with theirs, and speak favorably."[24] But Micaiah said, "As surely as the LORD lives, I can tell him only what the LORD tells me."[25]

Micaiah wasn't a court prophet. He delivered the bad news. Israel would be defeated, and King Ahab would be killed. Four hundred prophets were willing to compromise their integrity to stay in the king's good graces. Only one was willing to tell the truth regardless of the consequences. Same with Daniel, who delivered hard truth to Nebuchadnezzar about his pride at great risk to his own life. Advisors don't lie. They aren't cowards. They find tactful, wise, respectful ways to challenge the leaders they advise.

Christianity Today, the magazine Billy Graham founded, acknowledged the uneasy choice every advisor faces, in an editorial in 1972: "We grant there is risk involved when a clergyman becomes a confidant of powerful figures in the secular world. . . . But is not the risk far outweighed by the opportunity? Have not evangelicals long prayed for an entrée without compromise into the affairs of state?"[26]

Only those with wisdom and courage can take the risk—wisdom to know when to speak and courage to actually do it. Advisors must remember that it's better to keep your soul than sacrifice it for the sake of power.

Jockeying for Power

Alexander Hamilton and Aaron Burr's personal and political rivalry drives the plot of the musical *Hamilton*. Burr is the consummate politician. He relies on the breadth of his connections more than the depth of his convictions. When Hamilton arrives in the United States, Burr's advice to him is to "talk less and smile more. . . . Don't let them know what you're against or what you're for."[27] Hamilton tries to take the advice but in the end can't set aside his convictions.

As Hamilton's influence grows, Burr is none too happy to discover that he negotiated a significant behind-closed-doors deal with Thomas Jefferson and James Madison. It piques Burr's competitive nature. He doesn't care what decision was made; he simply cares that he wasn't the one to influence it. In retaliation he unseats Hamilton's father-in-law in a Senate run. Eventually, the rivalry leads to a duel that ends Hamilton's life.

An advisor's craving for influence easily turns collaborators into competitors. People become obstacles to climb over on your way to where you want to be. When this happens, an advisor looks more like the corrupt Persians trying to eliminate Daniel, than Daniel himself. The advisor sells his integrity for power. He loses his way and forgets whom he serves. As a result, he loses sight of the main task at hand. It's not power. It's not even influence. It's joyfully serving King Jesus as an outsider inside the halls of power.

Influencing the Influential

Advisors change the world by influencing the influential. Before they can do that, they must become the sort of people leaders seek: men and women who do their jobs with a high-degree of excellence and character. Those traits, not political adeptness, must distinguish them from others. But neither of those traits develops quickly. That's why the path to becoming an advisor is often long and comes without guarantees.

Even if an advisor gets into the room where it happens, the spiritual dangers of those places are real. Few people can touch power and remain unaffected. It's hard to be in Babylon's halls of power and not become Babylonian. The book of Proverbs says that wisdom begins with the fear of the Lord.[28] That is a fear the advisor can never leave behind: She will not have the requisite courage to stand and resist real evil otherwise. She will not have the requisite discernment to know when it's best to hold her tongue and live to fight another day.

If you aspire to be an advisor, don't be discouraged. Your labor is not in vain. If you're in the room with the decision-makers at your school, your business, or your local government, you *can* influence the room and work for the common good. If you do, you will play no small role in nudging Babylon closer to justice, closer to goodness, and closer to God. Babylon will never be perfect. But through your work, it can become a better place.

If you want to learn more about how to grow as an advisor, you can find additional practices and suggested reading at the end of the book.

Advisor Overview

Advisors recognize that elite institutions have the power to shape culture. They pursue professional excellence and personal character, hoping to be invited into important discussions within those institutions where they can exert influence to resist evil and cultivate good within Babylon.

Key Insight: On both a national and local level, particular individuals have an outsized influence. Their decisions affect more people than the average person's. Thus, advisors understand that access to the rooms where big decisions are made is necessary if you want to work for the common good.

Orientation toward Culture: Advisors recognize that they are outsiders in Babylon but can still influence outcomes if they are in the right room with the right people at the right time. Advisors seek to influence the influential, not for the sake of gaining power but for the sake of God's kingdom. They use their influence to encourage leaders to make choices that positively influence people's lives and resist ones that lead to injustice or harm.

Guiding Principles: Advisors know that only people who do their jobs with excellence, respect those in authority, and display character in their personal and professional lives get invited into the rooms where important decisions are made. Although they are personally above reproach, they know that Babylon doesn't share their values, so they develop the requisite wisdom to navigate morally ambiguous situations. When possible, they try to nudge Babylon toward the good, knowing that while perfection is never possible, *proximate* goodness is better than evil.

Shadow Side: The same competitive spirit that drives the advisor to pursue vocational excellence can lead them to put their personal priorities over the king's priorities. Seduced by power, many advisors become nothing more than court prophets who celebrate a leader's wrongheaded ideas and desires rather than courageously challenging them.

CHAPTER 8

The Artist

CHANGING BABYLON BY MAKING BEAUTY

———

A Christian should use these arts to the glory of God, not just as tracts, mind you, but as things of beauty to the praise of God. An art work can be a doxology in itself.

—FRANCIS SCHAEFFER

The books or the music in which we thought the beauty was located will betray us if we trust to them; it was not in them, it only came through them, and what came through them was longing. . . . For they are not the thing itself; they are only the scent of a flower we have not found, the echo of a tune we have not heard, news from a country we have never yet visited.

—C. S. LEWIS

Mahalia Jackson's world-famous contralto voice rung out over a silent crowd, "Tell 'em bout the dream, Martin!" Before her stood a crowd of 250,000 people at the Washington Monument. Across the country, television sets projected the image. At the center, behind a podium festooned with broadcast microphones, stood Dr. Martin Luther King Jr.

He had reached the end of his prepared remarks. What came before was melodic and beautiful. But the herculean effort required to organize hundreds of thousands of people gave King little time to prepare it. He'd arrived at his hotel the night before the speech at ten o'clock and only then began writing. Five hours later he finished, arriving at the march physically and mentally exhausted.

But when he reached the end of his prepared remarks, he didn't stop. He leaned toward the crowd. A long silence filled the airwaves. Some broadcasts cut their coverage. They thought he was finished. Then King said, "I still have a dream." Yes, he did. But what was it? With what words could he sing it? It took a gospel singer's croon—"Tell 'em bout the dream, Martin!"—to draw King's song into lyrical expression. He continued,

> I have a dream that one day this nation will rise up and live out the true meaning of its creed: We hold these truths to be self-evident, that all men are created equal.[1]

King's baritone hymn thrummed to the cadence of sermons by Black preachers from generations past, fraught with pain and taut with the impossible hope that things *could* be different.

> I have a dream that one day on the red hills of Georgia, the sons of former slaves and the sons of former slave owners will be able to sit down together at the table of brotherhood.

Jackson swayed and clapped. She called out and King responded. Her art generated his art. His art generated hers. Call and response until a fresh vision of the future snapped into focus:

> I have a dream that one day even the state of Mississippi, a state sweltering with the heat of injustice, sweltering with the heat of oppression

will be transformed into an oasis of freedom and justice. I have a dream that my four little children will one day live in a nation where they will not be judged by the color of their skin but by the content of their character. I have a dream today. . . .

King's poetry unveiled the beastly visage of Jim Crow, even as it revealed a beatific vision of ethnic unity. History and hope pulsed in every syllable. What *was*. What *is*. What *will be*.

I have a dream that one day every valley shall be exalted, every hill and mountain shall be made low, the rough places will be made plain, and the crooked places will be made straight, and the glory of the Lord shall be revealed, and all flesh shall see it together. . . . [We] will be able to join hands and sing in the words of the old Negro spiritual: Free at last. Free at last. Thank God almighty, we are free at last.

Before Jackson and King, the crowd roared with hope. Hundreds of thousands of people joined the joyful chorus. Jim Crow died that day. Beauty struck the final blow. Poetry gave flight to an impossible vision. Holy imagination drew a hoped-for future into the present.

This is the power of art. *This* is the strength of beauty. *This* is the calling of joyful outsiders who walk in the way of the artist. Like King and Jackson, they seek to change Babylon by creating beauty that both resists the ugliness of Babylon *and* cultivates hope for its true flourishing.

How Artists Change the World: From Culture War to Culture Care

In America most people think of culture as a war zone. It's an overheated, blasted, contended space where the elite battle for the minds, hearts, and habits of everyday people. In this battle, artists play a critical role, not as makers of beautiful art but as makers of useful *art*illery in the culture wars.[2] Art is useful as *advertising* in capitalistic battles to take market share. Art is useful as *media* in digital battles to capture attention. Art is useful as *entertainment* in consumeristic battles to seize subscription fees. In the battle for votes, money, institutions, and influence, art exists to shell the enemy and take their territory.

No one can blame artists for enlisting in the battle. Whether it's for a paycheck, fame, or a favored cause, we've all been trained to measure art by its usefulness in some greater battle. The question is whether this is God's vision for the arts. What if culture isn't a battlefront at all? Japanese American Nihonga artist Makoto Fujimura writes, "Culture is not a territory to be won or lost but a resource we are called to steward with care."[3] Culture isn't a war zone. "Culture is a garden to be cultivated."[4] Fujimura's words echo Jeremiah's exhortation to the exiles to "build houses" and "plant gardens" in Babylon.

Artists embrace this path. They pursue culture *care* instead of culture *war.* Politicians need sneering ads about *the other team,* but artists know we need soulful portraits that humanize both sides. Idealogues need propaganda to support their narrative, but artists know we need novels that make us circumspect about our parochial assumptions. Entertainment executives need music that appeals to our basest desires, but artists know we need music that softens our hard edges and surprises us with hope. Although Babylon may be an artist's employer, the artist must not forget that she serves a greater master, who taught that the world is changed not by spilling the blood of others but by spilling your own. So even as artists service the empire, they do so subversively, lacing their work with the self-giving beauty of Jesus and refusing work that leaves no space for it.

To do this well, artists must release themselves from Babylon's demands to be *useful.* When they do this, they mirror the creator God. After all, God's creation served no utilitarian purpose. Jesus did not *need* the world he made. It was not *necessary* for his well-being. He charged the world with grandeur simply because he is grand, gracious, generous, and overflowing with gratuitous creativity. The majesty of the mountains and the calmness of a still sea have no use to him. And yet when we encounter them, they reveal to us the nature of beauty itself. Beauty, in the words of poet T. S. Eliot, is "that which makes life worth living."[5] He continues, "If we take culture seriously, we see that a people does not need merely enough to eat . . . but a proper and particular cuisine."[6]

He's right. God feeds your soul with a particular kind of gratuitous beauty that he designed your soul to enjoy: the beauty of himself. And the beauty of the world through which we see him. He now invites joyful outsiders on the artist's path to do likewise: *to feed a beauty-starved culture with the cuisine of heaven.* In the words of Mahalia Jackson, artists tell 'em bout the dream. They allow the beauty of the dream to shatter what was already broken, and build anew what otherwise could not have been imagined. As C. S. Lewis once observed, it is often through such beauty that the world discovers the scent of a flower it has not smelled, the echo of a tune it has not heard, and news from a country it has not yet visited.[7] The artist's art carries the aroma, sounds, and good news of heaven to earth. How can earth remain the same?

Three Guiding Principles for Artists from the Lives of Zechariah and Haggai

When the first waves of exiles returned from Persia to Jerusalem, they found the city in ruins. There were no parades welcoming them home. Only rubble. So they collected their tools and began the long, expensive, arduous process of rebuilding. But in the end, it proved too heartbreaking. When the elders saw the foundation of the new temple, they wept because it was but a shadow of what Solomon built centuries earlier.

In despair, they gave up on the temple. They attended to their own homes instead. *Eat, drink, and be merry, for tomorrow we die.* Unmetabolized pain too easily becomes desperate self-preservation. But God didn't give up on them. He sent them two artists: the prophets Zechariah and Haggai. Together they used beautiful words to, in the words of Old Testament scholar Walter Brueggemann, "speak a new world beyond the loss."[8]

Through their art—the poetry and prose now collected in the books of Haggai and Zechariah—they called the people to see beyond despair. The artists gathered the fragments of their broken dreams and bound them together into something new. What they made did not deny the pain. Instead, they made something new and beautiful out of the pain—something that couldn't exist without the hurt but which did not allow the hurt to have the final say. Zechariah and Haggai walked the border between loss and hope, heaven and earth, present and future. Indeed, their art still guides artists in the present seeking to do likewise. Here are three guiding principles modern artists can learn from their ancient forebears:

1. Cultivate Skillfulness

For years, when I pictured the prophets creating, I imagined some form of automatic writing. *The prophet enters a trance. And the words of God flow from him perfectly in a single draft.*[9] But no place in the Bible suggests that this is how it worked—in fact, every prophetic book in the Old Testament shows signs of having been carefully written, edited, and organized. So the prophets weren't automatons. They were *poets* honing a craft. God prepared Zechariah and Haggai for their prophetic task by superintending over their entire lives, ensuring they would develop the skills needed to craft their art. They learned to read. They learned to write. They mastered Hebrew poetic tools like parallelism, couplets, alliteration, imagery, metaphor, chiasm, refrains, inclusios, and wordplay.

Much later Jesus would carry on their legacy as a *poet*-prophet by mastering the art of parables. While we don't know how he developed his skill, we do know he deployed it as a kind of performance art to challenge religious authorities. The parables were near the center of Jesus's teaching ministry, unveiling realities about the world, the human heart, and God's kingdom, which he claimed couldn't be revealed in any other way.[10] As theologian Paul Tillich wrote, "In the creative work of art we encounter reality in a dimension which is closed for us without such works."[11] But art can't have this effect if it is not practiced and deployed *skillfully*, as Jesus himself did.

Of course, mastering any art form is far from easy. But it's God's calling to artists. He commands musicians to "play skillfully."[12] God knows it takes years of hard work and practice to obey his command. But God is faithful: He works *through* your hard work to co-create sounds, words, and sights that challenge, console, and give hope to the world around you.[13] So artists must endeavor to rigorously hone their craft through practice.

2. Become a Border Walker

By centering the artist's calling on the cultivation of beauty, I don't mean to center a specific aesthetic. Nor do I mean to promote vacuous sentimentalism or to suggest that artists avoid the deepest places of pain and despair. To say so would cheapen the Bible's vision of beauty. No, beauty happens precisely at the *border* of hurt and healing. Haggai and Zechariah show us that artists are called to live on the *border* of heaven and earth. To create in the *in-between* places. To make lovely vases from sin-shattered jars of clay. They had the imaginative ability to live *between* pain and possibility. To draw hope from tragedy.

Thus, in Zechariah's poetry, a washed-up descendant of David (Zerubbabel) becomes a signet ring on God's hand. A filthy priest (Joshua) becomes a paragon of purity. A faithless city (Jerusalem) becomes a holy mountain called the "Faithful City."[14] An unprotected people without walls or armies become those shielded by Yahweh "so that the feeblest among them will be like David."[15] Repentance turns into holiness. Mourning into joy. Loss into possession.

The beauty of Zerubbabel, Joshua, and Jerusalem's hope is richer *because* Zechariah never blunts their despair. His poetry takes root in the borderland between *what is* and *what will be*. Zechariah was what Makoto Fujimura calls a "border walker," someone who lives in the in-between spaces. Between heaven and earth, life and death, hope and despair.

When an artist unveils heaven on earth, it's less like a cheesy Thomas Kinkade watercolor and more like Jesus weeping over Lazarus's body and then roaring him back to life. Without tears, triumph is cheap. Makoto Fujimura wrote, "Culture care starts with the identification and articulation of brokenness. It creates a safe space for truth telling. But it does not stop there. It starts with listening and then invites people onward toward beauty, wholeness, and healing."[16]

This movement from the bottom up characterizes how Jesus and all artists cultivate beauty. They walk the border, moving up *from* death *to* life. *From* earth *to* heaven. *From* despair *to* hope. In Christ, the artist takes up the crosses of this world, dies alongside the hurting, and then comes out the other side alive, bearing the nail-scarred marks of resurrection: wholeness and healing.

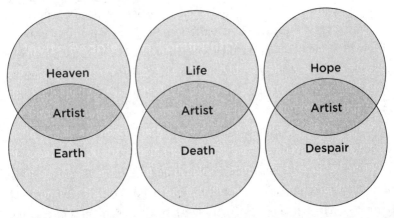

If you're an artist, you must learn to walk in the way of Jesus. You must tread the border between heaven and earth, life and death, hope and despair. If your art loses the odor of death, it will descend into sentimentalism. Conversely, if your art loses the aroma of life, it will descend into cynicism. But when you walk the border of death and life, descending into tragedy and then ascending to glory, you walk with the crucified king of heaven. There is nothing cheap or sentimental about it. By his grace you make hard-won beauty. Which is to say, true beauty.

3. Cultivate a Hopeful Imagination

Border-walking requires the artist to have a dexterous imagination. It requires what Brueggemann calls a "hopeful imagination."[17] This is precisely what Zechariah and Haggai had. Through their art, the people traveled through despair, sin, and remorse and emerged charged with hope—a robust vision of heaven on earth.

Contemporary culture leaves little space for robust hope. Temporary pleasure is the best it has to offer. In place of vision, it revels in irony, cynicism, and darkness. Our most popular and critically acclaimed TV shows explore the depths of human depravity. They revel in blood and sex and vulgarity. Because their creators lack a hopeful imagination, their art never rises from the casket. Border walkers don't fear the darkness or revel in it. Instead, they learn to speak the *whole* truth about darkness, as Jesus did. Although humanity walks through the valley of the shadow of death, God has prepared a table for the weak, lost castaways of Babylon who turn to him. Darkness never gets the last word.

Few lives illustrate how artists walk the border between heaven and earth better than that of Vincent van Gogh. In his story we'll learn how artists change Babylon by creating beauty.

The Man with a Double Soul

In the dim light of a cramped hut, Vincent van Gogh opened a letter from the Belgian Evangelization Committee, fearing the worst. When he had arrived as a missionary to coal miners at the Borinage, he looked the part: well-dressed, fed, and clean. But now things were different. He entered the lives of the people he evangelized—miners sent below the earth on twelve-hour shifts. The air was toxic. Explosions were frequent. Typhoid fever and tuberculosis took the lives of many. Alcoholism took those who survived the diseases. Vincent couldn't bear watching them descend into darkness from the safety of his pulpit in the light. So he went into the mines and into their homes. His clothes become sooty and filthy. He crafted bandages from his clean bedsheets to care for the sick. He emptied his pantries to feed the hungry, becoming malnourished himself. Over time his selfless devotion made him like them: unclean, unkempt, and underfed.

Vincent knew the Belgian missionary board would not approve. They believed that while the spiritual lives of the miners were valuable to God, their physical lives were filthy and ugly. But the young missionary saw differently. He walked the border between light and darkness in the mines and found Christ there with them. He wrote to his older brother Theo that, despite what others said, there is "so much that is picturesque in this region."[18] Beneath the soot there was beauty.[19] He yearned to capture that light in drawings and sketches—the pictorial language he learned to love during his brief time as an apprentice art dealer. Perhaps art would unveil the soulfulness and beauty of the miners. But Vincent never got far because he feared that drawing would distract him from his "real work" as a missionary.[20]

Eventually news of young Vincent's unconventional ministry traveled back to the missionary board that sent him. The letter he held in his hands said they found his approach too radical. They wanted respectable missionaries, not wild men walking the borders between the mines and civilization. So they unceremoniously dismissed him from his post.

The dismissal hit Vincent hard. He would need to return home and tell his parents that he'd failed *once again* to secure a vocation. This was his third attempt. First as an art dealer. Then as an aspiring seminarian. And now as a missionary. But his third dismissal was not an ending. On the next day something rose to life in Vincent. No longer a missionary, Vincent gave himself to a new calling. He filled scraps of paper with rudimentary charcoal drawings, inching ever closer toward capturing the light he saw in the miners, a light to which the ordinary world was blind. This was his final calling. This was Van Gogh's artistic genesis.

As the years rolled on, his subjects changed. Peasants and prostitutes. Sowers and reapers. Chasmic quarries and starry nights. His homes changed as well. For a time he lived in The Hague. He welcomed a prostitute, Sien, and her daughter into his home. He helped her survive her second pregnancy and kept her off the street for a year afterward. He worked from despair toward hope in his art.

One chalk portrait of Sien, called *Sorrow*, is angular and sharp with despair. "What I want to express, in both figure and landscape," Van Gogh wrote to his brother, "isn't anything sentimental or melancholy, but deep anguish."[21] With few exceptions, Van Gogh's paintings and drawings of Sien and her world communicate desperation. A spartan life spent in soup kitchens. A woman whose sagging face made her appear twenty years older than she was. A daughter's unkempt hair zigzagging in a tangle of impoverished anguish. In Sien, Van Gogh saw Jesus, "the man of sorrows," whom he envisioned "as a workman, with lines of sorrow and suffering and fatigue on his countenance."[22] Thus, his drawings humanized Sien by showing her likeness to Christ. Her pain hid beauty, a deep-down dignity that confronted Babylon's ugliness—for the ways it treated a daughter of God as a discardable object.

Vincent saw that life wasn't all suffering and pain. Jesus not only "knows our ills," he wrote, but also acts as "the great Healer of sick souls."[23] Sien's infant, Willem, became Vincent's pathway from sickness to healing. In one watercolor, Van Gogh depicts mother and son in profile. Willem's infant gaze transforms Sien. She is once again a young woman. She leans to kiss Willem's forehead with eyes shut. A tenderness in this painting transfigures a hungry family into a holy family, sanctified by ordinary love. Vincent wrote to Theo, "If one feels the need of something great, something infinite, something where one feels one can see God, one need not go far to find it. I think I saw something—deeper—more infinite—more eternal than the ocean in the expression of the eyes of a little baby when it awakes in the morning—or laughs because the sun is shining in its cradle. If there is a 'ray from on high,' it could be found there."[24]

Vincent had what he called a "double nature," both "that of a monk and that of a painter."[25] His double nature allowed him to walk the borders of darkness and light. Between the subterranean and the surface. Between the genteel salons and the squalid brothels. Between the sorrow and the tenderness. He lived between two overlapping worlds: heaven and earth. And that was the foundation of his artistic genius.

A Feast of Beauty beyond Death

Van Gogh found a happiness in domestic life with Sien that he would never again experience. He hoped to marry her, but his brother urged him to do otherwise. Sien's family pressed her back into prostitution. He left The Hague despondent.

After several years of wandering, he landed in Arles, France, a region known for spectacular ruins. But the acqueducts couldn't hold Vincent's attention. The weavers, peasants, and farmers stole his gaze. He planned to begin a small community for artists there and was briefly joined by the French postimpressionist Paul Gauguin. Their nine weeks together were stormy. Hours after Gauguin finally left, Vincent took a razor and mutilated his right ear. He was hospitalized, then later admitted himself to an asylum housed in an old monastery, Saint-Paul de Mausole.

After a year recovering in the monastery-asylum, he moved closer to his brother in Auvers-sur-Oise, where he lived in the attic of a local inn. One day, while painting a gold-flecked wheatfield, he was shot in the chest. Two days later, Vincent died. Local papers reported it as a suicide, but later evidence suggests that perhaps two impoverished boys, who habitually bullied Vincent, shot him. The dying painter did not tell the authorities because he wanted to protect them. It was, perhaps, one last act of mercy for those the world cast aside—one last way of finding the light in awful darkness.

The end of Van Gogh's life wasn't entirely tragic. During his final years, he created hundreds of paintings, including many of his best-known works. *The Starry Night. Wheatfield with Crows. Sunflowers. Self-Portrait with Bandaged Ear. The Bedroom. Wheat Field with Cypresses.* And the night before he died, *Irises.* These paintings churn with cosmic energy. They're charged with luminosity. The soulishness of things bubbles in every brushstroke of grass. The fullness of life blazes in every sun. Eternity swirls around every star. There is a madness in his paintings that makes their viewers sane. The world *is* enchanted in those paintings. The veil between the natural and supernatural is thin. And thus they unveil the shimmering, dancing, glorious beauty of the Creator in all created things.

Over a century later, people still seek out Vincent's paintings because, in the words of theologian Henri Nouwen, they "show that there is something more to life."[26] His art served no cause. It wasn't useful or even valuable in his life. He gave his art to us gratuitously, freely, and generously. It remains a feast of life after Vincent's death. That is how artists serve Jesus: *You walk the borders of hope and despair, allow your hopeful imagination to see what others can't, create beauty by moving from despair to hope, and then give your gift to the world around you.* What Nouwen wrote of Van Gogh must be true of all artists in the service of King Jesus: "In the midst of darkness he saw light. In the midst of ugliness he saw beauty. In the midst of pain and suffering he saw the nobility of the human heart. He saw it, and he burned with desire to make others see it."[27]

What would your life be like if you walked the borders between earth and heaven? Between sickness and health? Between despair and hope? How would your community change if your art created empathy for those the world discarded? If your art's beatification of the outcasts confronted Babylon's ugliness and lies? Let the beauty of your hard-won hope unveil a reality deeper than darkness: A kingdom *is* coming. So tell 'em bout the dream. Burn to make them see it.

The Shadow Side of the Artist

Vincent van Gogh's life offers you both a picture of the artist's calling and a warning about every artist's temptations. By the time he died, he'd abandoned Christian community and the church. It's not hard to understand why: They'd rejected him for his eccentricities. As a result, Vincent conformed to the world around him. Unfortunately, many artists experience similar rejections in the modern church and follow the same path. My friends ministering in the neighborhoods around Hollywood tell me that it's not uncommon for a young, talented artist to move to LA with hopes of changing Hollywood only to be changed by Hollywood instead. So let's look at three temptations artists must learn to resist.

Abandoning the Church

Artists fear being misunderstood in Christian community. Their habit of walking the borders makes them seem eccentric at best and a danger at worst. Sensing those fears, many artists do what Vincent did: They begin to see the church as a human construct, bereft of spiritual vitality. In *The Starry Night*, the light of the stars burns brightly, but the lights in the church are out—it's a picture of how Van Gogh saw the body of Christ.

What often begins as a rejection of the church develops into a rejection of Jesus himself. It's hard to love the groom (Jesus) if you hate his bride (the church). In Van Gogh's re-creation of Rembrandt's *The Raising of Lazarus*, Jesus is replaced by a blazing sun. While Van Gogh never rejected Jesus, he did transpose him into a lesser being who was less critical of Van Gogh's vices: heavy drinking and sexual immorality.

Artists must never allow the difficulties of communal life—the hypocrisy, snubs, squabbling, and unkindness—to unmoor them from Christ's bride. Why? Because the flawed, broken community of Jesus is the very place where the Spirit is at work generating new life, new beauty, and new hope. Though walking the border between the church's glorified future and its imperfect present may be painful, it is necessary if you want to remain connected to the One whose presence abides in the fellowship of redeemed sinners.

Self-Isolating

Just like Vincent, I've battled with depression my whole life. If you're an artist, you too may feel your emotions intensely. In some ways this is a superpower. It's what allows you to connect deeply with the emotions of others—to see light in darkness. So when an artist is healthy, she moves toward others. But when she's not, her keen emotional sensitivity can lead her to fixate on her own internal life, intentionally or unintentionally creating distance between herself and others.

Vincent's letters to his brother show that the more he isolated himself, the more self-obsessed and self-loathing he became. The late fiction writer David Foster Wallace described depression as a black hole with teeth.[28] It draws you in and chews you up. Thus, while battling with depression is no sin (the Bible is full of prophet-poets who knew despair), giving yourself to the black hole by isolating yourself is dangerous. Like too many other artists, Wallace ultimately took his own life. So you must never forget that you were made in the image of a triune God, whose eternal existence lives *in community*: Father, Son, and Holy Spirit. You deny the image of God in yourself when you cut yourself off from others and choose to wander into the darkness of loneliness.

Conforming to Babylon

As border walkers, artists often inhabit the places in Babylon that are most self-consciously opposed to Jesus and his kingdom. An artist begins with hopes of changing the world, breaking stereotypes about Christianity, and creating art for Jesus that isn't "Christian art." But he underestimates the influence of Babylon and, like Van Gogh, who later became a frequenter of brothels and alehouses, becomes like the world around him.

Sometimes this is for social reasons: No one likes being an outsider. An artist wants to fit in. His artistic peers reject Jesus, and so he wants to do likewise. But at other times artists conform for aesthetic reasons. The artist sees the skill and popularity of Babylon's artists, and that persuades him to disavow what he once hoped for—the return of King Jesus—as naive, ugly, or both.

To resist both conformity and isolation, artists must resist the first temptation: to abandon the church. When Jesus looks on his bride, he sees her not as she is but as she will be: good, beautiful, just, and true. Every time Jesus chooses to see the church this way, he deploys hopeful imagination. And his hope is not in vain! In a similar way, artists must use their imaginations to see beyond the church's failures and sin. After all, every artist shares the same weaknesses. How would your life change if you saw the church as the apostle John did: as a radiant bride dressed for her wedding day? Once you can see it, tell everyone about *that* dream.

Making Beauty to Remake the World

The arts aren't optional if Christians desire to both *resist* and *cultivate* Babylon. Art has the power to cut across the reasoning and self-justifications the world makes for its evil and injustice. Art has the ability to speak truths that can't otherwise be expressed. Art can reach across the borders of tribes, worlds, emotions, and realities that otherwise remain worlds apart. The artist's calling is to cultivate beauty in precisely this manner: as a border walker. She refuses to be co-opted by the culture warriors vying for power, prestige, and wealth. Instead, she cares for culture by empathizing with its pain, confronting its ugliness, and telling everyone about the beautiful dream: the coming kingdom for which all people long, even if they don't know it yet.

Jesus walked the path of the artist, crafting parables of the kingdom that challenged the world around him *and* cultivated the world to come. Now you are being invited into his way. So walk the borders. Develop a hopeful imagination. Hone your skill. And above all, trust that the Master Maker is working alongside you. By his grace, the beauty you create will not only be a gift to the beauty-starved world around you, it will also be the means by which he changes it.

If you want to learn more about how to grow as an artist, you can find additional practices and suggested reading at the end of the book.

Artist Overview

Artists are those who see light in darkness, beauty in ugliness, hope in despair. They walk the border of heaven and earth, life and death, health and sickness. Through rigorous training and practice, they hone their artistic skills to create beauty. Not the cheap beauty of sentimentalism but the rich beauty of imaginative hope rooted in an equally rich empathy for Babylon's castaways. Artists make beauty both to confront the world's ugliness and to cultivate the good within it.

Key Insight: Artists understand that God designed the human soul with a hunger for beauty. But evil and injustice have marred God's beautiful world and made much of it ugly. Thus, true beauty has the power not only to challenge the ugliness but also to paint a picture of our shared dream: God's kingdom on earth as in heaven.

Orientation toward Culture: Artists do not join forces with culture warriors who value art only if it is useful for their particular interests: commercial, political, or ideological. Instead of culture-warring, artists practice culture care, intentionally giving away the gift of beauty, just as God gave us the gift of beauty in his creation. They understand that when humans feed on beauty, it not only nourishes them but also confronts Babylon's ugliness and points all people toward the lovely kingdom of Christ.

Guiding Principles: Artists labor to practice and hone their craft, understanding that beauty can't be created without profound skill. They endeavor to live as "border walkers," those who live between heaven and earth, healing and pain. This allows them to empathize with the pain in the world (the opposite of sentimentalism) *and* project new possibilities for the world (the opposite of cynicism). To that end, they intentionally cultivate a hopeful imagination, which resists our modern penchant for irony and despair.

Shadow Side: Artists are often misunderstood in the church, which sometimes leads them to abandon the church. In their isolation, artists sometimes give themselves to their emotions, especially despair. If they do, they actively isolate themselves from others, giving in to the lies of self-loathing. In such a condition, they become easy prey for Babylon's artists, whose skill and influence sometimes persuade artists to leave behind not only the church but Jesus as well.

CHAPTER 9

The Ambassador

CHANGING BABYLON BY WINNING HEARTS

The evangelical task primarily is the preaching of the Gospel, in the interest of individual regeneration by the supernatural grace of God, in such a way that divine redemption can be recognized as the best solution of our problems, individual and social.

—CARL F. H. HENRY

I am deeply convinced that the greatest need of our time is spiritual awakening and revival.

—LUIS PALAU

Five passengers departed Honolulu for a three-hour sightseeing tour on a Wheeler Express Cruiser. While at sea the cruise encountered a sudden storm, and but for the two-man crew fearlessly navigating the rough water, the ship would have been lost. It ran aground on an uncharted island. The seven passengers were stranded. According to the ship's manifest, in addition to the captain and the first mate, the missing included Thurston Howell III and his wife Eunice, the actress Ginger Grant, professor Roy Hinkley, and Mary Ann Summers.

If you've ever seen *Gilligan's Island*, then you probably know this isn't a true story. It's the setup for the show, a weekly sitcom that ran on CBS from 1964 to 1967 before going into syndication. Undoubtedly, the person most important to the group's survival was the professor, who solved the problem du jour by building homemade contraptions from the boat's spare parts and the natural resources on the island. His most impressive inventions included a Geiger counter to determine whether a meteor was radioactive and a telegraph to try to reach a spacecraft orbiting overhead. After watching enough episodes, you'll ask the obvious question: If the professor can build anything and fix anything, then why doesn't he fix the hole in the boat, allowing them to return home?

How Ambassadors Change the World: Changing and Winning Hearts

We're tempted to do the same thing. We work on urgent secondary problems while ignoring less urgent primary problems. Ambassadors change the world by focusing on the central problem with the human condition: People have a hole in their hearts. They don't know and love Jesus. While ambassadors value changing laws and shaping culture, they refuse to build Geiger counters and neglect the hole in the hull. If you're drawn to the way of the ambassador, it's likely because you see that while a law can ban pornography, only the gospel can change people so they don't lust for illicit sexual material. While a law can ban racial discrimination, only the gospel can change hearts such that we love people who are different from us. While a law can declare abortion illegal, only the gospel can persuade people to give their children the gift of life. While a rehab clinic can offer addiction treatments, only the gospel deals with the problems at the root of addiction.

Ambassadors believe that if we share the gospel, more people will become Christians as a result, and many of the world's problems will be resolved. So they set to work changing the world by winning hearts to Jesus.

Jesus changed the world by forgiving sin, reconciling people to the Father, and transforming humans from the inside out. The primacy of forgiveness takes center stage in Jesus's interaction with the paralytic. The Gospels tell us that Jesus forgave the paralytic's sins even though that wasn't what the man or his friends wanted most. Only after the teachers of the law challenged Jesus's right to forgive sins did he heal the man of his paralysis. It begs the question: Why didn't Jesus immediately do what the paralytic wanted? Because Jesus knew that his paralysis was *a* problem, but his sin was *the* problem.

Jesus didn't *heal* every sick person he encountered. But he did *forgive* every person willing to turn to him. Again, it's not that physical needs are unimportant or that Jesus doesn't care about them. He does. They just aren't the most important problem we have. To paraphrase Jesus, what good is it for a person to have a healthy body, live in a crime-free neighborhood, and have access to clean water but forfeit their soul? This is why proclaiming the gospel was the central task of Jesus's three-year ministry *and* the ministry of his disciples after his ascension.

Ambassadors embrace Jesus's call to make disciples of all nations. They change the world by evangelizing. I don't mean giant crusades and altar calls (though both have been used effectively in the past). I primarily mean *relational* evangelism. Ambassadors build trusting relationships with those far from God, invite them into their homes, and share the gospel.

An ambassador emphasizes relationships and hospitality because they understand how people *actually* change. Conventional thinking is that if you want someone to fight for a cause, then you need to convince them intellectually of the cause's rightness. In this model, reason precedes action. Thus, if you want to change the world, you must aim for the mind. Write articles. Participate in debates. Distribute materials. Make arguments. People will join the movement only after they share your beliefs. But the truth is much more complicated.

Ziad Munson argues in *The Making of Pro-life Activists* that change works in almost the opposite direction. *Belonging precedes believing.* Our beliefs are shaped more by the people we spend time with than by abstract arguments. Munson's research of pro-life activists found that people's "beliefs about abortion are often undeveloped, incoherent, and inconsistent until individuals become actively engaged with the movement."[1] In other words, someone doesn't become a pro-life activist by reading a persuasive pamphlet. Instead, it usually starts with a personal connection. A friend asks you to attend a pro-life march or invites you to volunteer with them at a pro-life pregnancy center. First, you belong, then you believe, and finally, you behave differently.

This pattern permeates most movements, which explains why the early church put such a strong emphasis on hospitality and relationships. Jesus's ministry was a movable feast. All were invited to his table, but especially the hurting. At that table they not only heard the good news, they also tasted it.

Ambassadors understand that people change through relationships. Friendship precedes transformation. Often a person belongs to a Christian community and *then* comes to faith, experiences regeneration, and (sometimes much later) begins to care about social issues and work for a better world. Thus, ambassadors don't change the world by protesting. They change the world by cultivating relationships in Babylon. They seek those far from God, praying that God will heal the hole in their hearts, and then draw them into *his* vision of the good life through friendship. To learn how to live as ambassadors, we'll examine the life of the apostle Paul.

Three Guiding Principles for Ambassadors from the Life of Paul

Before Paul was an ambassador for Christ, he was an ambassador for Judaism. We meet Paul in Acts 8, when he becomes a coconspirator in the persecution and execution of Christians like Stephen. After Stephen's death Paul journeyed to Damascus to imprison followers of Jesus. But he met Jesus on the way, and his life turned upside down. The ambassador attacking Christ suddenly became an ambassador for Christ.

Jesus entrusted Paul with the message that God was reconciling the world to himself. And then, ironically, he made Paul the zealous Jew, his primary ambassador to the despised gentiles. As the story of Acts continues, Paul dedicates himself to sharing that message as widely as possible, even at great cost to his reputation and comfort. He built deep relationships across the Mediterranean basin. He shared meals. He shared his life. He shared his heart.

In Paul's story we find three guiding principles that can help you become an ambassador: redefine success, prioritize prayer for lost people, and live a life that makes following Jesus attractive to those who don't know him.

1. Redefine Success

Jesus dramatically redefined success for Paul. While imprisoned, Paul *rejoiced* because he was an "ambassador in chains."[2] Why? Because he saw his chains as an opportunity to share the gospel with the palace guard. Indeed, it seems that some of his Roman guards converted. At the conclusion of his letter to the Philippians, Paul includes greetings from "those who belong to Caesar's household."[3]

The mostly likely explanation for how they became Christians is that Paul led some of the palace guards to Christ and they in turn shared the gospel with the most powerful and influential family in the world. Paul didn't define success by worldly standards. He was imprisoned. He wasn't a power player in Caesar's court. Instead, he defined success as sharing and spreading the gospel in all circumstances. Ironically, the humble road of building relationships and persuading people of the truth of the gospel probably created more change in Caesar's household than a political figure could.

Paul was so committed to this definition of success that he even rejoiced when people preached the gospel out of impure motives.[4] Some preached out of envy. Others out of ambition. And others out of greed. But whatever the reason, Paul was encouraged because he—like all ambassadors—measured the success of his life by the gospel's progress, not his own freedom, power, or reputation.

A true ambassador seeks out opportunities to share Christ wherever she goes. She knows that she's not in the cancer ward only to get chemo.

She's also there to share Jesus. She knows she's not in the office just to pull a paycheck. She's also there to share about how Jesus changed her life. When she hears that churches and ministries in her town are growing, she rejoices, whether or not she's involved. If you want to be an ambassador, you have to redefine success in your life. No, the goal isn't to awkwardly hawk the gospel in every situation but instead to see every situation as a *potential* opportunity to share about Jesus. Your definition of success shouldn't be based on your reputation. Your definition of a good life shouldn't be measured by personal comfort. If it is, you'll never share the good news. You must redefine success as sharing the good news of the gospel, with the hope that many will put their faith in Jesus.

2. Pray for Lost People

If following Jesus landed you in prison, what would you ask others to pray for? I know what would be at the top of my list: getting me out of here! But Paul never did that. Despite multiple imprisonments he never prayed for release. And he never prayed for his health or comfort either. Instead, Paul prayed for the lost. He prayed that people's eyes would be opened. That they would comprehend spiritual truth.[5] That doors would open for an opportunity to share the truth.[6] That when he opened his mouth, he'd have the right words to "fearlessly make known the mystery of the gospel."[7]

Our prayers reveal what's most important to us. No one talks to God about things they don't care about. If prayer reveals our values, then I'm afraid my prayers reveal that what's important to me is, well, me. Specifically, my circumstances, my health, my safety, my comfort, my family, my possessions, and my success. My prayers center on my needs and my wants. But an ambassador longs for something more than his own comfort and reputation: He prays that God will empower the gospel to spread as far as possible. And God hears the prayers of ambassadors!

In 1934 an elderly woman named Clara Frasher began praying for the high school students in Gainesville, Texas. She invited a few friends to join her. For six years they got down on their knees in Clara's living room and prayed for the students attending the school across the street from her house. In 1939 Jim Rayburn, a seminary student in Dallas, drove seventy-five miles to Gainesville to start a new ministry at the local high school. Why did he choose that school when there were many closer ones that required less travel? The only answer that makes any sense is the prayers of those women. Once he heard about the prayer group, Rayburn joined them. Two years later those prayers birthed Young Life, a ministry that has led hundreds of thousands of students to Christ.

Clara Frasher was an ambassador. You can be an ambassador, too, if you remember that every human heart is in *God's* hands, so there is no greater evangelistic tool than prayer itself. It's better than a communication degree. It's better than good looks. It's better than a good sense of humor. Ambassadors pray with ferocity for the hearts and souls of those far from God.

3. Live in a Way That Makes Christ Attractive

Paul was deeply convinced that the way Christians lived would either draw people to Jesus or repel them. He told Titus to teach others to live such beautiful lives that they made "the teaching about God our Savior attractive in every way."[8] Paul himself was willing to give up his personal freedoms if any of them became a stumbling block inhibiting the spiritual journey of others.[9] Ambassadors understand that their lives often speak louder than their words and that their words can be heard most clearly when their lives are most consistently aligned with Jesus.

In 1994 Mother Teresa spoke at the National Prayer Breakfast in Washington, DC, where she gave a blistering speech on abortion.[10] In attendance were many pro-choice politicians, including President Bill Clinton. When a reporter asked how he felt about what Mother Teresa had said, Clinton remarked, "How do you argue with a life so well lived?" Mother Teresa's life gave her message credibility. Paul said the same is true for every Christian.

Do you realize that your life will either repel or attract people to the gospel? An ambassador who verbally abuses his employees, neglects his children, speaks self-righteously, or attacks his enemies is repellent. No one wants to follow his God. So our lives must taste of the King's savor and shine with the King's beauty so that the King himself is present to the world through us. Only then will others be persuaded to follow him.

Changing the World One Heart at a Time

In 1966 the question "Is God Dead?" appeared on the cover of *Time* magazine. Pundits opined about the decline of Christianity. But five years later the opposite happened. A revival was taking place within California's hippie communities. *Time* magazine yet again released a cover about God, but this time it was a psychedelic Jesus announcing the revival. Apparently God didn't die. Or maybe he did and rose again in a kibbutz. What happened in the five years between those very different magazine covers is simple: A group of ambassadors got to work building relationships, sharing the gospel, and changing lives. One of those ambassadors was a man named Bill Bright.

While studying for a Greek exam as part of his coursework at Fuller Seminary, Bill Bright received a vision from God to launch a nationwide ministry to college students. That ministry, Campus Crusade for Christ (CCC, now known as Cru), became the largest nonhumanitarian Christian ministry in the world, with five thousand staff serving in the United States, thirty thousand serving internationally, and a $500 million budget.

It all began when Bright and his wife, Vonette, were personally mentored by Henrietta Mears, a Bible teacher whose Sunday school class at the First Presbyterian Church of Hollywood regularly drew six thousand people.[11] As part of the ministry, Mears regularly took teams from the church to the nearby UCLA and USC campuses to sharpen their evangelistic skills. Mears wasn't motivated only by evangelistic zeal. She wanted to recapture the universities from secularizing influences, including communism. Convinced that America was joining Europe in turning away from God, Mears believed the answer was personal evangelism and worldwide missions.

Bill Bright was initially scared to share the gospel with a stranger, but the first person he spoke to became a Christian and later went to seminary. Bright concluded that if the gospel was powerful enough to change lives, it was powerful enough to change the world. Communism didn't stand a chance when confronted with the gospel's power.[12] All of this could give the impression that politics were a central concern of Mears and her acolytes. But the truth is that politics were rarely discussed—even after the Brights moved into Mears's house and launched Campus Crusade at UCLA. While Bright was aware of communist influence on UCLA's campus, he didn't engage in voter drives or protest marches. Instead, Campus Crusade focused on what Bright thought mattered most: sharing the good news of Jesus with as many people as possible.

What happened at UCLA served as a paradigm for CCC's future ministry. Bright and his team focused on fraternities, sororities, athletes, and campus leaders. In the first several months, 250 people became Christians, including an all-American linebacker, the student body president, and the editor of the campus newspaper. Bright believed it was leading people to Christ that would can change the world.

As the ministry grew, CCC's national leaders connected their evangelistic initiatives more explicitly to cultural change. In 1975 CCC launched a new ministry called Christian Embassy in Washington, DC. It began with only one staff member and a big vision: evangelize the nation's capital. The Embassy's first president, Rolfe McCollister, said, "We want a more Christian government. We plan to do that by evangelizing official Washington."[13] Swede Anderson, a Bright confidant, said the intention was to "lead these people to Christ," which "would also affect how they would think politically."[14] Bright's ambitions were even larger. He hoped that more conversions would decrease the divorce rate, curtail the sexual revolution, reduce addiction, and create solutions to racial inequities.

Yet in the late 1970s and early 1980s, when many evangelical leaders became more explicitly involved in traditional politics, Bright never joined their ranks. Decades later many leaders regretted their choice, believing it compromised their prophetic voice and turned evangelicalism into a useful tool for right-wing politicians. But because he'd never joined them, Bright never had those regrets. Campus Crusade remained steadfast in its commitment to evangelism. As burdened as he was for social issues like abortion, he said, "I have not felt that fighting abortion is my number one priority, for I try to evaluate everything I do each day in light of the Great Commission."[15]

While the Brights and Campus Crusade for Christ staff cared deeply about the cultural and moral issues affecting people's lives, they never lost sight of their primary calling to share the gospel's good news. They were convinced that if you win people to Christ, then you can win culture to Christ. Today ambassadors cultivate and resist Babylon in a similar fashion. They build relationships, share the gospel, and trust that if God heals the hole in more human hearts, it will have an impact on our collective life together in Babylon.

The Shadow Side of the Ambassador

Campus Crusade was instrumental in my (Keith's) own conversion. It's where I learned to read the Bible, confess sin, and share my faith. I saw myself as an ambassador for much of my Christian life. I avoided cultural and political issues, convinced that evangelism was the *only* way to change Babylon. While I don't think that's the case anymore—as this book shows, there are *many* ways to change Babylon—I've never stopped believing that the world won't change without more people following Jesus. During my time as a student and staff member with Campus Crusade, I saw the beauty of this approach. But I also saw the shadow side. Ambassadors are tempted to turn people into projects, fall prey to easy believism, and underestimate the importance of systems.

Treating People like Projects

In one of the Crusade discipleship groups I attended as a college student, members were expected to share their faith weekly and turn in the names of the people they had talked to. One week I hadn't shared the gospel with anyone, so I left that section of the accountability form blank. When others in my group found out that I hadn't shared Christ with anyone, I was embarrassed and determined not to feel that way again.

So the next week I cornered a first-year student who had the audacity to leave the door to his dorm room open. I went through the Four Spiritual Laws with him, not because I loved him but because I loved myself. To me that student wasn't a person. He was a project. He was a way to fill a blank on a spiritual worksheet and make me look good.

Sharing the gospel shouldn't be a means to a self-serving end. Trying to impress others, grow your ministry, or even change the culture are the wrong reasons to talk to people about Jesus. We will never draw people to the one person who never used people by using them. Jesus didn't love people because it was his job. He just loved them. He enjoyed being with them. They weren't projects. And maybe that's why no one could keep lost people from him.

People can tell when you're genuinely interested in them and when they've become your project. When we see people as Jesus does, we love them. And out of love for them, we share with them the love of God in Christ.

Falling Prey to Easy Believism

In the Great Commission, Jesus didn't call his disciples to tally "decisions for Christ." He called them to make disciples, teaching them to obey his commands. Jesus values *disciples* over *decisions*. This is because praying the sinner's prayer doesn't make a person a Christian. Only faith does. And Jesus says the evidence of genuine faith is a *changed life*. So he's less interested in altar calls and magic prayers. He wants transformed disciples.

One of the most tragic illustrations of why easy believism *isn't* enough took place in the spring and summer of 1994 in Rwanda. Hutu militants murdered between five hundred thousand and eight hundred thousand Tutsis. Many of the victims were killed in their own homes by their own neighbors and villagers. As many as five hundred thousand women were raped. What should shock us is that Rwanda was one of the most Christianized countries in Africa, with upward of 90 percent of the country identifying as Christians. Hutus and Tutsis attended the same churches. Many of the deaths occurred on church property. How could something like this happen? The answer is easy believism: Christians emphasizing one-time intellectual assent to orthodoxy over obedience to Jesus.

Anytime an ambassador reads about "decisions" and "conversions," she should ask, *What happened next?* How are they growing? Are they connected to a Christian community? Even the best evangelists don't always produce the best long-term results. One report shows that only 6 percent of those who came forward at a Billy Graham Crusade "are any different in their beliefs and behavior one year later."[16]

John Heyman, the creator of Campus Crusade's *Jesus Film*, saw the issue with such problems: "They accept commitments but do nothing to nurture the commitments, and people are left out there dangling and still looking."[17] An ambassador's goal isn't to tally numbers. It's to build *life-changing* relationships that draw people into *lifetime* discipleship.

Underestimating the Importance of Systems

Ambassadors are tempted to put too much faith in the power of the individual to change the culture. One more person fighting racism might change racism. One more person mitigating climate change may change the climate law. One more person refusing to abort a child might change abortion law. It's intuitive to believe that the world improves every time another individual follows Jesus, but is that true?

During a speech at UCLA, Dr. Martin Luther King Jr. addressed the primary objection moderate white Protestants had toward civil rights legislation. They were for desegregation but said that discrimination is a *heart* issue, not a law issue. They wanted King to slow down and focus on the heart, not to pass legislation. Dr. King told the crowd that he could affirm some truth in that argument but that there was more to say.

It may be true that you can't legislate integration, but you can legislate desegregation. It may be true that morality cannot be legislated, but behavior can be regulated. It may be true that the law cannot change the heart, but it can restrain the heartless. It may be true that the law can't make a man love me, but it can restrain him from lynching me, and I think that's pretty important also. So while the law may not change the hearts of men, it does change the habits of men. And when you change the habits of men, pretty soon the attitudes and the hearts will be changed. And so there is a need for strong legislation constantly to grapple with the problems we face.[18]

While the ambassador rightly notes that individuals sometimes shape the law, the inverse is also true. Systems of laws and economics have the power to shape (and oppress) individuals. Some things are both heart issues *and* legal issues. Some changes need both individual *and* systemic transformation. In the 1950s and 1960s, a person coming to authentic faith in Christ would most likely, over time, make their sphere of influence less racist and more accepting. But such changes would not stop lynchings, integrate lunch counters, enfranchise Black voters, or allow interracial couples to thrive.

Ambassadors may be sheepish about confronting controversial cultural issues—often because they don't want to lose the opportunity to speak to both sides of the debate—but Jesus invites us to do more than preach good news. When he began his ministry, he said,

> [God] has anointed me
> to proclaim good news to the poor.
> He has sent me to proclaim freedom for the prisoners
> and recovery of sight for the blind,
> to set the oppressed free,
> to proclaim the year of the Lord's favor.[19]

In response, everyone in his hometown tried to run him off a cliff. So it's true that seeking justice might make our evangelistic calling more challenging. Still, ambassadors must not succumb to the temptation to separate the good news of forgiveness from the good news of justice—which often means attending to the systems around us.

Start with the Heart

If you want to change the world, you must deal with the hole in every human heart. Forgiveness and transformation were central to Jesus's ministry not because physical and social needs are unimportant but because they are *secondary* to our spiritual needs. Therefore, ambassadors take to heart Jesus's commission to make disciples and proclaim the gospel. They build relationships, invite people into their homes, and—when the time is right—share the gospel.

In today's world we need more ambassadors. Evangelism has fallen on hard times. Some Christians even think it's *wrong* to share the gospel. But what could be wrong about inviting others to encounter the King of joy and life? Nothing!

If God is calling you down this path, redefine success in your life. Every time and every place is an opportunity to build a relationship, love a person, and share about Jesus. Pray for the lost with fervor. Live an attractive life, seasoned with goodness, generosity, and kindness. By these ordinary means, God may use you to change individual lives. And as individual lives change, families change. And as families change, neighborhoods change. And then cities. And states. And even nations. Evangelism isn't all we need to cultivate and resist Babylon, but there's no hope if we don't share the gospel. So, ambassadors, reach out for the lost, invite them into your homes, share the good news, and rejoice when our world grows closer to God's kingdom.

If you want to learn more about how to grow as an ambassador, you can find additional practices and suggested reading at the end of the book.

Ambassador Overview

Ambassadors find great joy in sharing the gospel with people and seeing them come to faith in Jesus. They know they represent Jesus to the people in their lives, so they are careful to live in a way that makes the gospel attractive and does not hinder their neighbor's faith journey. By leading people to Jesus, ambassadors hope to bring fundamental change to Babylon one heart at a time.

Key Insight: Ambassadors believe that apart from Jesus, every human has a hole in their heart. So rather than fixating on all the secondary issues that plague humanity, they address the fundamental problem by sharing the gospel. This requires them to build bridges, make friendships, and practice hospitality.

Orientation toward Culture: Ambassadors know that until we address the hole in every human heart, all our attempts to solve social problems will fall short. Genuine cultural change can't just be legislated. Therefore, ambassadors believe the best way to change Babylon is to help people develop a relationship with God.

Guiding Principles: Ambassadors don't measure success by their personal comfort and reputation but by the gospel's progress in the world. They fervently pray for the lost, asking God to give them opportunities to talk to their neighbor about Jesus. They keep careful watch over their lives to ensure that they attract people to Jesus rather than repelling them with immorality or self-righteousness.

Shadow Side: An ambassador's enthusiasm to see people become Christians can lead them to treat people like projects. Likewise, it can cause them to water down the gospel message, emphasizing decisions for Christ over discipleship. They sometimes overemphasize the importance of the individual and minimize the ways in which legal and cultural systems harm others.

CHAPTER 10

The Protester

CHANGING BABYLON BY CHALLENGING INJUSTICE

*To enact a vision of human flourishing based on the
qualities of life that Jesus modeled will invariably
challenge the given structures of the social order. In this
light, there is no true leadership without putting at risk
one's time, wealth, reputation, and position.*

—JAMES DAVISON HUNTER

*Come dream with me. Dream of a fight for something
bigger, something more important and worthwhile. We
need to fight for justice and peace, for the walls between
us to come crashing down.*

—JOHN M. PERKINS

Shawn Fain looks more like a high school biology teacher
than a union boss. But the deeply religious man raised in a Missionary
Baptist church in Indiana is the president of the United Auto Workers, one
of America's largest and most powerful unions. Fain was elected to the
position on the promise to employ a more aggressive negotiating strategy

with the big three automakers. This led to a successful strike, resulting in sizable employee pay raises.

A few days before launching the strike, Fain shared how his Christian faith informs his leadership. He told union members that he begins every day by reading from a devotional and praying. Then he shared an entry he'd read earlier in the week:

> Great acts of faith are seldom born out of calm calculation.
>
> It wasn't logic that caused Moses to raise his staff on the bank of the Red Sea.
>
> It wasn't common sense that caused Paul to abandon the law and embrace grace.
>
> And it wasn't a confident committee that prayed in a small room in Jerusalem for Peter's release from prison.
>
> It was a fearful, desperate, band of believers that were backed into a corner.
>
> It was a church with no options, a congregation of the have-nots pleading for help, and never were they stronger.
>
> At the beginning *of every* act of faith, there is often a *seed of fear*.[1]

Later in the same speech, Fain turned to Matthew 19:23–24 to paint an earthly vision of the kingdom of God:

> Why is it easier for a camel to pass through the eye of a needle than for a rich man to enter the kingdom of God? I have to believe that the answer, at least in part, is because in the kingdom of God, no one hoards all the wealth while others suffer or starve. In the kingdom of God, no one puts themselves in a position of total domination over entire communities. In the kingdom of God, no one forces others to perform endless, backbreaking work just to feed their families or put a roof over their heads.[2]

Shawn Fain rooted the UAW strike in a biblical vision for a better world.

He is a protester, and he's hardly the first. The book of Exodus records the oldest example of protest in human history: Shiphrah and Puah, the midwives who refused Pharaoh's order to execute Hebrew babies. One could easily argue that the biblical tradition *invented* the concept of protest. The Bible is a minority report on the empire. In it stirs a spirit of protest. A voice that can't remain silent in the presence of Babylon's evil. Since the days of Shiphrah and Puah, God has called many protesters to resist *and* cultivate Babylon by boldly challenging its injustice.

How Protesters Change the World

Marches. Sit-ins. Picket lines. Open letters. Civil disobedience. Protests take many forms, but they all share one thing in common: They interrupt society's natural rhythms. Shouts interrupt silence. Public letters interrupt hierarchies. Picket lines interrupt business operations. Bodies interrupt traffic. The interruptions issue a message: *We are discontent with the status quo, and we will interrupt it until it changes.* Or as they say, "No justice, no peace."

Depending on your temperament (or ideological bent), you may find these interruptions heroic or frustrating. But the *reason* people protest is because protests work. Or, more aptly, *some* protests work. If you want to walk the path of the protester, you must start by wrestling with the truth that many protest movements lead to nothing. Initially, the Occupy Wall Street movement intrigued me. But my interest quickly soured when I realized all they had were grievances against Wall Street and no positive plan. Their protests led to *nothing.* So why do some protests create change, while others cause no effect? Let's look at three key components:

1. **Successful protests require a critical mass of diverse people.** According to Erica Chenoweth, professor of public policy at the Harvard Kennedy School, 3.5 percent of the population is the magic number. No protest movement with that participation rate has ever failed.[3] When a movement gains that much momentum, it is difficult to stop. That means the moment a protest gets riotous or violent, it defeats itself. Fewer people will participate.

The elderly, children, the disabled, and the risk-averse will not feel safe joining.

2. **Successful protests undermine the authority of the powerful.** Leaders have power only so long as people obey the rules. But once a critical mass of people refuse to do so, the powerful lose legitimacy. Zeynep Tufekci, associate professor at the University of North Carolina, writes, "The Soviet Union did not fall because it ran out of tanks to send to Eastern Europe when the people there rebelled in the late 1980s. It fell, in large part, because it ran out of legitimacy and because Soviet rulers had lost the will and the desire to live in their own system."[4] When enough people refuse to comply with the policies, the institution loses the ability to function and unjust leaders eventually find leadership impossible.

3. **Successful protests change the Overton window.** The Overton window is the range of beliefs considered acceptable by most of the population. For example, in the 1940s most white Americans thought that being prosegregation was an ethically, socially acceptable position—even if they didn't hold that position themselves. By the 1990s the opposite was true: Most white Americans would consider a prosegregation stance barbaric and unacceptable. The Overton window shifted dramatically. Such rapid changes are rare and often driven by protest movements. If a protester wants to participate in large-scale social change, they must keep this long game in mind. If she wants to create small-scale or local change, the same applies: She must shift the window of what people *locally* find morally acceptable.

Protests are Christian to the extent they are shaped by Christian virtues. This means fighting for causes aligned with God's values. But it also means fighting God's *way*. Remember, Jesus rejected the path of the Zealots. You can't bring in God's kingdom through Babylon's methodologies. That's why joyful outsiders who walk the path of protest follow the footsteps of Shadrach, Meshach, and Abednego.

Four Guiding Principles for Protesters from Shadrach, Meshach, and Abednego

King Nebuchadnezzar did what all megalomaniacs do: He made a statue of himself. And then he said the quiet part out loud: *I made it so you would worship me.* He called together government officials from across the empire to gather before the golden statue, and then he ordered them—and the entire population of Babylon—to bow down to it whenever they heard music playing. His guards would, quite literally, incinerate anyone who resisted.

What would you do if a despotic, violent, and volatile pagan king told you to worship him *or else*? Shadrach, Meshach, and Abednego chose civil disobedience. They publicly and nonviolently refused to bow before the idol. As officials in Nebuchadnezzar's government, they weren't naive about the consequences. They knew their peers would notice and report their insubordination to Nebuchadnezzar. When they did, the king hauled them in for questioning. They met Nebuchadnezzar's overheated rage with serene confidence. They had counted the cost. And they chose joy over conformity.

So the king tossed them into the furnace. But God protected them. Jesus was with them in the flames. When they emerged with no smell of fire on them, their protest had its intended effect: Nebuchadnezzar was chastened and worshiped their God. In Shadrach, Meshach, and Abednego's story, we learn what all protesters need: moral clarity, courage, hope, and a commitment to nonviolence.

1. Develop Biblical Moral Clarity

Shadrach, Meshach, and Abednego weren't seeking a fight with King Nebuchadnezzar. They willingly participated in the same leadership development program Daniel did. They took on Babylonian names without protest. When they felt they couldn't eat Babylonian food, they didn't picket or draw attention to themselves. Instead, they respectfully asked for permission to abstain and received it. But when Nebuchadnezzar ordered the whole nation to worship him, they knew they couldn't remain silent.

This couldn't be handled privately or quietly. It was a public issue. It was a public command. It required public defiance. It required public interruption. The differences in their approach to the various situations show discernment. Breaking the first three commandments publicly is far more grievous than a name change. That kind of moral clarity is rare.

Similarly, a protester must develop the wisdom required to navigate complicated moral issues. They can't object to everything in Babylon and hope to have any influence. To know when the stakes are high, and a protest is necessary, they need a mind trained by Scripture. God's Word alone defines good and evil. A quote apocryphally attributed to Dr. King gets it right: "One has not only a legal but a moral responsibility to obey just laws. Conversely, one has a moral responsibility to disobey unjust laws." The problem is that most people lack the moral clarity to tell the difference. They rely on their feelings and intuition. But a protester *must not* do this. We serve not ourselves but King Jesus. So if you haven't worked hard to develop a theologically rich and ethically sound vision of God's world according to God's Word, then you aren't ready to protest. Protesters have moral clarity *because* they have a firm grasp on the Bible's vision of right and wrong.

2. Show Courageous Conviction

Without courage there is no protest. Those in power don't loosen their grip willingly. The fingers of unjust leaders must be pried open. The protester must have enough courage to risk her reputation, her job, her freedom, her family, or even her life. Shadrach, Meshach, and Abednego didn't know God would save them from the furnace. More likely, they'd feel the furnace melt and peel their skin until they suffocated and then died. So resisting the king took courage. They were willing to die to stay true to their convictions.

Most of us *assume* we'd show courage in the decisive moment. Had you been a soldier in Nazi Germany, you would've rescued Jews, not executed them. Had you been a housewife in Selma, Alabama, you would've courageously marched alongside King on Bloody Sunday, not cheered as the dogs tore their bodies. Had you been with Jesus at his arrest, you would've had the courage to stand by him, not deny him.

Of course, that's exactly what Peter thought too. When Jesus told him that he lacked courage, Peter responded, "Lord, I am ready to go with you to prison and to death."[5] A few hours later he denied Jesus three times. If Peter lacked courage in the decisive moment, why do we assume we're any different? We're not. Which means courage is something we must *develop*, not *assume*.

The problem is that the most popular form of protest—social media slacktivism—develops vanity, not courage. It's hardly an act of bravery to post about a popular cause on your social media account. Such "protests" accomplish little but self-adulation. Rather than training yourself to show courageous conviction, you're training yourself to protest when it makes you look good. Your protest might not be a protest if it doesn't require you to risk anything but a mouse click. Protest requires bravery.

That said, a protester's courage does not, ultimately, come from herself. When she experiences fear—and she will!—she doesn't say to herself, "Self, please stop being afraid." Instead, she takes hold of God's promise "Do not be afraid. I am with you."[6] She draws strength from the stories of those who showed bravery before her. Moses confronted Pharaoh. Esther interrupted Xerxes. Daniel prayed to God, not Darius. Only then does the protester step out in courage and act. *That* is how you develop courage.

3. Display Radical Hope

Before Shadrach, Meshach, and Abednego were interrogated, they knew what awaited them. The most powerful king in the Middle East was about to vent his fury on them—and yet they never lost hope. When he threatened them with death, they responded calmly, tactfully, *and* defiantly, "King Nebuchadnezzar, we do not need to defend ourselves before you in this matter. If we are thrown into the blazing furnace, the God we serve is able to deliver us from it, and he will deliver us from Your Majesty's hand. But even if he does not, we want you to know, Your Majesty, that we will not serve your gods or worship the image of gold you have set up."[7]

Contrary to how things looked, God was in control, not King Nebuchadnezzar. So their hope was in God. He would rescue them either from the furnace or in the life to come.

The opposite of hope is cynicism. And cynics make for terrible protesters for one simple reason: The only logical reason to make a sacrifice is because you believe something better is possible. Why risk your personal welfare if you have no hope for change? To the cynic, the powers are invincible, so resistance is futile.

In *I Am Not Your Negro*, James Baldwin recounted how in 1968, Robert Kennedy said it was conceivable that in forty years, America would have a Black president. Baldwin dismissed the comment out of hand. He had good reason to be cynical. Even after the passage of the Civil Rights Act, Black leaders were being assassinated. Racism continued to churn through bodies. But his cynicism clouded the future. Forty years later Barack Obama was elected president. Indeed, he enshrined the possibility of a better world in the White House by weaving Dr. King's words "The arc of the moral universe is long, but it bends toward justice" into a rug in the Oval Office.

King didn't root this hope in the secular myth of progress. He rooted it in the Bible's promise. The Bible is a book of hope because it is the story of God's plan to set this broken world back into joint. To confront every evil. Right every wrong. Wipe away every tear. King remembered what we too easily forget: Christianity is a *hopeful* faith. Unlike the Greeks and Romans in the first century, Christians weren't fatalists. Unlike the Babylonians, the exiles didn't see history as a repeating cycle. No, Christians believe history *does* have a trajectory. King said,

> The method of nonviolence is based on the conviction that the universe is on the side of justice. It is this deep faith in the future that causes the nonviolent resister to accept suffering without retaliation. He knows that in his struggle for justice he has cosmic companionship. This belief that God is on the side of truth and justice comes down to us from the long tradition of our Christian faith. There is something at the very center of our faith which reminds us that Good Friday may reign for a

day, but ultimately it must give way to the triumphant beat of the Easter drums. Evil may so shape events that Caesar will occupy a palace and Christ a cross, but one day that same Christ will rise up and split history into A.D. and B.C., so that even the life of Caesar must be dated by his name. So in Montgomery we can walk and never get weary, because we know that there will be a great camp meeting in the promised land of freedom and justice.[8]

Apart from the Christian story, hope is naive. Who could hope that justice will prevail in such a broken world? No one except those like Shadrach, Meshach, and Abednego—those who trust in the goodness and sovereignty of God.

4. Commit to Nonviolence

When Nebuchadnezzar ordered everyone to bow down to the golden statue, Shadrach, Meshach, and Abednego didn't take up arms. If resistance resulted in death, why not die fighting? Why not die starting a rebellion? But they weren't combatants. Instead, they walked in the way of Jesus. They loved their enemies. They turned the other cheek. They took up their cross. They peacefully resisted and then willingly submitted to the punishment for their act of civil disobedience.

Similarly, protesters must commit to nonviolence. Not just for moral reasons but for practical ones too. Omar Wasow, a political science professor at UC Berkeley, examined Black-led protests during the Civil Rights Movement to determine the political consequences of protest marches. He concluded that whether a protest was peaceful or violent, it shaped the media coverage and affected subsequent elections.[9] Peaceful protests resulted in headlines highlighting the concerns of the protesters. But violent protests were framed as riots. Peaceful protests led to favorable elections for politicians supporting the protesters, while violent protests did the opposite.[10]

After Bloody Sunday on March 7, 1965, images of state troopers bludgeoning unprotected protesters with clubs, whips, and rubber tubing wrapped in barbed wire filled TV screens and newspapers. They shocked the nation's conscience and led to an increase of support for civil rights legislation. If the protesters had retaliated, the opposite may have happened.

But King would be the first to tell you that the reason protesters adopt nonviolence is *not* just practical. It's moral. In his Nobel Prize acceptance lecture, he said, "We adopt the means of nonviolence because our end is a community at peace with itself."[11] Jesus concurred, commanding his people to live at peace with those who seek us harm: "I tell you, do not resist an evil person. If anyone slaps you on the right cheek, turn to them the other cheek also. . . . I tell you, love your enemies and pray for those who persecute you."[12]

Civil rights activist Clarence Jordan was right: "We cannot enter the kingdom of peace with a six-shooter on our hip."[13] The means of our protest must correspond to the character of our community. God wisely designed the world such that nonviolent means have a tremendous power to change it. Jesus's nonviolent church changed Rome's landscape, and modern nonviolent protests can do the same.

Few lives show the power of moral clarity, courage, hope, and nonviolence like the life of Fannie Lou Hamer. In her story, all joyful outsiders find a model of how to cultivate and resist Babylon by means of loving protest.

The Protest That Changed the Delta

Fannie Lou Hamer is the civil rights champion every historian celebrates but too few Americans know. Born a sharecropper in 1917, she died a saint in 1977. Hamer was six years old when she started picking cotton as a sharecropper in the Mississippi Delta. Like most Black Americans in the South, she regularly saw terrible violence against her people. Between the end of Reconstruction in 1877 and the beginning of the Civil Rights Movement in 1954, four thousand Black people were lynched across the South. Two hundred fifty-five of those lynchings occurred in the Delta's nineteen counties. Civil rights activists decided that made it a critical location for a voter registration drive. If they broke the Delta, they could break the Jim Crow South.

In August 1962, Hamer heard pastor James Bevel preach a sermon connecting faith and social action. Bevel asked, "How can we not recognize that the hour has arrived for black men and women to claim what is rightfully their own—the right to vote?"[14] In the call for justice Hamer heard the call of Jesus.

"When they asked for those to raise their hands who'd go down to the courthouse the next day, I raised mine," Hamer later explained. "Had it up as high as I could get it. I guess if I'd had any sense I'd a-been a little scared, but what was the point of being scared? The only thing they could do was kill me and it seemed like they'd been trying to do that a little bit at a time since I could remember."[15]

With nothing to lose but her life, she boarded a bus with seventeen others. It took them to the county courthouse to register. But by the time the bus stopped, fear had already gripped the travelers. "[When] we got there most of the people were afraid to get off the bus," said civil rights worker Charles McLaurin. "Then this one little stocky lady just stepped off the bus and went right on up to the courthouse and into the circuit clerk's office."[16] It was Fannie Lou Hamer.

She quickly learned that getting off the bus wasn't the biggest hurdle. The Sworn Written Application for Registration asked for the applicant's name, place of residence, and employer.[17] The not-so-subtle hint was that both their employer and the Ku Klux Klan would be alerted. Jobs would be lost. Houses might burn down. But even if Hamer withstood the raw intimidation, she still had *legal* obstacles. The application required prospective voters to produce an assigned section of the state constitution from memory and then provide a "reasonable interpretation" of it. Hamer was assigned a passage about de facto laws. "I knowed as much about a facto law as a horse knows about Christmas Day," she said. That was the point. The literacy test wasn't designed to encourage informed voting but to prevent Blacks from voting. Whites were exempt from the test if the registrar deemed them of high moral character.[18]

After Hamer filled out the form and failed the test, she returned home to find that the plantation owner, B. D. Marlowe, was on his way to talk to her about her trip to the courthouse. She met him on the front porch. More than a little heated, Marlowe told her, "You'll have to go back down there and withdraw that thing, or you'll have to leave."[19]

Unperturbed, Hamer responded, "Mr. Dee, I didn't go down there to register for you. I went down there to register for myself." B. D. Marlowe gave her until morning to choose. She left that night. Hamer later said, "I had been workin' at Marlowe's for eighteen years. I had baked cakes and sent them overseas to him during the war; I had nursed his family, cleaned his house, stayed with his kids. I had handled his time book and his payroll. Yet he wanted me out. I made up my mind I was grown, and I was tired. I wouldn't go back."[20]

She understood how the system worked and was determined that it wouldn't defeat her. So she returned to the courthouse and told the registrar, "Now, you cain't have me fired 'cause I'm already fired, and I won't have to move now, because I'm not livin' in no white man's house. I'll be back here every thirty days until I become a registered voter."[21] On her third attempt, she succeeded. Fannie Lou Hamer's protest broke the Mississippi Delta.

This Little Light of Mine

The following summer, Hamer's courageous protesting took the form of a sit-in at a "whites only" lunch counter in Winona, Mississippi. When the restaurant owner alerted the authorities, officers arrived to forcibly remove the protesters from the premises. Fannie Lou was one of the women arrested. "They carried us on to the county jail," Hamer said. "It wasn't the city jail, [but] the county jail, so we could be far enough out. [They] didn't care how loud we hollered, wasn't nobody gon' hear us."[22]

In the prison, Hamer listened to Annell Ponder's and June Johnson's screams before it was her turn. The severe beating she received at the hands of two Black men—who themselves were under the threat of physical punishment if they refused to cooperate—resulted in permanent physical damage. After the beating, she sang,

Paul and Silas was bound in jail, let my people go.

Had no money for to go their bail, let my people go.

Paul and Silas began to shout, let my people go.

Jail doors open and they walked out, let my people go.[23]

She later explained, "When you're in a brick cell, locked up, and haven't done anything to anybody but still you're locked up there, well sometimes words just begin to come to you and you begin to sing."[24] And she never stopped singing. Hamer knew she sung to the God who delivered Israel from slavery and believers from sin. She knew he'd rescue her too.

Yet there was a dissonance in her faith. She never understood how white Christians could read the same Bible and justify the mistreatment of their brothers and sisters. "Christianity is being concerned about [others], not building a million-dollar church while people are starving right around the corner," said Hamer. "Christ was a revolutionary person, out there where it was happening. That's what God is all about, and that's where I get my strength."[25]

Hamer's faith led her to cofound the Mississippi Freedom Democratic Party, in opposition to the all-white, anti–civil rights Mississippi Democratic Party, for the right to represent the state at the Democratic National Convention. By the time the DNC's Credentials Committee was scheduled to hear Hamer's testimony asking them to reject Mississippi's all-white delegation, it became a national news event. President Lyndon B. Johnson, fearful that he'd lose the Southern vote if civil rights became a central issue in the election, called an impromptu press conference to draw attention away from the hearing. Having realized they'd been duped by the president, the television networks later replayed Mrs. Hamer's testimony. The president tried again to quiet her by dispatching a team of trusted advisors, including Walter Mondale, J. Edgar Hoover, and vice-presidential candidate Senator Hubert Humphrey, a well-known civil rights advocate. Senator Humphery relayed the national party's final compromise to the Mississippi Freedom Democrats. Hamer wasn't impressed and warned him that the vice presidency wasn't worth his soul. She later recalled what she told him:

> Senator Humphrey, I been praying about you; and I been thinking about you, and you're a good man, and you know what's right. The trouble is, you're afraid to do what you know is right. You just want this job as vice president. I know a lot of people have lost their jobs, and God will take care of you, even if you lose out on this job. Mr. Humphrey do you mean to tell me that your position is more important to you than 400,000 black people's lives? Mr. Humphrey, I'm going to pray for you again.[26]

After that, no one in Democratic leadership scheduled meetings with her. They knew she was a force that couldn't be stopped.

Hamer died of complications from breast cancer on March 14, 1977, aged sixty. She was buried in her hometown of Ruleville, Mississippi. Andrew Young, the United States ambassador to the United Nations, spoke to an overflow crowd. After Young's eulogy, Hamer kept singing—this time through a crowd stricken by grief. The mourners sang Hamer's favorite song: "This Little Light of Mine."

Before she died, she had explained why she loved the song: "[In] the fifth chapter of Matthew, [Jesus] said, 'A city that's set on a hill cannot be hid.' And I don't mind my light shining; I don't hide that I'm fighting for freedom because Christ died to set us free. And he stayed here until he got thirty-three years old, letting us know how we would have to walk."[27] Hamer let the light Jesus gave her shine in protest. You can do the same. And the darkness cannot overcome it.

The Shadow Side of the Protester

A protester's strong sense of right and wrong sometimes makes him blind to his own shortcomings and mixed motivations. It's only natural. When you are busy fighting the evil in the world, you sometimes forget about the evil in every human heart. Protesters aren't perfect, and their imperfections are often used to discredit their cause. It's more politically expedient to hide your sin than share it and risk jeopardizing the cause. But what do you gain if you win a legal war but lose your soul in the process? To that end, protesters must actively resist three temptations that derail their ability to do good in Babylon: participating in virtue signaling, seeking personal gain, and demonizing opponents.

Participating in Virtue Signaling

In the spring of 2021, audio surfaced of a phone call between Rachel Nichols, one of ESPN's NBA reporters, and Adam Mendelsohn, LeBron James's advisor. During the call, Nichols indicated that she thought Maria Taylor got the coveted host position for *NBA Countdown* during the Finals because she is Black. Nichols, who is white, was known for being a public supporter of diversity, but her private comments demeaned Taylor as a diversity hire. After the call was leaked to the public a year later, Kevin Draper wrote in the *New York Times*, "Multiple Black ESPN employees said they told one another after hearing the conversation that it confirmed their suspicions that outwardly supportive white people talk differently behind closed doors."[28]

Rachel Nichols was guilty of virtue signaling. She cultivated a public persona that was inconsistent with her private self.

While social media allows protests to rapidly expose injustices and mobilize supporters, it also allows people to project a positive image without taking effective action or making costly choices. People who make their profile pictures a black square aren't necessarily trying to be dishonest, but many have bought into the "highly online" lie that putting something on the internet makes it real and causes change. In truth, it just excuses people from taking risks. And without risk there can be no change. Virtue signaling isn't a protest, it's a performance. So protesters walking in the way of Jesus should be cautious about social media posts that make them look more virtuous than they truly are. They must heed Jesus's warning about doing good works to be seen by others. Better for your work to go unnoticed than to be noticed for work you haven't done.

Seeking Personal Gain

Ibram X. Kendi's *How to Be an Antiracist* was published in 2019 but didn't become a bestseller until George Floyd was murdered in 2020. Kendi was named a MacArthur Genius the following year and received a $625,000 no-strings-attached grant. After learning of the grant, he told the *Guardian*,

> When inequality is normal, and you're doing nothing to challenge that inequality, you're complicit in its maintenance. . . . To be antiracist is to actively challenge the structures of racism in this country. If we're truly serious about dismantling racism, we have to figure out a way to both analyse and study the structure of racism, while also providing a pathway for individuals to dismantle that very structure that we're seeking to eliminate. Some people would call this idealistic, I don't think it's idealistic. I think it's the world that we should be focused on creating.[29]

Kendi hit the speaking circuit, started a podcast, and launched the Center for Antiracist Research in partnership with Boston University.[30] But by the fall of 2023, the *Boston Globe* reported that the center was undergoing a reorganization and cutting staff. Some former employees leveled charges of financial mismanagement. As much as $55 million in donations was unaccounted for. Under Kendi's leadership no degree programs had begun, and the center produced little research. The media pundits who once applauded Kendi now called him a grifter—someone who swindles people out of money through fraud or deceit. And our fractured political environment is ripe for grifters to prosper.

Michael Flynn launched the ReAwaken America Tour to protest the 2020 election results. The speakers on the nationwide tour riled up disaffected Trump voters before appealing for financial donations. It's difficult to believe that Flynn, a retired general, believes the conspiracy he's selling. But, to paraphrase Upton Sinclair, it's difficult for a general to be honest about an election when thousands of people are paying to hear him lie about it. Journalist Tim Alberta visited the tour in Branson, Missouri. He wrote about the ways people were profiting:

Not all swindles were spiritual in nature. One person was screening trailers for his forthcoming documentary about education. Another was raising money for his fight against election fraud. Yet another was pushing his specialty diet and warning about the dangers of "big agriculture." My personal favorite was the guy peddling "Kingdom Fuel," a powdered shake mix, which he pitched as a means of staying healthy, living longer, and defying the malevolent medical regime. (It comes in two flavors, vanilla and chocolate.)[31]

As both of these examples show, successful protests can generate tremendous revenue. The grift happens when protesters realize they can personally profit off of injustice. To keep up the grift, they no longer need to protest genuine injustice but instead only need to gin up fear over make-believe grievances.

Jesus shows us a better way. His ministry also depended on donations, but he did his best (Judas notwithstanding) to steward those resources toward the cause he promoted: the proclamation of the kingdom, the healing of the sick, and the ending of oppression. Christian protesters refuse to inappropriately profit off their cause. Instead, they set up systems of financial accountability to ensure donations are used responsibly.

Demonizing Your Opponents

When you're fighting for a just cause, it's easy to slap unflattering labels on anyone who opposes you. They aren't just wrong. They're wicked. You begin to believe the lie that the line between good and evil cuts between "us" and "them," not down every human heart. Left unchecked, smug self-righteousness builds walls instead of bridges—the very bridges that might bring about the change protesters seek.

In 1957 Dr. King preached one of his most famous sermons, "Loving Your Enemies," at Dexter Avenue Baptist Church. After decades of Jim Crow and thousands of lynchings, it wasn't hard to justify hate. But King refused to give in to the false dichotomy that anyone was purely good or evil. He preached,

[One must] discover the element of good in his enemy, and every time you begin to hate that person and think of hating that person, realize that there is some good there and look at those good points which will over-balance the bad points. . . . Within the best of us, there is some evil, and within the worst of us, there is some good. When we come to see this, we take a different attitude toward individuals. . . . And when you come to the point that you look in the face of every man and see deep down within him what religion calls "the image of God," you begin to love him in spite of [his weakness and evil]. No matter what he does, you see God's image there.[32]

Fannie Lou Hamer would agree. During Freedom Summer in 1964, some civil rights groups didn't welcome the involvement of white college students. But Hamer insisted on an integrated protest movement. She said, "If we're trying to break down this barrier of segregation, we can't segregate ourselves."[33] This is exactly what the apostle Paul told Jews and Gentiles in Ephesus. They couldn't build walls, because Jesus tore down "the dividing wall" with his own blood.[34]

You can't demonize your opponents when you see their humanity. You can't build walls when you worship a king who tore them down. So endeavor to see the image of God in your opponents. Work to see the good. Seek to build bridges, not walls. Resist the temptation to demonize those who oppose you.

Let Your Light Shine

Christians have a rich tradition of protesting injustice. Shiphrah and Puah. Moses. Nathan. Elijah. Daniel. Shadrach, Meshach, and Abednego. And, of course, Jesus. Entire chapters of the Bible are protest literature—railing against the evils of Babylon! That's why it's so surprising that many Christians are hesitant to adopt the posture of a protester—especially when that means breaking laws or interrupting the status quo. The simple truth is that God's people have done this for millennia, and they must continue doing it until Christ returns.

While protest is clearly an act of resistance, it's also an act of cultivation. It clears the ground of the weeds of injustice that choke out goodness, wholeness, and the flourishing of beautiful, beloved communities.

So if you see an injustice, don't be afraid to let your light shine. Find moral clarity in God's Word, take courage from God's promises, and set forward in the hope that because Jesus is king, the arc of the moral universe bends toward justice.

If you want to learn more about how to grow as a protester, you can find additional practices and suggested reading at the end of the book.

Protester Overview

Protesters know God opposes injustice and invites his people to join their voices with his. They have sensitive consciences and deeply feel the plight of those in need. Thus, they speak courageously on behalf of the powerless, knowing they will often suffer as a result. They protest with words and actions, both public and private, knowing that the only way to cultivate justice in Babylon is by first resisting injustice.

Key Insight: God wants his creation to flourish, but corruption and oppression jeopardize his good plans. Protesters are strengthened by God's beautiful vision, knowing that the moral arc of the universe bends toward justice. They participate in God's mission by bending history toward God's ends with both words and actions that show the evil of injustice.

Orientation toward Culture: Protesters change Babylon by challenging injustice. They understand that those in power rarely change without external pressure. But exerting pressure requires a critical mass—people must be rallied. Once enough people join a cause, it's possible to generate legal and cultural change.

Guiding Principles: Protesters have a strong sense of moral clarity, rooted in biblical ethics, which allows them to discern when it is right to actively resist those in power. Doing so comes with great risk, which means protesters must be courageous. But they don't need just *any* kind of courage. They need the kind of courage that comes from confidence in God's promises. They commit themselves to Jesus's ethic of nonviolence, not only because it's effective but also because they seek to create communities that love their neighbor and their enemy. Above all else, they are hopeful: The world *can* change, and that means their work is not in vain.

Shadow Side: Protesters are tempted by easy, costless ways to protest online. When this happens, their protest becomes a performance. It's more about their reputation than the cause itself. Sometimes they go one step further, using the cause for personal gain: fame or fortune. In such scenarios, they have to gin up more grievances, and demonize their opponents, just to keep their protest running. God's cause fades into the background, and the protest is all that matters.

CHAPTER 11

The Builder

CHANGING BABYLON BY BUILDING INSTITUTIONS

*We share in doing the things that God has done in
creation—bringing order out of chaos, creatively
building a civilization out of the material of physical and
human nature, caring for all that God has made.*
—TIMOTHY KELLER

*Perhaps a new generation of leaders will arise who
want to build for posterity, to plant seeds that will take
generations to bear fruit, to nurture forms of culture that
will be seen as blessings by our children's children. If we
are serious about flourishing, across space and through
time, we will be serious about institutions.*
—ANDY CROUCH

Allan Tibbels dribbled the basketball, went for an easy
layup, and tripped. He flew headfirst into a concrete wall. His neck broke
on contact. At age twenty-six he was now a quadriplegic. He wouldn't walk
his daughters down the aisle. He couldn't teach his son to throw a ball. His

wife would need to dress and bathe him. But Allan never gave in to despair. He told his wife, Susan, "Breaking my neck is God's will for my life."[1] He had no idea how right he was.

Eventually Allan returned to his job as a youth worker with troubled kids from suburban Baltimore. Life was a carousel of hardship. Learning to remove a toothpaste cap was such an enormous achievement for Allan that Susan scrapbooked it. Then Allan and a friend, Mark Gornik, began to read the writings of John M. Perkins, a Christian civil rights activist who challenged suburbanites like Allan and Mark to live among those in poverty.

So in 1986 Allan broached the idea with Susan: *What if we embraced a little more tension?* He asked Susan to move with him to Sandtown—the most drug-addled, poverty-stricken neighborhood in all of Baltimore. Despite her initial hesitations, Susan agreed. After they moved, Allan and Mark asked God to show them how they could love their neighbors, and one night Allan shared his vision. He used his mouth to scrawl a drawing of Sandtown with crayons. Instead of tenements with absentee landlords, broken windows, and trash heaps on the sidewalks, he drew fifteen square blocks of clean, beautiful homes owned by local residents. Allan drew his future.

Working alongside Mark, Allan planned the renovation of Sandtown. He founded a Habitat for Humanity chapter and began fundraising. Eventually he scraped together enough funds to build the first house. Sandtown residents made up his work crews, which meant most were ex-convicts, recovering drug addicts, or reformed drug dealers. It was rehabilitation in disguise.

The houses they built had mortgages *half* as expensive as what residents had previously paid in rent. As the years passed, the neighborhood slowly grew stable and beautiful. Before his passing in 2010, Allan built 286 houses from his wheelchair—almost 75 percent of the fifteen square blocks he had dreamed of in crayon decades earlier.

When people claimed he saved Sandtown, Allan would demur. God saves, not him. Allan just shared what he had with his neighbors. Of course, the truth is more complex: God transformed Sandtown through Allan and Mark's efforts. They built houses, churches, gardens, and social programs—in other words, *institutions*—that cared for the holistic needs of their community: material, social, spiritual, vocational, educational, and aesthetic.

Allan was a *builder*. He prayed, "Your kingdom come on earth as in heaven," and then built like God expected him to be the answer to that prayer. All builders seek to change Babylon by building institutions that make Jesus's jubilant dream "to proclaim good news to the poor," give "freedom for the prisoners," and "set the oppressed free," a *reality*.[2] While institutions aren't the hottest topic today, builders understand that institutions are the basic building block of a culture. Princeton professor emeritus of religion Jeffrey Stout wrote, "A culture is an enduring collection of social practices, *embedded in institutions*, reflected in specific habits and intuitions, and capable of giving rise to recognizable forms of human character."[3] In other words, culture is transmitted through institutions. Builders change culture by building and changing institutions. They aren't just charity workers and church planters. Builders are all institutional stewards and leaders. They're entrepreneurs, business owners, investors, politicians, city officials, police officers, managers, doctors, lawyers, principals, and teachers. They're the people who construct and preserve *life-giving* institutions that seek to make Jesus's dream a reality, thereby cultivating the common good in Babylon.

How Builders Change the World: Building toward a Better Dream

Unfortunately, most Western institutions don't pursue Jesus's dream. Instead, they chase the *American* dream. Corporate institutions grow profits and shareholder value so that owners, employees, and shareholders can *enjoy* the American dream. Charities supply material needs like food and housing so that the materially poor can *achieve* the American dream. According to Brian Fikkert, Covenant College professor of economics and community development, the American dream is to become a "purely material, individualistic, self-interested, consuming machine."[4]

American institutions make wealth and consumption their bottom line because that's the bottom line for most Americans. A Pew Research Center study found that parents care far more about their child's bank account than anything else—including marriage and family.[5] My point *isn't* that marriage should be the center of reality but that Americans put little ahead of material prosperity.[6]

The question is whether the American dream is a worthy bottom line for builders. A look at the data suggests the answer is no. In Harvard's seminal, longitudinal study on human happiness, they discovered that while economics *do* play a role in overall happiness and lifespan, the single most important factor is simple: *you need warm relationships to live a happy, long life.* So if you have to choose between the riches of the American dream and the riches of community, you should choose the latter. Unfortunately, we're doing the opposite. The US surgeon general declared that we have a "loneliness epidemic."[7] We're rich in stuff, but we're poor in relationships. So we're deeply unhappy.

Our institutions *must* be built to pursue more than wealth and consumption. The American dream is the wrong dream for both the materially wealthy and the materially poor.[8] The American dream is Babylon's dream. It's full of Babylon's lies. Builders see that if we want to cultivate Babylon, we need institutions that pursue *more* than material prosperity. We need institutions that chase Jesus's vision of the good life.

Allan Tibbels and Mark Gornik built institutions where people could find *holistic* flourishing. Yes, this included housing and food—material needs are real and important! But it also included vocational training, work, community, gardening, art, discipleship, and worship. They didn't build institutions that churned out "wealthy, autonomous consuming machines."[9] They built institutions that changed and challenged Babylon by pursuing a holistic vision of the good life. All builders share that same calling.

Four Guiding Principles for Builders from the Life of Nehemiah

When Jesus walked the streets of Jerusalem, he walked on stones laid by builders before him. One of those builders was Nehemiah, who served as a cupbearer to the Persian king Artaxerxes. At the time, Jerusalem was inhabited but remained in ruins. Most importantly, there was no wall. In the ancient world, unwalled cities were not merely an eyesore. They were architectural invitations to raiders and thieves. A city without walls had no way of stopping violent marauders from sacking, stealing, raping, and pillaging.

So Nehemiah asked the king for a leave of absence, traveled to Jerusalem, and oversaw not only the reconstruction of its walls but also the reformation of its legal and bureaucratic institutions. While far from perfect, Nehemiah sought to construct institutions that not only protected people and supplied material needs but also allowed them to thrive socially, spiritually, and vocationally. He made Jerusalem a place where families could raise their children safely, find work, worship God and no longer needed to sell their property and bodies to others just to survive.[10] In Nehemiah's life we discover four guiding principles for all builders seeking to change Babylon by building institutions.

1. Build Durable Institutions

Nehemiah built a *physically* durable wall and a *socially* durable taxation structure that helped the *whole* community flourish. Durability mattered in part because Nehemiah knew he couldn't remain in Jerusalem forever. Whatever the reason, durability is a key, definitional component of every healthy institution. Scholar Yuval Levin defines institutions as "the durable forms of our common life."[11] This is a spacious definition designed to include charities, businesses, government, education, family, marriage, and much more besides. Like Nehemiah, builders build not for the present but for the future. They construct not for themselves but for others. This requires durable structures, both physical and social.[12]

For example, a builder in private equity must resist the temptation to focus on the short term. Normally, a private equity firm buys a business, strips it, loads debt onto it, and then sells it for a quick profit. This is the opposite of durability. While it might help investors at the firm enjoy the American dream, it ignores the long-term good of the business's employees.

As my friend Brent Beshore jokes, "You should be long-term greedy." He's not actually encouraging greed. He's pressing back against the short-term mindset of his industry. When his private equity firm buys a business, they don't use debt but instead try to create a win-win for all the stakeholders and then hold the business *long term*. During that time, his firm helps the business to flourish holistically, trusting that in the long run healthy people will create healthy organizations and that such businesses will be more valuable—not just materially but also spiritually and socially—in the long term.

Cultivation takes time, and institutions take time to change Babylon. Thus, builders build with durability in mind.

2. Build Communal Institutions

When Nehemiah returned to Jerusalem, he immediately understood that he couldn't rebuild the wall alone. Instead, he gathered laborers from every class and invited them to build for God's glory. The building project was Nehemiah's first step toward creating several institutions within which the community could find not only work but also a common life with common goals.

Compare Nehemiah's approach with the highly individualistic digital culture of social media influencers and celebrities. Or to the federal institutions captured by presidential personality cults. They all build institutions around *individuals*, for the *individual's* benefit. My friend Elizabeth Neumann described the difference between working under President George W. Bush and President Donald Trump in precisely this way. When she told President Bush that she enjoyed serving him, he corrected her and told her that she served the American people. But toward the end of her tenure with Trump, she was put through "loyalty tests" that quizzed her on her knowledge of Trump's life and history. She served *him*, not the people.

I don't share that to make a political point. Instead, I'm trying to highlight a problem crippling Babylon's institutions. Healthy institutions exist for the community, not for an individual. They can't be built without a leader's blood, sweat, and tears. In healthy institutions, individual leaders lay down their lives for their people, not the other way around. Thus, builders build institutions to glorify God and serve others, not to glorify self and serve self. What about you? How does your institution glorify God and serve your community? Find an answer to that question and remain true to it.

3. Build Institutions That Promote Virtue in Its People

Nehemiah cared deeply about the Jewish people's fidelity to God's law, which led him (alongside Ezra) to lead a covenant renewal ceremony. When the people agreed to the covenant, they agreed to follow not only the ten commandments but also the Deuteronomic case laws built around them. Nehemiah built legal structures to enforce the covenant, hoping to form the people into a holy, virtuous people.

Yuval Levin writes that every institution has "frameworks and structures" that govern space (where we interact), time (the schedules of our common life), and practices (the normative behaviors and ethics of our interactions).[13] This is why managers can speak of "workplace environments," "operating hours," and "professionalism." Builders understand that none of these things are morally neutral—they can be designed to inculcate a love of God or a love of Babylon. When you read stories of entire corporations of apparently normal people collectively choosing to lie or that harm others, you should recognize that this happens in part because institutions have an incredible power to shape individuals. Institutions can normalize evil *or* normalize good. Thus, builders seek to design their institutions to foster holiness and virtue, critically evaluating whether an institution's *space*, *time*, and *practices* point toward Christ's vision or away from it.

4. Define and Pursue Your Institution's Purpose

When Nehemiah arrived in Jerusalem, he had a clear sense of purpose: to rebuild Jerusalem's infrastructure and government. But he didn't come to that purpose lightly. He spent days in intense prayer and fasting to discern his purpose. Once he had clarity, he prayed again, and then approached

Artaxerxes to secure the resources necessary to accomplish his purpose.[14] When Nehemiah arrived in Jerusalem, he analyzed the situation and *stated* his purpose to the people in the form of an aspirational story: *We are disgraced and in danger, but God's hand is on us, so let's build this wall.* He spoke with such clarity about his purpose that the people of Jerusalem joined his cause *joyfully.* They worked hard because a clear mission is the key not only to institutional productivity. It's the key to institutional joy.[15]

To do this well, a builder's purpose must have *clarity* and *character.* If he can't state his institutional purpose in one (highly condensed!) sentence, then he lacks *clarity.* Jeff Bezos repeated "Put the customer first" so frequently that it not only became annoying to his employees, it became their way of life. While complexity is good for planning, it's bad for purpose. *Character* also matters. If you can't confidently say that your institutional purpose glorifies God, serves the institution's internal and external community, and pursues a Christ-centered bottom line, then your institutional purpose lacks character.

Lastly, builders understand that purpose is not created *ex nihilo.* Purpose is generated in communion with the creator God, through prayer, reflection, and action.

Clarence Jordan, a New Testament scholar and founder of Koinonia Farm, wrote, "Promised lands of any kind are not . . . ready-made and waiting to be occupied; they are essentially institutions to be painstakingly and eventually achieved by folk who . . . have had some practice in pioneering and in conceiving and constituting new institutions to implement a new and higher way of life."[16] He's right. Institutions aren't just clumps of humans who happen to work together. They're organized, well-led collectives of individuals coordinating their efforts toward a higher cause.[17] Prayer-soaked purpose is the engine that drives a healthy institution. When its purpose is unclear, a business grows rusty, apathetic, and unproductive. When its purpose is aimed toward the American dream, a charity does evil, not good.[18] But when an institution's purpose is oriented toward God's higher ends by God's higher means, it has the power to change Babylon.

Jesus was a builder. And he changed the world by launching a small church of builders. Now he invites you to walk in his way. To show you what that looks like in the world of business, I want to introduce you to an entrepreneur named Pete Ochs.

American Nightmare

Pete Ochs would be the first to tell you, "I love to build things."[19] He grew up on a farm in Hoisington, Kansas. "You had very little money," Pete said, "and when things go wrong, you just had to learn to fix them." Pete also grew up in the church. In sixth grade he was catechized and could tell you the chief end of man by memory: "to glorify God and enjoy him forever."[20] But what that meant in daily life was a mystery to him. *His* chief end was starting a business and living the American dream.

So when he turned thirty, Pete left a high-paying job as a banker to start his own investment banking company. Six years later his company made its first business acquisition. Every year after that, it acquired a new business, and Pete did what most investors do: "Back then, it was the philosophy everybody had," Pete said, "buy a business, put as little down as you can, leverage it, make as much money as you can, and flip it."[21] Longevity and durability weren't his bottom line. Profits were. Even though he was a legally ethical business owner, he wasn't building institutions for the common good.

Pete kept attending church and called himself a "ninety-ten guy." He thought that integrating faith and work meant giving a tithe on Sundays. If Pete grew his wealth, then God would be happy because Pete's tithe would grow. Of course, Pete was excited about what he could do with the remaining 90 percent. It could buy a *lot* of American dream.

By the time Pete reached his forties, he was wealthier and more successful than he ever imagined. But he was empty and unsatisfied. He worked seven days a week. His wife was at a breaking point. Something was missing. Then the Twin Towers fell, and his businesses lost 50 percent of their value. In a single year, everything he had built broke apart into a living nightmare. Pete prayed in anger to God, "Don't you understand what

I've done for you?" But God didn't issue him an apology. Instead, Pete heard God say back, "Pete, I don't want your money. I want your heart."

That revelation made Pete do a one-eighty. He suddenly realized that everything he built wasn't his. It was all God's. And God was asking him to steward it all for a different bottom line: Jesus's vision of the common good. Pete asked, "If we're going to impact *people*, what would that business need? And what would that business look like?" He formulated a new approach to business unlike anything he'd seen in investment banking. He imagined buying companies with the goal of keeping them and developing them not only to produce a profit but also to transform lives.

The story of Adam and Eve became the center of his new vision. In the story of Eden, he found three key insights about what kind of capital a healthy business could produce. First, God put humans on earth to work and produce. This is *economic* capital. Second, God put humans together in relationship with each other and himself. This is *social* capital. Third, God gave Adam and Eve a moral calling to obey him. This is *spiritual* capital. Pete explained in an interview, "We would say the purpose of business is *not* to maximize shareholder value per Milton Friedman and a bunch of others. We would say the purpose of business is to be a catalyst for flourishing. And we would define flourishing as economic, social, and spiritual capital."[22]

Pete had a new business philosophy, one in which his faith and the values of God's kingdom were woven seamlessly into his work. Now he needed to find a company he could purchase, based on his new sense of purpose, and transform it into a new catalyst for human flourishing.

Seat King

Not long afterward, Pete found a struggling industrial chair manufacturer called Seat King. The business would've been profitable but for one problem: They couldn't find enough labor. Pete thought he could solve that problem, so he purchased the business and began the hunt. But the solution he arrived at wasn't what he expected: a maximum-security prison.

Inmates at Hutchinson Correctional Facility in Hutchinson, Kansas, had committed some of the most violent and grievous crimes imaginable.

It wasn't a safe place. But it made good *economic* sense because the inmates needed work, and Pete needed workers. The question was whether building a factory in the prison could meet Pete's other bottom lines: *social* and *spiritual* capital.

At the time, the prison was a social and spiritual desert. Gangs. Drugs. Violence. Pete understood that creating social and spiritual capital would require more than a factory. It would require a vision. "The vision we casted was this," Pete explained, "we want to have the best prison in the United States of America, and to have the best prison, we needed to have the best prisoners, the best inmates." The inmates weren't so sure. "They looked at me like I was some kind of man from outer space."

But Pete had a clear sense of purpose. He would build an institution that changed the lives of prisoners and turned a profit. The inmates changed their minds when they learned that Pete was ready to put his money where his mouth was. Whereas most inmates make fifty cents a day, Pete promised to pay them fair market wages; provide job training in skills like needlework, gluing, and welding; and hold weekly classes on life lessons about fatherhood, leadership, finances, and generosity. Later he invested a million dollars to build a seminary in the prison and develop a curriculum now used across the country.

But the greatest gift Pete gave was himself. He didn't lead from a safe distance. He got to know the guys working on the floor. They could tell he loved them. By personal example Pete created an institutional culture that cultivated virtue, love of others, and excellence. To stay on the floor, inmates needed to practice virtue on and off the clock. Once they entered this institutional greenhouse, the men began to change and grow, shaped by Seat King's institutional norms.

A former employee of Seat King explained that most people end up in prison because they don't know how to make good choices. Prison rarely helps, because everyone is the same. But Seat King was different. "When I had my job at Seat King, I started hanging around more people that knew how to make good decisions," he said, "because to have that job you couldn't get into any trouble." The institution was changing him, and when people gave him a hard time about "hanging around that white dude," he responded, "Why would he want to hang around someone like me? I'm an ex-gang member. I'm a murderer. I'm in prison with a life sentence. Why would he even want to take a chance with me? And that had a huge impact on my life."

In the years since he bought Seat King, Pete has continued to refine his institutional model, applying it in other prisons and deploying it in other countries. He's no longer a ninety-ten guy who thinks God *merely* wants a tithe. He's a builder called to steward *100 percent* of what God has given him. That is what it means to "glorify God and enjoy him forever." The American dream lost its luster for Pete. He regularly gathers with other business owners who voluntarily take significantly lower salaries than they could otherwise because they believe there is such a thing as too much. Babylon might claim otherwise, but Jesus taught that "life does not consist in an abundance of possessions."[23]

For Pete, true life is found in God and shared in a common life for the common good. True life flourishes when builders build healthy institutions designed to last, not to turn a quick profit. True life is cultivated when followers of Jesus live their whole lives for God's great glory, not the American dream. True life is found when God's kingdom is "on earth as in heaven" because people built institutions that care for the *whole* person, not merely their material needs.

How would your life change if you built for better bottom lines? If you rejected the American dream and took hold of Jesus's dream? When builders do this, they're laughed at and treated as outsiders. But give them time and they will do more to care for Babylon's lost and hurting than the scoffers. They'll be the ones who transform Babylon and build things that last.

The Shadow Side of the Builder

In 1932 *New York Times* reporter Walter Duranty won the Pulitzer Prize for his coverage of Stalinist Russia. At the time, there were widespread rumors that Soviets were engineering a famine to kill millions of Ukrainians by starvation. But Duranty claimed he "made exhaustive inquiries about this alleged famine situation"[24] and found that "conditions are bad, but there is no famine."[25] In truth, the Holodomor (Ukrainian for "death by hunger") took millions of Ukrainian lives.

The entire story ended up being a case study in institutional abuse. Stalin used institutional power to kill Ukrainians. Decades after Duranty won the Pulitzer, evidence surfaced that he *willingly* lied for the Soviets. Doing so preserved his connections with Stalin and gave him special access to the regime so he could write *more* award-winning pieces and grow his celebrity.[26] Duranty manipulated his journalistic institution, the *New York Times*, for the sake of personal gain. As he wrote in his prize-winning piece, "You can't make an omelet without breaking eggs."[27] That old cliché summarizes the temptations of every builder: First, the temptation to harm others for the sake of the institution. Second, the temptation to manipulate the institution for personal gain.

Nehemiah knew this temptation all too well. After returning to Persia, he heard reports that Jerusalem had fallen back into idolatry, so he returned and "cursed them and beat some of them and pulled out their hair."[28] His end (stopping idolatry) justified his means (physical and verbal abuse).

Unfortunately, stories of charity leaders, CEOs, and pastors using their institutional authority to abuse others are all too common. If builders aren't careful, they bully. They gaslight. They manipulate. They justify their misdeeds by pointing to all the good they're doing. Mark Driscoll, disgraced former pastor of Mars Hill, once bragged to a group of pastors, "There is a pile of dead bodies behind the Mars Hill bus and by God's grace, it'll be a mountain by the time we're done. You either get on the bus or get run over by the bus. Those are the only options. But the bus ain't gonna stop."[29] He's not the first builder to think this way, and he won't be the last. If you're a builder, you must attend to these stories and soberly realize, *I can become that.*

Therefore, a wise builder sets up accountability systems to protect the institution from current and future abuse—including abuse from the builder herself. This can be scary for builders because they know those systems may very well harm them. But they must ask what's better: becoming a belligerent bully who is far from Christ or a humbled leader who stays close to God?

Left unchecked, bully builders tend to redirect an institution's purpose away from the common good and toward personal gain. They build a cult of personality. They seek celebrity. Again, Nehemiah shows this temptation. Throughout the book, he breaks into first-person celebrations of his work—sometimes taking credit for God's work![30] His self-glorifying refrains grow in frequency as time goes on, suggesting that in Nehemiah's later years he began to see what he built in Jerusalem as a platform for his own renown. His original purpose (to glorify God and serve the community) recedes over time.

Nehemiah's temptation has only accelerated today because of social media and celebrity culture. Yuval Levin warns that in such a society "we will find that the people who occupy our institutions increasingly understand those institutions . . . as platforms that allow them greater individual exposure and enable them to hone their personal brands."[31]

Builders can easily use churches, charities, and businesses to magnify their own name rather than the name of God. If they do this, they begin to make decisions that benefit their short-term interests and hurt the long-term aims of the institution.[32] Yet again, accountability is the best way to resist this temptation. Builders must find trusted friends and advisors—ideally, people they don't pay or manage—who will confront them when they're using the institution for personal gain. Additionally, they should actively avoid drawing attention to themselves and instead make much of God's work and the good work others do.

Build for Heaven on Earth

When Jesus began his public ministry, he unrolled the scroll of Isaiah and read these words to his local synagogue:

> The Spirit of the Lord is on me,
>   because he has anointed me
>   to proclaim good news to the poor.

He has sent me to proclaim freedom for the prisoners
and recovery of sight for the blind,
to set the oppressed free,
to proclaim the year of the Lord's favor.[33]

His proclamation was a confrontation with Babylon. Its institutions had not only failed to care for people, they had oppressed them. But Jesus's proclamation was also a jubilant vision of hope! Prisoners *can* be freed. The blind *can* recover sight. The oppressed *can* be defended. His vision looked forward toward an eternally durable city—the city of God, where all will be as it should be.

In the interim, Jesus invites and graciously empowers builders to make his proclamation a reality on earth as it is in heaven. You are being invited to walk the path of the builder if God has put it in your heart to lead and build. To preserve and upkeep. To start or maintain the businesses, churches, schools, hospitals, and city halls that—if led with wisdom—can become durable and purposeful institutions that cultivate the common good.

If you want to learn more about how to grow as a builder, you can find additional practices and suggested reading at the end of the book.

Builder Overview

Builders are individuals whom God has gifted to lead and preserve institutions like businesses, charities, schools, hospitals, churches, and governmental offices. Rather than chasing the American dream, they build institutions that seek Jesus's vision of the common good. This entails *wholistic* human flourishing, not just *material* human flourishing. Builders try to construct social structures that are durable and communal, not short-term and individualistic.

Key Insight: Builders understand that God designed humans to share a common life inside institutions. When that common life is aimed toward the common good, those institutions become catalysts for human flourishing.

Orientation toward Culture: Most institutions in America direct themselves toward the American dream: an individualistic life accompanied by material wealth and material consumption. But such institutions lead to loneliness, disconnection, and ugliness. Thus, builders construct their institutions both as an act of resistance (they reject the American dream) and as an act of cultivation (they build toward Jesus's dream).

Guiding Principles: Builders construct durable institutions designed to provide long-term wholeness, healing, and prosperity not only for those inside the institutions but also for those outside. They ensure that their institutions are communal. They value the good of the community over the builder's personal interests or the interests of a small group inside the institution. Builders use the space, schedule, and norms of their institution to inculcate virtue. They carefully and prayerfully define the purpose of their institution to ensure it's directed toward God-glorifying ends.

Shadow Side: Builders face the temptation to bully people inside and outside the institution in service of the institution's goals. They take an "ends justify the means" approach to leadership that turns them into narcissists and manipulators. If their behavior goes unchecked, they direct the institution toward their personal interests, using it as a platform for personal gain or celebrity.

Conclusion

A UNIFIED WITNESS

In Kazuo Ishiguro's Nobel Prize–winning novel, *The Remains of the Day*, a butler named Mr. Stevens reflects on the meaning of *dignity*. He recalls the story of a different butler serving in India who found "a tiger languishing beneath the dinner table."[1] Rather than shouting or losing his composure, the butler quietly made his way to his employer and requested permission to use a shotgun in the house.

His employer obliged, and a few minutes later he and his guests heard three shots. Sometime later the butler emerged to serve tea, and when asked if all was well, he replied, "Dinner will be served at the usual time, and I am pleased to say there will be no discernible traces left of the recent occurrence by that time."[2]

In Mr. Stevens's view, this butler's behavior perfectly embodied the meaning of *dignity*. He explains,

"Dignity" has to do crucially with a butler's ability not to abandon the professional being he inhabits. Lesser butlers will abandon their professional being for the private one at the least provocation. For such persons, being a butler is like playing some pantomime role; a small push, a slight stumble, and the façade will drop off to reveal the actor underneath. The great butlers are great by virtue of their ability to inhabit their professional role and inhabit it to the utmost; they will not be shaken out by external events, however surprising, alarming or vexing.[3]

I know it's rather old-fashioned to write about dignity, much less about manservants, and yet every time I read this quote, I am reminded of my calling as a joyful outsider in Babylon. After all, I am also a servant of a king, and he calls me to inhabit a way of life in both public and private that honors and glorifies him no matter what circumstances I encounter.

Of course, this is not a professional responsibility. It is a *vocation*, a life calling for all of life. Jesus does not want us to compartmentalize our discipleship—following him on Sundays but ignoring him in our personal affairs or at work—but instead to lead seamless lives of devotion in all things.[4]

It has been the great labor of this book to enable you to do just that. I want you to live with dignity. And I want you to know that fear has a habit of making seams. I may be a Christian during my quiet time but not when injustice threatens those I love. I may be Christian at small group but not when an unbelieving friend needs to hear the gospel. I may be Christian in prayer but not in the art studio. It is only when you receive and experience the joy of God as an outsider that you can set aside fear and muster the courage to take the next right step.

While the next step is not always clear, I hope that by the close of this volume, many seeds have been planted in your mind. Perhaps some of them germinate even now. I hope you feel freedom knowing that there is not one rigid approach to Babylon but many faithful approaches. I pray that as you face the challenges ahead, you will learn to practice all six ways, putting on whatever outfit the moment calls for: the trainer, the advisor, the artist, the ambassador, the protester, or the builder.

Although you live in a disorienting world, you don't follow a disorienting king. Give him your heart, improvise his story with gusto, and I believe you will discover a deeper coherence running through the grain of everything. Steven Garber writes,

There is an intended seamlessness to human life under the sun. If we have eyes to see, there is congruity, and our task is to make sense of what is there. Life is meant to be coherent—but we don't experience it that way. All day long we live with incongruity and incoherence, with fragmentation across the whole of life. . . . [And yet] rather than accepting fragmentation as normative, we should do the harder work of discovering and discerning the integral character of life and learning.[5]

I hope that the stories and practices I've shared have helped you move one step closer toward understanding the good, beautiful, and coherent fabric of God's Word. I hope it's helped you make sense of the tension you feel and to develop the wisdom you need to navigate with joy. Together, we can resist Babylon's efforts to tear the fabric of reality, even as we work to repair it. In Jesus there is a common life to be lived for the common good, and until he returns, I hope we all seek it as outsiders with joy.

A Unified Body

For too long, Christians have argued for singular approaches to culture. Perhaps it's a symptom of our technique-obsessed age, with its naive faith in technocratic, managerial solutions. Or perhaps it's because an individual has only one subjective window on life—her own—and this often leads her to believe that her perspective must be the best.

Whatever the reason, I hope you received this book as a humble call for Christians to return to one of Paul's central metaphors for the church: a unified body with diverse parts. We live *together* as outsiders in Babylon, and only *together* can we embody Christ's mission to confront and heal the world.

And we must not forget that we aren't *a* body. We're *the* body of Jesus. Everywhere Jesus walked, shalom followed in his steps. Bodies were healed. Darkness were cast out. Injustice was confronted. Relationships were restored. Truth was proclaimed. Beauty was unfurled. Couldn't the same be true of his body today? If we have any hope of answering yes to that question, it will come only when the hands of God's body stop judging the feet, and the feet stop judging the eyes, and the eyes stop judging the ears.

We need trainers to change Babylon by changing habits. We need advisors to change Babylon by influencing leaders. We need artists to change Babylon by making beauty. We need ambassadors to change Babylon by winning hearts. We need protesters to change Babylon by challenging injustice. We need builders to change Babylon by constructing institutions.

We need each other if we want to resist Babylon. We need each other if we want to cultivate Babylon. We need to learn to embrace all six ways. And we need to learn *not* to judge those who walk in a different way than we do.

Of course, I that sometimes joyful outsiders will still find themselves crossways with one another. An advisor frustrated by a protester's demands. A builder frustrated by an artist's border-walking. An ambassador frustrated by a trainer's disciplines.

But it is precisely at those moments that I hope you'll think of this book and remember: We're all one body. Perhaps the protester's pressure will give the advisor leverage to push for good *from the inside*. Perhaps an artist's border-walking will bring new insights and people to the builder's institution. Perhaps a trainer's emphasis on discipleship will ensure that an ambassador's converts grow in faith. Joyful outsiders need one another. Though we have different callings at different times, we serve the same kingdom.

So together, let's live as outsiders, encouraging one another in the tension. Let's live like foreigners *and* love like natives. Let's build houses *and* never make homes. Let's live loosely to the powers of the world and serve them with excellence. Let's plant vineyards *and* wait for the wine of God's kingdom. Above all, let's fix our eyes on Jesus *and* remember the joyful outsiders who came before us. As the author of Hebrews reminds us, "Since we are surrounded by so great a cloud of witnesses, let us also lay aside every weight, and sin which clings so closely, and let us run with endurance the race that is set before us, looking to Jesus, the founder and perfecter of our faith, who for the joy that was set before him endured the cross, despising the shame, and is seated at the right hand of the throne of God."[6]

Never forget that life comes out of death. So in distress, look to our Savior. Look to our outsider king. He was crucified *outside* Jerusalem. But he was also resurrected *outside* its gates. He will one day return from *outside* Babylon to bring lasting justice, to heal all creation, and to make a forever home with all his joyful outsiders. And in an instant we will be *insiders* with him. Yes, in the future our long pilgrimage will end, but until then, trust him, abide in his presence, and walk by faith.

So choose joy today. And join *him* as an outsider.

Key Practices and Suggested Reading for Joyful Outsiders

If you've begun your journey toward one of the six ways, you'll quickly discover that our chapters are like small streams winding toward far greater rivers. While a stream is a great place to get comfortable with water, the *real* swimming starts in the river. You must learn to move with the current.

To that end, I've provided additional practices you can implement on top of the guiding principles in each chapter. We hope they deepen your joy. We hope they deepen your love for Jesus. Through them, ask God to strengthen you by his grace to answer his call to be a joyful outsider.

At the end of each set of key practices, I've also provided a suggested reading list. Consider those your introduction to the great rivers. Now that you've finished *Joyful Outsiders*, we'd encourage you to pick up one and continue your journey.

Key Practices and Suggested Reading for Trainers

In the chapter on trainers, we explored four guiding principles based on the life of Ezra: practicing abstinence to learn resistance, embracing personal sacrifice and trusting prayer for renewal, practicing rigorous study, and pursuing countercultural holiness. But we never discussed what it looks like to train *others*. We saw that Bonhoeffer established a residential seminary to train others in the way of Jesus. Likewise, Ezra taught the people.[1] But our context is quite different from theirs. Bonhoeffer's approach required shared living arrangements for single men with minimal familial demands. Ezra's efforts took place in a confined geographical area and were financially resourced by the Persian government.

So what do you do today when Christians are geographically dispersed across the suburbs, countryside, or city? When some are married and others are not? When some have strict vocational and familial demands? Our context makes training harder than ever. So while there's no perfect model, here are three common practices you can apply today.

1. One-on-One Training

Find someone who is eager to grow closer to God, and read through a book on the spiritual disciplines together (see the end of this section for recommendations). Then create a list of disciplines you want to practice together, and integrate them into your lives one at a time. Most habits take thirty days of continual practice to form, so don't add more than one per month. I recommend starting with silence and solitude, moving to the daily office, adding in fasting, and lastly, adding rigorous Bible study. Remember, the disciplines of abstinence function as spiritual inhalation. Breathe first. Then act.

2. Group Training

Gather a group of people within a geographical region to pray, either in the early morning, at noon, or at any time that works for everyone. Rather than emphasizing extemporaneous prayer, read through prayers in a prayer manual (see the end of this section for recommendations). Encourage people to use that same manual privately throughout the week to instill a practice of prayer. During your group prayers, leave space for silence. Setting a timer for two minutes can help. Lastly, observe a collective fast once a month. Remember, you should keep your expectations low—just like it's difficult to return to the gym after a long hiatus, so it is with spiritual disciplines. Seek to be a gracious trainer who is patient with failure.

3. Intensive Training

For people in your church, plan a weekend retreat oriented around spiritual disciplines. On the retreat, create space for people to share their stories and confess their sins, then schedule times of solitude and silence, Bible study, and prayer. Providing people with prayer manuals (or asking them to purchase one ahead of time) will guide their meditations and relieve stress. After all, most of us aren't prepared to pray for a whole day. Practice a day-long fast that ends with a celebration—food and drink—centered on thanking God for the goodness of his creation and friendship. These weekends will be most effective if you follow up with either group or one-on-one training.

If you're a trainer, Jesus is calling you to make disciples. Do so in his way. Walk through life with others, model spiritual disciplines, show mercy to those who struggle, and practice humility by confessing your own shortcomings. This takes time and the Holy Spirit's power, so be gracious to yourself and others. After three years with Jesus, Peter still lacked the strength to pray with him for a night. But a few years later, he was not only strong enough to do this, he was also trained others to do likewise. The people Peter trained became the earliest Christian counterculture, and while they were far from perfect, the beauty of their life together attracted those Rome had discarded and showed the Romans a better way. I pray that through your efforts and by God's grace, something similar might be true in your town, suburb, or city.

RECOMMENDED READING FOR TRAINERS

The Spirit of the Disciplines by Dallas Willard
The Ruthless Elimination of Hurry by John Mark Comer
Invitation to Solitude and Silence by Ruth Haley Barton
Beautiful Resistance by Jon Tyson
Praying like Monks, Living like Fools by Tyler Staton
Habits of the Household and *The Common Rule* by Justin Whitmel
   Earley

Key Practices and Suggested Reading for Advisors

Prayer is a political act. We call on the *king* of heaven to enact his divine will on earth—regardless of the earthly powers at large. When Paul instructs Christians to pray for "kings and all those in authority," he puts the political authorities in their proper place.[2] They derive their authority from God and would have no power had he not given it to them. Advisors understand the importance of influence, and thus they never forget that the people they advise are always a secondary power compared with the God who has influence over everything. Compared with him, the most influential people of our world are like dust in the wind.

Advisors seek to practice prayer in all of life, but especially *before they seek to influence leaders and in times of great distress.* Lastly, they should seek opportunity to glorify God, not themselves.

1. Pray before You Seek to Influence Others

The need to pray before seeking to influence others is seen in the life of Esther, a Jewish queen in the Persian Empire. While her position might lead you to believe she had guaranteed influence, that wasn't the case. The king had a harem of women, including Esther, to choose from. In the Persian court, no one, not even the queen, was permitted to enter the king's presence without his direct request. Archaeologists discovered Persian art showing a soldier standing behind the king with a sword drawn, ready to kill anyone interrupting the king—unless he pardoned them by extending his scepter. And yet Esther needed access to the king to persuade him to allow the Jews to protect themselves from a genocide.

Before her terrifying visit, Mordecai tells Esther that perhaps God has made her an insider in the Persian court "for such a time as this."[3] That forces her to decide who she fears most: God or King Xerxes? She chooses God. But how does she choose him? Through prayer and fasting. She instructs Mordecai to gather the Jews in Susa to join her and her attendants in praying and fasting for three days. Only after that will she approach the king. In a book that never mentions God, this is a crucial moment. The prayers make a political statement. Yahweh is the true king who rules over King Xerxes.

Advisors must remember God's sovereignty when they seek to influence leaders, whether they're governing officials or business executives. Because God is the one actually in charge, advisors seek his counsel, provision, and help. This can be as simple as a prayer before a meeting. *God give me wisdom and discernment. Give me favor in the eyes of others. Help me say words and share ideas that nudge us closer to your kingdom.* Also, to seek God first each morning, advisors can look through their schedule for the day—not to worry about what's to come but instead to pray for meetings and ask for God's provision. Given the temptation of some advisors to grow proud or power hungry, such prayers create humility and remind them whom they serve chiefly.

2. Pray under Great Distress

Esther's life was on the line the minute she stepped into Xerxes's chamber. While modern advisors may rarely face life-and-death situations, they do face innumerable circumstances where pressure is high and the tension between God's kingdom and Babylon is taut to the point of snapping.

Daniel faced similar pressures. One is recorded in Daniel 2, when Nebuchadnezzar commands that the wisemen (Daniel was in their ranks) not only interpret his dreams but also supernaturally discover what his dreams entail without him explaining. What is Daniel's first response? *Prayer.* He gathers his friends to ask for wisdom from the God who "deposes kings and raises up others."[4] He isn't confused about who's ultimately in charge.

I realize this story might feel distant from what modern advisors face. But it's not. Dream interpretation was a key part of Babylonian governance. They believed the dream realm connected to the spiritual realm and thus used their dreams as guides for strategy and policy decisions. In a similar way, modern leaders often expect their lieutenants to grasp impossibly complex situations. To cut gordian knots. To try to see into the future and strategize accordingly. We may use computations, AI models, or best practices—but they're all means of managing the future, just like dreams.

Daniel knew he lacked the ability to accomplish what the king requested. He was humble. But he also knew God saw all. He could do what was otherwise impossible. Thus, when advisors find themselves in intractable pressure cookers, they too must turn to God in prayer. For him the impossible is possible. Just as Daniel gathered friends to join him, advisors should do likewise. These may be friends inside or outside your organization. You may, like Esther, ask people to join you for a prayer vigil or fasting. Indeed, prayer and fasting are precisely the means by which Nehemiah later prepares himself to stand before a different Persian king.

The point is *not* that God will guarantee you success but that an advisor's faith in God's sovereignty will make her quite unlike all the Babylonian advisors around her. For one thing, she'll be a nonanxious presence. She knows that the king of heaven is with her. She knows that he's in charge. Even if she loses her livelihood, there's nothing that the powers can do to take away her eternal life. So while the wise men and women of Babylon scramble to preserve themselves and protect their reputations, the advisor is freed to nonanxiously work on the problem at hand.

3. Glorify God, Not Yourself

If God sees fit to guide you to the best solution, you should not hesitate to tactfully give him glory. When Daniel comes before Nebuchadnezzar, describes his dream, and explains it, Nebuchadnezzar calls him the wisest man in Babylon. But Daniel demurs. He declares that God is worthy of praise because *he* "made known to us the dream of the king."[5] While Daniel and the king shared a supernaturalist worldview, there was nothing kosher about discussing a backwater's god in the palaces of Marduk. Daniel could have easily kept the credit and said, "It would've been too weird to speak of Yahweh." But he didn't take credit for God's work.

In a similar way, while leaders in your organization might not believe in the supernatural, they may very well be opened to it when you share that your work is not generated by mere hard work. The Divine One is at work through you. More importantly, when you reflect the praise others give you to the God you serve, you not only make clear where your deepest political allegiances lie, you also practice humility before your Creator.

Thus, advisors must make a practice of regular prayer both in the ordinary trenches of life *and* in moments of great distress. They should transcend the politics of their businesses and government offices—King Jesus is their Lord and no one else. Yet, as Paul commands the early Christians, they seek to advise the leaders around them with the excellence and fidelity they would give to Jesus himself. That means enlisting Jesus himself in the process and glorifying Jesus when the opportunity arises.

RECOMMENDED READING FOR ADVISORS

Preacher and the Presidents by Nancy Gibbs and Michael Duffy
Blinded by Might by Cal Thomas and Ed Dobson
To Change the World by James Davison Hunter
The Seamless Life by Steven Garber

Key Practices and Suggested Reading for Artists

In the chapter on artists, I suggested that the most common temptations for artists are abandoning the church, isolating themselves, and being conformed to the artistic world around them. Unfortunately, these temptations exist precisely because the modern church has been suspicious of the artists in their midst, treating them as eccentrics at best and dangerous thinkers at worst. Thus, the following practices focus on bringing artists into community—specifically, into God's triune community (sanctified making), the historic community (meditation on the tradition), and the present community (collaboration).

1. Sanctified Making

Bezalel and Oholiab were Israelite slaves in Egypt, where they spent years learning art forms under the tutelage of Egyptians: goldsmithing, weaving, dying, carpentry, and much more. After the exodus God filled them with his Spirit "to make artistic designs" in the tabernacle.[6] The Creator thus sanctified their many years of artistic training. Artists should follow in their steps by laying down their brushes, chisels, pens, pencils, violins, guitars, thread, needles, cameras, keyboards, mice, and bodies before their Creator and asking him to sanctify their creative work.

For example, Makoto Fujimura imaginatively imbued his materials with the presence of Jesus: "In the slow process of preparing the pigments and glue . . . I realized that I was practicing a devotional liturgy of sorts. I imagine my water-based paint to possess the tears of Christ. . . . By faith, I began to imagine painting with Christ's tears—began to see that the very materials I use, extravagant, water-based materials, are mixed with Christ's tears."[7]

I call this *sanctified making*. It is the prayerful act of submitting your skill, imagination, and materials to God, then inviting his creative presence into your creative process. By doing this, you enter into the triune community, generating new things under the tutelage of the Father, Son, and Holy Spirit. This practice will transform your acts of creation into almost sacramental realities that unveil the beauty of Christ on earth.

2. Meditation on the Tradition

If you read the prophetic art of Zechariah, one thing becomes blazingly clear: he steeped himself in the sacred writings of Israel.[8] He weaved echoes of the Torah and the Prophets into his work with incredible ease, suggesting that his continual meditation on the tradition gave him a fluency with it that freed him to give that tradition fresh expression in his own day.

The same pattern permeated Jesus's creative work. His parables rarely quote the Old Testament, but allusions to it are so thick that a skilled reader can't miss the connections. The prodigal son alludes to the story of Israel's exile and return. The parable of the sower weaves together the prophecies and parables of Isaiah.

When Roman soldiers crucified Jesus, he bled the tradition, crying out Psalm 22: "My God, my God, why have you forsaken me?"[9] Does your art bleed the tradition? Artists must join the community of ancient artists by meditating on the poems, stories, and songs of Israel. They must learn the sacred rhythms so that the tradition permeates their own work with subtly, not clumsiness. After all, God calls us to sing *new songs*, not mediocre covers.[10] To do this, artists must develop a daily practice not only of reading Scripture but also of attending to its artistic structure and comprehending its themes. If artists do this, they will enter the community of ancient biblical mentors. If *you* do this, you'll add a fresh chapter to Israel's story and songbook.

3. Collaboration

In the West, art is often viewed as an individualistic endeavor. But a different pattern permeates the Old Testament. Collaboration and community are the norm. Oholiab and Bezalel. Micah and Isaiah. Zechariah and Haggai.[11] This pattern of collaboration suggests it's not merely a personal preference. It's a regular means by which God's Spirit stirs us and stretches us to create new things.

In my own experience as a lyricist, my best work was written not alone but alongside musicians who pressed me to write with a rhythmic quality they could turn into singable melodies. This doesn't mean that *all* creation needs to be done with others. Much of it is not. But without a community of some sort—be it editorial or collaborative—our art grows stale and insular.

To do this, artists must cultivate relationships inside the church. Find other Christians who share your passion, and seek out ways to create alongside them. There are many ways to do this. Creative retreats. Regular gatherings to share works in progress. Viewing, reading, or listening parties in which artists engage the art of others. Churches can actively cultivate such communities by sponsoring studios and making spaces for creative collaboration. For example, Redeemer Church in Indianapolis rents out well over half of its historic building to artists who need studio space. While many aren't Christians, some are, and this creates natural opportunities for collaboration. Artists hang their works in the church's halls, creating community (and patronage!) between churchgoers and creators.

RECOMMENDED READING FOR ARTISTS

Culture Care by Makoto Fujimura
Art and Faith by Makoto Fujimura
Rembrandt Is in the Wind by Russ Ramsey
Adorning the Dark by Andrew Peterson
A Prayer Journal by Flannery O'Connor
Art and the Bible by Francis A. Schaeffer
Vincent Van Gogh: His Spiritual Vision in Life and Art by Carol Berry
Four Quartets by T. S. Eliot

Key Practices and Suggested Reading for Ambassadors

Even if you feel a *passion* for evangelism, it doesn't mean you practice the *action* of evangelism. It's not uncommon for Christians to feel uncomfortable sharing their faith with others—either because they fear rejection or simply don't know how to do it. We've become like the characters in *The Parable of the Fishless Fisherman*. It's the story of several fishermen who host meetings about fishing, study fish, develop training centers to teach people to fish, and attend conferences about fishing.

There's just one problem: they never fish. The parable ends, "Imagine how hurt some were when one day a person suggested that those who didn't catch fish were really not fishermen, no matter how much they claimed to be. Yet it did sound correct. Is a person a fisherman if, year after year, he never catches a fish?"

Jesus promised the first-century fishermen who followed him that they would become "fishers of men."[12] Before his ascension he called us to "make disciples of all nations."[13] So why are our nets empty? Why do many who claim to follow Jesus refuse to fish?

Ambassadors must help the church recover its evangelistic calling. They do this not just by *talking* about the importance of evangelism but also by *practicing* evangelism. Here are two practices they can deploy to ensure they do so:

1. Invest in Long-Term Relationships

Some people feel like they haven't shared their faith unless they've fully explained the gospel and invited the person to become a Christian. But the New Testament doesn't describe evangelism as a one-time event. Jesus and Paul both used the image of sowing and reaping to explain how Christians help people come to faith. Only a foolish farmer would return to his field a day after seeding it and be disappointed that none had sprouted. First comes sowing, and much later, reaping.

Ambassadors should embrace the entire process of cultivating a relationship and seeing it grow from a seed to a full head of grain. In some cases they may invest in someone at the beginning of their journey. In other cases they may be the one who reaps the harvest, seeing the conversions themselves. Either way, they keep the long-term in mind— understanding that if they reap, it's only because someone else sowed. And if they sow, they do so in order that others might reap. Paul reminded the Corinthians that he planted the seed of faith, Apollos watered it, and God would reward each one so that "the sower and the reaper may be glad together."[14]

This means you don't have to get through a fifteen-minute gospel presentation to say you're sharing the gospel—although sometimes you may do this! Sowing can take the form of asking good questions, showing hospitality, and displaying kindness. If a person shares a challenging situation they are going through, ask them how you can pray for them, then follow up to find out how they are doing. Ambassadors understand that spiritual growth takes time. They don't try to force a harvest before it's ready. Instead, they invest in long-term relationships.

2. Invite People into Community

We tend to imagine evangelism as an individual task. Sara makes a friendship with Shelly. Eventually Shelly becomes a Christian. Then Sara brings her into community. Of course, this does happen sometimes. But more often people are invited into a community of faith *before* they come to personal faith. Ambassadors must remember that they aren't alone; God wants to use the entirety of his people to change the lives of lost people.

Consider this example from outside the world of evangelism: in his book *The Making of Pro-life America*, Ziad Munson tells the story of Linda, a woman who transitioned from being a pro-choice feminist who financially supported the American Civil Liberties Union to a pro-life activist. How did it happen? Through community. Linda's first step to becoming pro-life wasn't by reading a book or having conversations with a friend. Instead, it was a visit to her ob-gyn, who invited her to legislative hearings about liberalizing the state's abortion laws. Even though she wasn't opposed to abortion, she went out of respect for her doctor, who had helped Linda navigate difficult pregnancies. As she attended the hearings, she found herself surrounded by a community of people committed to the pro-life cause. Slowly that community changed how she thought. Research shows that statistically Linda isn't an outlier. Community is often the gateway to faith—whether it's faith in a cause or faith in Jesus.

Thus, while ambassadors *should* seek out one-on-one time with those far from God, it's also important to introduce them to your Christian friends. You could also consider inviting someone to a small group or book club. Perhaps as they get to know other Christians, they will be attracted to Jesus. Lastly, you can invite them to church. Research shows that many people far from God are open to attending church. Most of them say all they need is a personal invitation.[15]

The gospel is best shared over time in the context of loving relationships. People aren't projects. There's no need to force a seed to harvest, nor is there a need to try to share your faith on your own. Ambassadors may take the lead on evangelism, but they must never be alone in it. Others will do the sowing or the reaping. And others must warmly welcome an ambassador's non-Christian friends into their circles. If you're an ambassador, remember that God isn't asking you to be his salesperson. He's asking you to do something far more meaningful and far more difficult: Get to know people. Show them the hospitality he's shown you. Love them the way he loves you. And then share with them the good news that his love is for them too.

RECOMMENDED READING FOR AMBASSADORS

How to Talk about Jesus (Without Being That Guy) by Sam Chan
Finding Common Ground by Tim Downs
Evangelism in the Early Church by Michael Green
Learning Evangelism from Jesus by Jerram Barrs
Sent: Living a Life That Invites Others to Jesus by Heather Holleman
  and Ashley Holleman

Key Practices and Suggested Reading for Protesters

It's easy for anyone to idealize their heroes. The truth is always more complicated. Dr. Martin Luther King Jr. has long been a hero of protesters, and thus it's easy to imagine that he was born with an innate distaste for violence. But in his younger years, he wasn't a staunch defender of nonviolence. He grew up in a church that, like many today, divided the world into sacred and secular realms. In the sacred realm, it is wrong to do violence. After all, Jesus said so. But in the secular realm, violence is not just normal—it's sometimes necessary. King wrote of his perspective at that time, "The 'turn the other cheek' philosophy and the 'love your enemies' philosophy are only valid, I felt, when individuals are in conflict with other individuals; when racial groups and nations are in conflict a more realistic approach is necessary."[16]

During seminary King encountered the writings of Walter Rauschenbusch and was particularly affected by his book *Christianity and the Social Crisis*. Rauschenbusch argued that the gospel has social implications, not just spiritual ones. Religion isn't merely a private affair. It has public implications. That insight began King's pilgrimage toward nonviolence. Soon after, he learned about Mahatma Gandhi and his nonviolent resistance against British colonial rule. Gandhi's teaching and successful resistance gave King hope that the power of love could bring about social and systemic change, even in America.

The Montgomery bus boycott allowed King to test his intellectual commitments. In his retelling, being named the boycott's leader and spokesman forced him to commit to a strategy for social change. He combined what he had learned from the Sermon on the Mount and Gandhi, writing that "Christ furnished the spirit and the motivation while Gandhi furnished the method."[17] He put that method into writing by creating a pledge all protesters were required to sign. Creating a pledge is a key practice for all protesters because it not only focuses their strategy but also articulates the character and means by which they challenge injustice.

Creating a Pledge

King's pledge for the Montgomery boycott is a fantastic place to start. Protesters could copy or adapt his words, knowing that King's reputation might even allow them to convince those who are skeptical. Here's the pledge in its entirety:

1. Meditate daily on the teachings and life of Jesus.
2. Remember always that the nonviolent movement in Birmingham seeks justice and reconciliation—not victory.

3. Walk and talk in the manner of love, for God is love.
4. Pray daily to be used by God in order that all men might be free.
5. Sacrifice personal wishes in order that all men might be free.
6. Observe with both friend and foe the ordinary rules of courtesy.
7. Seek to perform regular service for others and for the world.
8. Refrain from the violence of fist, tongue, or heart.
9. Strive to be in good spiritual and bodily health.
10. Follow the directions of the movement and of the captain on a demonstration.[18]

Here's what a new pledge might look like:

1. I commit to seeing the humanity of my opponents and refuse to demonize them.
2. I commit to speaking the truth in love. I refuse to use my words to demean or belittle people made in God's image.
3. I commit to living by the fruit of the Spirit. I refuse to fight the way the world does.
4. I commit to Christlike behavior. I refuse to disobey Jesus in pursuit of social change.
5. I commit to praying for my enemies every day. I refuse all forms of hatred.
6. I commit to meditating on Scripture daily and surrendering to its definition of good and evil.

This pledge ensures that protesters don't forfeit their eternal life for temporal gain. It calls them to resist the temptation to abandon Christ's teachings and instead to fight for Christ's kingdom in Christ's way. His kingdom is a kingdom of justice, love, and mercy, and this pledge reminds protesters that it can't be ushered in by anger, hate, and deception.

How would your protests change if you created a personal pledge? What would happen if you invited other joyful outsiders to sign on with you? Doing so would set your protests apart from the protests of Babylon, where violence, destruction, anger, and hatred run amok. More importantly, it would ensure your own fidelity to a higher God than the cause itself: Jesus.

RECOMMENDED READING FOR PROTESTERS

King: A Life by Jonathan Eig
The Montgomery Bus Boycott and the Women Who Started It by Jo
  Ann Robinson
A Knock at Midnight, edited by Clayborne Carson and Peter Holloran
"Letter from Birmingham Jail" by Martin Luther King Jr.
The Inconvenient Gospel by Clarence Jordan
Let Justice Roll Down by John M. Perkins
God's Long Summer by Charles Marsh

Key Practices and Recommended Reading for Builders

Builders can exist at almost every level of an institution. Nehemiah wasn't the king of Persia, but he still exercised leadership in Judea. In a similar way, a teacher may not be a principal or a superintendent, but they can still be builders in their spheres of influence. The same applies in a business setting, where managers and team leaders may not set the vision and strategy for the entire company but *do* have latitude on their own teams.

Thus, the following two practices focus on two broad leadership skills builders must develop. Professors Bob Burns, Tasha Chapman, and Donald Guthrie write, "Leadership requires *both* creative art and methodical tasks."[19] The art of leadership "involves ambiguity, imagination, innovation, emotional engagement and improvisation."[20] The methodical tasks of leadership require attention to "technical details, repetitive chores, organization, administration, plans, orderly procedures and perhaps even restroom repair."[21]

James March, named the most admired management expert by the

Harvard Business Review, calls the imaginative, innovative, visionary aspects of institutional leadership "poetry."[22] He calls the methodical, managerial, technical aspects of leadership "plumbing." Let's look at both.

1. The Poetry of Leadership

As poets, builders use the power of words to give tasks meaning and purpose. This is the most neglected aspect of leadership in highly managerial, technique-driven environments. But without it, institutions suffer mission drift. People working in poetry-less institutions aren't just uninspired, they're bored. They pull a paycheck. They do a job. But they don't really care.[23]

Leadership expert Simon Sinek says this is why the first job of every leader is to accomplish the poetic task of articulating an organization's "why." He writes, "Very few people or companies can clearly articulate WHY they do WHAT they do. When I say WHY, I don't mean to make money—that's a result. By WHY I mean what is your purpose, cause or belief? WHY does your company exist? WHY do you get out of bed every morning? And WHY should anyone care?"[24]

Instead of beginning with the *why*, most leaders start with *what* they do and *how* they do it. For example, if you work at a support center for unhoused families, you might be tempted to say that the core of your work is what you do: We help families find homes. Or how you do it: We provide short-term housing and job training. But few leaders start with the why: Because God sheltered us with his love, we shelter others.

This is why builders must be great sloganeers—individuals who can capture the why in clear, repeatable language. During Steve Jobs's tenure at Apple, he practiced this kind of thinking relentlessly. They didn't focus on what they did (we make computers) or how they did it (with elegant design). Instead, they focused on why they existed (we disrupt the status quo in the tech world). That idea became a slogan in their ads: "Think different." Apple employees understood their *why*, which not only guided their *how* and their *what* but also motivated them to get up and go to work every morning.

Depending on the kind of institution you work in and where you are in the org chart, your why may be broad or narrow, outward facing or inward facing. Whatever your situation, as a builder you must ensure that your why is aligned to Jesus's vision of the good life, explicitly or implicitly. By focusing on the poetry of leadership, you give your employees and coworkers the opportunity to do something more than a job—you invite them into a divine calling and a purpose bigger than themselves.

2. The Plumbing of Leadership

All leaders take on the ordinary managerial tasks associated with leadership: organizing and prioritizing tasks and then deploying other people to execute them. As poets, builders tell people *why* their corner of the institution exists. As plumbers, builders tell people *how* to do it and *what* they need to do. James March writes that successful plumbing requires at least four components:

1. **Hiring Competent People:** Builders must hire or train people to do their jobs with skill and excellence.
2. **Task Delegation:** Builders must resist the urge to solve every problem themselves and instead push work down, trusting their coworkers and employees to do the work. They do this by clearly delegating responsibilities to others based on their competencies.
3. **Institutional Culture Making:** Builders clarify and enforce the ethical norms of the institution. They clearly define the values they expect others to abide by, define the character they expect others to cultivate, and set the rules by which everyone will be held accountable. Additionally, they structure the institution to reinforce those values through rituals, practices, and meetings that habituate members of the institution into the institution's ethical norms.
4. **Coordination:** Builders develop systems that create clear lines of communication, define processes and procedures, and prioritize critical activities.[25]

Of course, entire books have been written on management, so a four-point list is hopelessly reductionistic. But here's the main takeaway: Institutions are communal organisms, which means that accomplishing any sort of common good for God's kingdom requires the skilled delegation of tasks to competent people whose work is carefully coordinated and characterized by a common culture. If you're a more poetic leader, you can't neglect the plumbing of your institution. Systems, structures, hiring, culture, and coordination are all ways you make your why a reality. If you're a more managerial leader, you can't ignore the poetry of leadership. Institutions need a clear *why* to drive systemic decisions.

RECOMMENDED READING FOR BUILDERS

Becoming Whole by Brian Fikkert and Kelly M. Kapic
Practicing the King's Economy by Michael Rhodes, Robby Holt, and Brian Fikkert
Managing Leadership Anxiety by Steve Cuss
The 4 Disciplines of Execution by Chris McChesney, Sean Covey, and Jim Huling
The 6 Types of Working Genius by Patrick Lencioni
A Time to Build by Yuval Levin

The Six Ways Personal Inventory

To help you determine which of the six ways best fits your personality, I've put together a simple inventory that can be finished in ten to twenty minutes. I recommend doing it with a group of friends who can help evaluate your results. After the inventory, you'll have a space to tabulate your results, followed by a brief overview of each way.

Step 1: Rate Each Statement

In this section you will find six sets of eighteen statements. *Rate how strongly you agree with each statement on a scale of 1 to 5.*

Scaling System

1 = Strongly disagree

2 = Disagree

3 = Neutral or no feelings

4 = Agree

5 = Strongly agree

Note: Remember that your goal isn't to game the system and get the result you want. The goal is to be honest and allow the results to guide you toward a way of cultural engagement that fits your temperament.

SET 1

____ I'm excited when I get to study the Bible, read Christian books, and practice spiritual disciplines.

____ I'm frustrated when people don't take my advice.

____ I love helping others deepen their faith.

____ I feel misunderstood when people think I'm being judgmental.

____ I admire people with deep Bible knowledge, an active prayer life, and a passion for holiness.

____ I change the world around me by helping others grow in holiness and wisdom.

____ People get frustrated when I'm too serious.

____ I try to avoid using my time on frivolous things that distract me from Jesus.

____ I seek new ways to practice my faith and grow in holiness.

____ I enjoy spending my time in prayer and personal study.

____ I seek churches that are theologically deep, value discipleship, and emphasize spiritual disciplines.

____ My friends would say I'm disciplined and serious about my faith.

____ My friends seek my help when they have Bible questions or want to discern wise choices.

____ People say I'm good at helping people who want to deepen their love of Jesus.

____ God has given me a passion for helping others grow in holiness through Bible study, friendship, and prayer.

____ I am sometimes tempted to be self-righteous toward those who don't match my discipline.

____ I am sometimes tempted to be proud of my discipline.

____ I am sometimes tempted to make legalistic demands of others.

____ **Set 1 Total**

SET 2

____ I'm excited when I get to be in the rooms where decisions are made.

____ I'm frustrated when Christians aren't in rooms where decisions get made.

____ I dream about how to influence big decisions in my local sphere for the common good.

____ I feel misunderstood when people think I'm power hungry or jockeying for prestige.

____ I admire people who can build relationships with influential people.

____ I change the world around me by influencing decision-makers.

____ People get frustrated because they think I'm a compromiser.

____ I try to avoid doing low quality work.

____ I seek to learn whatever is necessary to do my work with excellence.

____ I enjoy spending time building trust with leaders.

____ I seek churches that positively influence local businesses or government.

____ My friends would say I'm comfortable discerning my way through morally ambiguous situations.

____ My friends seek my advice when they want to influence change in their organization.

____ People say I'm good at disagreeing tactfully and persuading others to my position.

____ God has given me a passion to grow my influence through excellent work.

____ I am sometimes tempted to use people for my own ends.

____ I am sometimes tempted to compromise my convictions to gain influence.

____ I am sometimes tempted to flatter people insincerely.

____ Set 2 Total

SET 3

_____ I'm excited when I get time to read fiction, watch a movie, listen to an album, or visit a gallery.

_____ I'm frustrated by the lack of creativity in the church.

_____ I dream about someone appreciating and understanding my art.

_____ I feel misunderstood when people see my curiosity as a threat.

_____ I admire people who can express their emotions and experiences artistically.

_____ I change my environment by trying to make it more expressive and beautiful.

_____ People get frustrated when I'm critical of the way Christians make art.

_____ I try to avoid inauthenticity.

_____ I seek truthful, authentic expressions of pain and hope in art.

_____ I enjoy spending my time creating art in my preferred medium.

_____ I seek churches that value artistic expression in worship.

_____ My friends would say I'm a bit eccentric.

_____ My friends seek my help when they want to discover new art (music, film, fiction, etc.).

_____ People say I'm good at creative endeavors.

_____ God has given me a passion to make the world more beautiful and empathic.

_____ I am sometimes tempted to stop going to church.

_____ I am sometimes tempted to isolate myself from others.

_____ I am sometimes tempted to copy the lifestyles and values of non-Christian artists.

_____ **Set 3 Total**

SET 4

____ I'm excited when I get to talk to someone about Jesus.

____ I'm frustrated when Christians don't want to share the gospel with others.

____ I love showing hospitality to non-Christians.

____ I feel misunderstood when people think I don't care about big social issues.

____ I admire people who build friendships with non-Christians.

____ I change the world around me by helping others develop a relationship with God.

____ People get frustrated when I want to share the gospel more quickly than they would.

____ I try to avoid superficial conversations.

____ I seek new ways to communicate the gospel to people far from God.

____ I enjoy spending time talking with people and deepening relationships.

____ I seek churches that focus on reaching lost people.

____ My friends would say I'm not afraid to bring up Jesus.

____ My friends seek my help when they have a friend they want to share the gospel with.

____ People say I'm good at building bridges with people outside the church.

____ God has given me a passion to see people get saved.

____ I am sometimes tempted to treat people as projects.

____ I am sometimes tempted to minimize the cost of discipleship.

____ I am sometimes tempted to minimize the importance of laws and systems in shaping culture.

____ **Set 4 Total**

SET 5

_____ I'm excited to rally people to a cause.

_____ I'm frustrated by Christians who are afraid to speak up about injustice.

_____ I dream about a world where people don't take advantage of each other.

_____ I feel misunderstood when people accuse me of just liking to argue.

_____ I admire people who are courageous enough to take risks for the powerless.

_____ I change my environment by calling out injustice.

_____ People get frustrated when I won't let problems go.

_____ I try to avoid treating my faith as though it's just _personal_, not having public implications.

_____ I seek justice for the weak, poor, oppressed.

_____ I enjoy spending time learning about solutions to injustice.

_____ I seek churches that care about social justice.

_____ My friends would say I speak the truth.

_____ My friends seek my help when they aren't sure what the moral thing to do is.

_____ People say I'm good at getting people to care about causes.

_____ God has given me a passion for standing up for the vulnerable.

_____ I am sometimes tempted to build my reputation around my cause.

_____ I am sometimes tempted to personally benefit from my protests.

_____ I am sometimes tempted to verbally attack those I think are doing bad things.

_____ **Set 5 Total**

SET 6

____ I'm excited when I lead and set direction in my organization.

____ I'm frustrated by organizations that only pursue wealth as their bottom line.

____ I dream about using charities, businesses, and institutions to do good in the world.

____ I feel misunderstood when people mistake my drive for pride.

____ I admire people who build and expand organizations.

____ I change my environment by building organizations that help people flourish inside and outside its walls.

____ People get frustrated when I get fixated on work or institutional culture.

____ I try to avoid getting sucked into materialism and consumerism.

____ I seek jobs that allow me to work with a sense of purpose.

____ I enjoy spending time thinking through my organization's strategy and purpose.

____ I seek churches that integrate faith and work.

____ My friends would say I work hard and am passionate about my workplace.

____ My friends seek my help when they want advice on how to effectively lead in their workplace.

____ People say I'm good at coming up with fresh ideas to improve my organization.

____ God has given me a passion to help people through business, charity, healthcare, or education.

____ I am sometimes tempted to manipulate people to buy into my plan.

____ I am sometimes tempted to pressure people into agreeing with my direction.

____ I am sometimes tempted to use my organization to bolster my own reputation.

____ **Set 6 Total**

Step 2: Tally Your Results

Tally the results in each set and then transfer your totals from each set into the following blanks. To the right of your totals is the way associated with that set. The highest scores reveal which way(s) fit you best.

Total for Set 1 ＿＿ The Trainer
Total for Set 2 ＿＿ The Advisor
Total for Set 3 ＿＿ The Artist
Total for Set 4 ＿＿ The Ambassador
Total for Set 5 ＿＿ The Protester
Total for Set 6 ＿＿ The Builder

Step 3: Find Which of the Six Ways Fits You Best

Start by focusing on the way(s) in which you scored the highest. Most people find that one or two ways resonate with their personality, interests, and talents most closely. For practical reasons, I suggest focusing on developing a primary way before moving to a secondary way. If you're unsure which to focus on, read through the following overviews of your top two results and ask yourself: Which way most piques my interest? Which way most fits with my aspirations? Which way describes me best in the present? Which way describes a temptation I've experienced as I've sought to engage the world around me?

Overviews of the Six Ways

The Trainer

Trainers are people who take deep joy in spiritual disciplines. They help others do likewise through one-to-one discipleship, small groups, teaching, or prayer. They have a passion for personal holiness and understand that spiritual practices are a key means by which God conforms us to the image of Christ. They earnestly want to help the church become a holy counterculture that attracts those whom Babylon discards and shows Babylon a better, more beautiful way to be human.

Key Insight: Trainers see that *all* humans share an internal readiness to do evil. But Jesus forgives us and promises to transform us. Thus, his Spirit can cultivate a readiness to do good in each of us when we structure our lives around the spiritual disciplines he practiced.

Orientation toward Culture: Trainers see that the church can change the world only if it is a holy counterculture, exemplifying life, goodness, kindness, justice, and generosity where Babylon does the opposite. To help the church become that sort of counterculture, trainers commit themselves to spiritual disciplines, which are the means by which God graciously transforms us.

Guiding Principles: Trainers understand that if we want to resist Babylon when the stakes are high, we must practice saying no when the stakes are low. Thus, they commit themselves to disciplines of abstinence like fasting, solitude, silence, and sabbath-keeping. They have a passion for renewal and revival but understand that it comes only by God's power. Thus, they embrace trusting prayer and personal sacrifice, waiting on him to act. Additionally, they're committed to the rigorous study, application, and teaching of God's Word, seeing it as the ethical and theological cornerstone of the church's countercultural witness. Lastly, they seek to help the church become a holy counterculture, understanding that the church changes the world by being a beautiful church.

Shadow Side: Trainers are often tempted by pride, believing that their superior discipline makes them superior followers of Jesus. If left unchecked, that pride bubbles into legalism. The trainer begins to create rules that others must follow to be serious themselves. Eventually legalism leads to judgmentalism. At this point trainers often become cloistered Christians, judging other followers of Jesus as half-hearted and uncommitted. They search for a more serious church with more serious Christians, rather than serving churches in need.

The Advisor

Advisors recognize that elite institutions have the power to shape culture. They pursue professional excellence and personal character, hoping to be invited into important discussions within those institutions where they can exert influence to resist evil and cultivate good within Babylon.

Key Insight: On both a national and local scale, certain individuals have an outsized influence. Their decisions affect more people than the average person's. Thus, advisors understand that access to the rooms where big decisions are made is necessary if you want to work for the common good.

Orientation toward Culture: Advisors recognize that they are outsiders in Babylon but can still influence outcomes if they are in the right room with the right people at the right time. Advisors seek to influence the influential, not for the sake of gaining power but for the sake of God's kingdom. They use their influence to encourage leaders to make choices that positively influence people's lives and resist choices that lead to injustice or harm.

Guiding Principles: Advisors know that only people who do their jobs with excellence, respect those in authority, and display character in their personal and professional lives get invited into the rooms where important decisions are made. Although they are personally above reproach, they know that Babylon doesn't share their values, so they develop the requisite wisdom to navigate morally ambiguous situations. When possible, they try to nudge Babylon toward the good, knowing that while perfection is never possible, *proximate* goodness is better than evil.

Shadow Side: The same competitive spirit that drives the advisor to pursue vocational excellence can lead them to put their personal priorities over the king's priorities. Seduced by power, many advisors become nothing more than court prophets who celebrate a leader's wrongheaded ideas and desires rather than courageously challenging them.

The Artist

Artists are those who see light in darkness, beauty in ugliness, hope in despair. They walk the border of heaven and earth, life and death, health and sickness. Through rigorous training and practice, they hone their artistic skills to create beauty. Not the cheap beauty of sentimentalism but the rich beauty of imaginative hope rooted in an equally rich empathy for Babylon's castaways. Artists make beauty both to confront the world's ugliness and to cultivate the good within it.

> **Key Insight:** Artists understand that God designed the human soul with a hunger for beauty. But evil and injustice have marred God's beautiful world and made much of it ugly. Thus, true beauty has the power not only to challenge the ugliness but also to paint a picture of our shared dream: God's kingdom on earth as in heaven.

> **Orientation toward Culture:** Artists do not join forces with culture warriors who value art only if it is useful for their particular interests: commercial, political, or ideological. Instead of culture-warring, artists practice culture care, intentionally giving away the gift of beauty, just as God gave us the gift of beauty in his creation. They understand that when humans feed on beauty, it not only nourishes them but also confronts Babylon's ugliness and points all people toward the lovely kingdom of Christ.

> **Guiding Principles:** Artists labor to practice and hone their craft, understanding that beauty can't be created without profound skill. They endeavor to live as "border walkers," those who live between heaven and earth, healing and pain. This allows them to empathize with the pain in the world (the opposite of sentimentalism) *and* project new possibilities for the world (the opposite of cynicism). To that end, they intentionally cultivate a hopeful imagination, which resists our modern penchant for irony and despair.

> **Shadow Side:** Artists are often misunderstood in the church, which sometimes leads them to abandon the church. In their isolation, artists sometimes give themselves to their emotions, especially

despair. If they do, they actively isolate themselves from others, giving in to the lies of self-loathing. In such a condition, they become easy prey for Babylon's artists, whose skill and influence sometimes persuade artists to leave behind not only the church but Jesus as well.

The Ambassador

Ambassadors find great joy in sharing the gospel with people and seeing them come to faith in Jesus. They know they represent Jesus to the people in their lives, so they are careful to live in a way that makes the gospel attractive and does not hinder their neighbor's faith journey. By leading people to Jesus, ambassadors hope to bring fundamental change to Babylon one heart at a time.

> **Key Insight:** Ambassadors believe that apart from Jesus, every human has a hole in their heart. So rather than fixating on all the secondary issues that plague humanity, they address the fundamental problem by sharing the gospel. This requires them to build bridges, make friendships, and practice hospitality.

> **Orientation toward Culture:** Ambassadors know that until we address the hole in every human heart, all our attempts to solve social problems will fall short. Genuine cultural change can't just be legislated. Therefore, ambassadors believe the best way to change Babylon is to help people develop a relationship with God.

> **Guiding Principles:** Ambassadors don't measure success by their personal comfort and reputation but by the gospel's progress in the world. They fervently pray for the lost, asking God to give them opportunities to talk to their neighbor about Jesus. They keep careful watch over their lives to ensure that they attract people to Jesus rather than repelling them with immorality or self-righteousness.

> **Shadow Side:** An ambassador's enthusiasm to see people become

Christians can lead them to treat people like projects. Likewise, it can cause them to water down the gospel message, emphasizing decisions for Christ over discipleship. They sometimes overemphasize the importance of the individual and minimize the ways in which legal and cultural systems harm others.

The Protester

Protesters know God opposes injustice and invites his people to join their voices with his. They have sensitive consciences and deeply feel the plight of those in need. Thus, they speak courageously on behalf of the powerless, knowing they will often suffer as a result. They protest with words and actions, both public and private, knowing that the only way to cultivate justice in Babylon is by first resisting injustice.

> **Key Insight:** God wants his creation to flourish, but corruption and oppression jeopardize his good plans. Protesters are strengthened by God's beautiful vision, knowing that the moral arc of the universe bends toward justice. They participate in God's mission by bending history toward God's ends with both words and actions that show the evil of injustice.

> **Orientation toward Culture:** Protesters change Babylon by challenging injustice. They understand that those in power rarely change without external pressure. But exerting pressure requires a critical mass—people must be rallied. Once enough people join a cause, it's possible to generate legal and cultural change.

> **Guiding Principles:** Protesters have a strong sense of moral clarity, rooted in biblical ethics, which allows them to discern when it is right to actively resist those in power. Doing so comes with great risk, which means protesters must be courageous. But they don't need just *any* kind of courage. They need the kind of courage that comes from confidence in God's promises. They commit themselves to Jesus's ethic of nonviolence, not only because it's effective but also because they seek to create communities that love their

neighbor and their enemy. Above all else, they are hopeful: The world *can* change, and that means their work is not in vain.

Shadow Side: Protesters are tempted by easy, costless ways to protest online. When this happens, their protest becomes a performance. It's more about their reputation than the cause itself. Sometimes they go one step further, using the cause for personal gain: fame or fortune. In such scenarios, they have to gin up more grievances, and demonize their opponents, just to keep their protest running. God's cause fades into the background, and the protest is all that matters.

The Builder

Builders are individuals whom God has gifted to lead and preserve institutions like businesses, charities, schools, hospitals, churches, and governmental offices. Rather than chasing the American dream, they build institutions that seek Jesus's vision of the common good. This entails *wholistic* human flourishing, not just *material* human flourishing. Builders try to construct social structures that are durable and communal, not short-term and individualistic.

Key Insight: Builders understand that God designed humans to share a common life inside institutions. When that common life is aimed toward the common good, those institutions become catalysts for human flourishing.

Orientation toward Culture: Most institutions in America direct themselves toward the American dream: an individualistic life accompanied by material wealth and material consumption. But such institutions lead to loneliness, disconnection, and ugliness. Thus, builders construct their institutions both as an act of resistance (they reject the American dream) and as an act of cultivation (they build toward Jesus's dream).

Guiding Principles: Builders construct durable institutions designed to provide long-term wholeness, healing, and prosperity not only for those inside the institutions but also for those outside. They ensure that their institutions are communal. They value the good of the community over the builder's personal interests or the interests of a small group inside the institution. Builders use the space, schedule, and norms of their institution to inculcate virtue. They carefully and prayerfully define the purpose of their institution to ensure it's directed toward God-glorifying ends.

Shadow Side: Builders face the temptation to bully people inside and outside the institution in service of the institution's goals. They take an "ends justify the means" approach to leadership that turns them into narcissists and manipulators. If their behavior goes unchecked, they direct the institution toward their personal interests, using it as a platform for personal gain or celebrity.

Acknowledgments

Firstly, thank you to our wives: Emily and Christine. You know that writing a book is no small task, and you willingly gave of yourselves to create the time we needed to finish this labor. No one but God knows how your faithfulness and selflessness made this book possible. So thank you for letting us work early in the mornings, retreat for days into writing cabins, and supporting us when we wondered if this project would ever come together as it has.

Secondly, thank you to our church. We love pastoring at The Crossing. It's full of joyful outsiders in businesses, homes, schools, and charities. You've inspired us and much of this book. But more importantly you've cultivated our local community to be a bit more like God's kingdom. We hope what we share here helps other churches become more like you all. A special thank you goes to my (Patrick's) Bible study, which graciously read through and discussed the first (and much poorer) draft of this book. Your feedback was invaluable. Similarly, thank you to the churches and Christian groups in Seattle, St. Louis, and the Bay Area for allowing us to teach the content in this book at an early stage—again, your feedback helped us hone our message.

Thirdly, thank you to our friends. Anna Lynne Frazier helped us develop the structure of the book and gave feedback on early drafts. Other friends talked us through the ideas in this book and provided insights that shaped its final form: Josh Butler, Brad Edwards, Michael Graham,

Ian Harber, Samuel James, Jake Meador, Brett McCracken, Peter Ostapko, Preston Sprinkle, Trevin Wax, and Sarah Eekhoff Zylstra. Also, thank you to a small circle of joyful outsiders whose friendship embodies joy and whose wisdom is found on more pages than not: Brent Beshore, Carl Edwards, Adam Guy, Tyler Jenkins, and Kyle Richter. Choose joy, brothers.

Fourthly, thank you to Don Gates, Paul Pastor, and the team at Zondervan. Don, your passion for great books that help people love God never ceases to amaze us. Paul, thank you for your probing questions and gentle critiques. Without your editorial labor, *this* book wouldn't exist. And it certainly wouldn't be as elegant, simple, or approachable as it has become. To the team at Zondervan, thank you for taking the risk on two unknown authors with a big idea. It's been a joy to work with you all.

Most importantly, thank you to Jesus, our king. You are the *true* joyful outsider. Though your creation treated you like an outsider, you died to rescue it for the *joy* set before you. May this book make everyone who reads it a bit more like you: joyful outsiders.

Notes

Preface

1. Heb. 12:2 NIV, emphasis added.
2. Heb. 12:2; 13:13 NIV.
3. Heb. 13:14.
4. One final note: You probably noticed this book has two authors. We chose not to announce the specific author behind every story because this book isn't about us (and trust us, it would get annoying). So from this point forward, we will use *I* in every chapter. If curiosity about who wrote what is killing you, hit one of us up on X: @PatrickKMiller_ or @KeithSimon_. We'll respond.

Chapter 1: Outsiders

1. Brian Yearwood, "Letter from Dr. Brian Yearwood, Superintendent of Columbia Public Schools, to Governor Michael L. Parson of Missouri," January 22, 2023, https://storage.googleapis.com/pt05-1/messages /attachments/8bf59a0a881b9f78c9e97aa54ae136a8/01.22.23_Governor _Parson_Letter.pdf.
2. Patrick Miller and Keith Simon, "A Public School District Took Middle Schoolers to a Drag Show Without Telling Their Parents | Opinion," *Newsweek*, January 25, 2023, https://www.newsweek.com/public-school -district-took-middle-schoolers-drag-show-without-telling-their-parents -opinion-1776503.
3. Dietrich Bonhoeffer, *Discipleship*, DBW Vol. 4: Dietrich Bonhoeffer Works, Volume 4 (Fortress Press, 2000), 250. Kindle.
4. Deut. 26:5.
5. Ex. 1:9–10.
6. 2 Kings 17:13.
7. Jer. 52:27–30.
8. 1 Pet. 1:1.
9. Matt. 2:13–15.

10. Heb. 13:12 NIV.

11. Matt. 26:31; 27:22, 37; Mark 15:34; John 18:30; Heb. 13:12–14.

12. Heb. 12:2 NIV, emphasis added.

13. Heb. 13:12–13, emphasis added.

14. 1 Pet. 1:1.

Chapter 2: The Wrong Kind of Outsiders

1. We've changed the details of this story and other stories to protect the identity of those involved. Many of the stories in this book are deeply personal, challenging, and ongoing.

2. Lesslie Newbigin, "Unfaith and Other Faiths," unpublished lecture given as one in a series of three to the Twelfth Annual Assembly of the Division of Foreign Missions, National Council of the Churches of Christ in the USA, 1962.

3. John 18:11.

4. Matt. 26:53.

5. Matt. 11:19.

6. Luke 5:31–32 NIV.

7. Eccl. 7:10 NIV.

8. Lesslie Newbigin, *The Gospel in a Pluralist Society* (Eerdmans, 1989), 153.

9. Neh. 8:10 NIV.

Chapter 3: Naming the Tension

1. Aaron M. Renn, *Life in the Negative World: Confronting Challenges in an Anti-Christian Culture* (Zondervan, 2024), 6.

2. "From 1870 to 1895, church attendance more than doubled, from 13.5 million people to 32.7 million, as the general population grew from 38.6 million to 69.6 million people. The net result was a 12 percent increase in churchgoers. Because this growth happened in the short span of only twenty-five years, it became the largest religious shift in the history of our country until now. What we have witnessed in the last twenty-five years is a religious shift about 1.25 times larger but going in the opposite direction." Jim Davis, Michael Graham, Ryan P. Burge, *The Great Dechurching: Who's Leaving, Why Are They Going, and What Will It Take to Bring Them Back?* (Zondervan, 2023), 4–5.

3. Davis, Graham, Burge, *The Great Dechurching*, xv.
4. Davis, Graham, Burge, *The Great Dechurching*, 4–5.
5. Gallup, Inc., "Religion | Gallup Historical Trends," Gallup.com, April 10, 2024, https://news.gallup.com/poll/1690/religion.aspx.
6. Ibid.
7. Tara Isabella Burton, *Strange Rites* (PublicAffairs, 2020), 15.
8. Ibid.
9. "Few Americans Blame God or Say Faith Has Been Shaken Amid Pandemic, Other Tragedies," Pew Research, November 23, 2021, https://www.pewresearch.org/religion/2021/11/23/few-americans-blame-god-or-say-faith-has-been-shaken-amid-pandemic-other-tragedies.
10. Throughout the 1990s, 42 percent of Americans said they believed premarital sex was immoral. "Changing Attitudes about Premarital Sex, Homosexuality," CBS News, May 6, 2015, https://www.cbsnews.com/news/changing-attitudes-about-premarital-sex-homosexuality/.
11. Travis Mitchell, "Attitudes on Same-Sex Marriage," Pew Research Center, May 6, 2024, https://www.pewresearch.org/religion/fact-sheet/changing-attitudes-on-gay-marriage/.
12. Gallup, Inc., "LGBTQ+ Rights | Gallup Historical Trends," Gallup.com, July 2, 2024, https://news.gallup.com/poll/1651/gay-lesbian-rights.aspx.
13. Statista, "Opinions on Sex between an Unmarried Man and Woman in the United States 2022," July 5, 2024, https://www.statista.com/statistics/1367103/us-opinions-on-sex-before-marriage.
14. *Sex Education in America*, The Henry J. Kaiser Family Foundation, January 2013, https://www.kff.org/wp-content/uploads/2013/01/sex-education-in-america-summary.pdf.
15. "Americans' Trust of Pastors Hovers Near All-Time Low," Lifeway Research, January 22, 2021, https://research.lifeway.com/2021/01/22/americans-trust-of-pastors-hovers-near-all-time-low.
16. Alexandria Ocasio-Cortez, quoted in Anthony Leonardi, "White Supremacists Have Done It: AOC Compares Religious Liberty Advocates to Racists Using Bible 'To Justify Bigotry,'" *Washington Examiner*, February 28, 2020, https://www.washingtonexaminer.com/news/white-supremacists-have-done-it-aoc-compares-religious-liberty-advocates-to-racists-using-bible-to-justify-bigotry.

17. John M. Perkins, *Let Justice Roll Down* (Baker, 2012), 158.

18. This isn't merely true for Christians who fought for abolition and the Civil Rights Movement. You can find followers of Jesus who lived as outsiders in every decade of America. They experienced terrible fear and an almost unbearable tension between their faith and their cultural environment, between the values of the kingdom of God and the decadence around them, between their hope for a beloved community and those who vandalize God's shalom.

    Whether it was the evangelicals fighting for women's suffrage, or the devout Baptists battling against rampant alcoholism, or the faithful Methodists resisting unsafe factory conditions and child labor, or the established Presbyterians challenging entrance into World War I because they feared it would corrupt the character of young men, or the passionate evangelists of the post-war era fighting the influence of Communism, or the heady leaders of the L'Abri fellowship awakening Americans to the evils of abortion, or the thoughtful Christian professors critiquing American greed during the booming markets of the mid-nineties—they all felt *profound* tension between their faith and their culture.

19. When we begin to buy into the lie that we can create a fully (or nearly) Christianized culture, we repeat the errors of the past. Oliver O'Donovan writes, "The ambiguities of Christendom, meanwhile, arose from a loss of focus on the missionary context. Once the two societies of Church and nation came to be seen as a single society, it was more difficult to frame the Church-state partnership in terms of the coming kingdom. It could seem, by a kind of optical illusion, that there was no more mission to be done. The peril of the Christendom idea—precisely the same peril that attends upon the post-Christendom idea of the religiously neutral state— was that of negative collusion: the pretense that there was now no further challenge to be issued to the rulers in the name of the ruling Christ." Oliver O'Donovan, *The Desire of the Nations: Rediscovering the Roots of the Political Theology* (Cambridge: Cambridge University Press, 1996), 212–13.

20. Nimrod is introduced in Genesis 10. He is described as the founding figure of several kingdoms including Babylon (Gen. 10:8–10).

21. Bruce K. Waltke and Cathi J. Fredricks, *Genesis: A Commentary* (Zondervan, 2001), 178.

22. Tremper Longman writes, "This tower was where earth touched heaven; in this sense, it is correct to see this building as a type of assault on heaven." Tremper Longman III, *Genesis,* Story of God Bible Commentary (Zondervan, 2016), 150.

23. J. Richard Middleton, *The Liberating Image* (Baker Publishing Group, 2005), 222–24.

24. Ibid.

25. Ibid.

26. In the original, Sayers uses "Strongholds" instead of "Babylon," but he is articulating the same point. Mark Sayers, *A Non-Anxious Presence* (Moody Publishers, 2022), 59.

27. 1 Pet. 5:13 NIV, emphasis added.

28. Philosophers prefer the term "as-structures." In a personal conversation with Christopher Watkin, he used a simpler phrase to express the same idea, "this-is-thatness." If you want a deeper exploration of "as-structures," see Christopher Watkin, *Biblical Critical Theory* (Zondervan Academic, 2022), 5–6.

29. Ibid.

30. 1 Cor. 1:22–29 NIV.

31. Michael W. Goheen, "The Surrender and Recovery of the Unbearable Tension," 3, https://missionworldview.com/wp-content/uploads/2020/06/ea8a85_25676f9a09904642bdbbacdaec231b11.pdf.

32. The Hebrew word *ʿĒden* could be translated as "delight" or "pleasure."

33. Hendrik Kraemer, *The Communication of the Christian Faith* (Lutterworth, 2002), 36.

Chapter 4: Joyful Outsiders

1. Luke 12:15 NIV.

2. Luke 16:13 NIV.

3. 2 Pet. 1:3–4 NIV, emphasis added.

4. Acts 20:35 NIV.

5. Heb. 12:2 NIV.

6. Ibid.

7. Ezek. 2:1 NIV.

8. Isa. 41:10 NKJV.

9. Ezek. 37:11–12 NIV.

10. The choice is made more acute by the fact that the Chinese Communist Party (CCP) operates the most sophisticated civilian surveillance system in the world. Using AI-powered cameras and internet tracking, they record where you go, what you buy, what you look at online, and whom you associate with. They compile your activities to generate a "social credit score," which determines whether an individual is "untrustworthy."

    Those deemed untrustworthy are doxed. The CCP posts their personal information and photos online, on buses, and even shows it before movies. You can lose your job, be passed over for a promotion, or not be hired at all because of a low social credit score. Your children can be prevented from entering higher education. The system is draconian. Your social credit score can be reduced for inane behavior, like jaywalking or playing your music too loudly on a train. And it can be utterly decimated for ideological divergence from the CCP—including worshiping in an orthodox, non-state-sanctioned house church.

    Chinese Christians not only face the ordinary costs of having low social credit scores but also can be fined exorbitantly for hosting Christian worship gatherings or owning properties where Christian gatherings take place. In some cases, the state even seizes properties. Chinese Christians carefully monitor all communication so as not to alert the party (which uses AI to read and report everything) to their faith or gatherings. They use USB thumb drives to store all their Christian resources and books so that if the CCP shows up, they can drop them into water, destroying the evidence to avoid the consequences. Josh Rogin, *Chaos under Heaven: Trump, Xi, and the Battle for the Twenty-First Century* (Mariner Books, 2021), 222, 262.

11. Nik Ripken and Gregg Lewis, *The Insanity of God: A True Story of Faith Resurrected* (B&H Publishing Group, 2013), 262–263.

12. Ibid.

13. Ibid.

14. Ibid.

15. 2 Cor. 4:17.

16. 2 Cor. 4:18.

17. Ezek. 34:28, 31 NIV.

18. Karen Abbott, "The Daredevil of Niagara Falls," *Smithsonian Magazine*,

November 8, 2023, https://www.smithsonianmag.com/history/the
-daredevil-of-niagara-falls-110492884/.

19. Ibid.

20. Ezek. 36:25–27 NIV.

Chapter 5: Finding Your Way

1. Amy Howe, "In The Case of the Praying Football Coach, Both Sides Invoke Religious Freedom," SCOTUSblog, April 25, 2022, https://www.scotusblog.com/2022/04/in-the-case-of-the-praying-football-coach-both-sides-invoke-religious-freedom/.

2. Bremerton School District, "Letter From Bremerton School District to Mr. Kennedy," Bremerton School District, September 17, 2015, https://firstliberty.org/wp-content/uploads/2022/01/20200722_Kennedy_Excerpts-of-Record_ER298-301.pdf.

3. Kennedy ultimately won the case, but not without a personal toll. At the time of this writing, he no longer attends church.

4. "Bremerton, WA Religion," n.d., https://www.bestplaces.net/religion/city/washington/bremerton.

5. In 1962, the SBC's president celebrated *Engel v. Vitale*, a case that banned school prayers, declaring that "we should be eternally grateful to [the Supreme Court]." W. Barry Garrett et al., "Baptist News Service," July 12, 1962, http://media.sbhla.org.s3.amazonaws.com/1611,12-Jul-1962.pdf.

6. Matt. 6:5–6 NIV.

7. Matt. 5:14–16; Luke 9:26 NIV.

8. Julia Duin, "Praying Coach Joe Kennedy's Comeback After Supreme Court Win," *The Free Press*, September 1, 2023, https://www.thefp.com/p/praying-coach-joe-kennedy-comeback.

9. Charles Marsh, *Strange Glory: A Life of Dietrich Bonhoeffer* (Knopf, 2014), 165.

10. From King's 1964 Nobel lecture. "The Nobel Peace Prize 1964," NobelPrize.org, n.d., https://www.nobelprize.org/prizes/peace/1964/king/lecture/.

11. Adapted from Saint Teresa of Calcutta's 1979 Nobel acceptance speech:

> And this is what I mean, I want you to love the poor, and never turn your back to the poor, for in turning your back to the poor, you are turning it to Christ. For he had made himself the hungry one, the naked one, the homeless one, so that you and I have an opportunity

to love him, because where is God? How can we love God? It is not
enough to say to my God I love you, but my God, I love you here. I
can enjoy this, but I give up. I could eat that sugar, but I give that
sugar. If I stay here the whole day and the whole night, you would
be surprised of the beautiful things that people do, to share the joy
of giving. And so, my prayer for you is that truth will bring prayer in
our homes, and the fruit of prayer will be that we believe that in the
poor, it is Christ. And if we really believe, we will begin to love. And
if we love, naturally, we will try to do something. First in our own
home, our next door neighbor, in the country we live, in the whole
world. And let us all join in that one prayer, God give us courage to
protect the unborn child, for the child is the greatest gift of God to a
family, to a nation and to the whole world. God bless you!

"The Nobel Peace Prize 1979," n.d., https://www.nobelprize.org
/prizes/peace/1979/teresa/acceptance-speech/.

12. I am well aware that I dramatically oversimplified various approaches
to cultural engagement here, but given that *Joyful Outsiders* is a practical
theology, I don't aim to make a contribution to the broader academic
field of cultural apologetics or ethics, nor to argue for one approach in
particular. This chapter and the six that follow it collectively summarize my
perspective on cultural engagement *not* in the abstract but in the concrete.

For those who wish to know my position: I am downstream from the
gilded age Calvinists (Kuyper, Bavinck, Warfield) and thus lean heavily on
a transformationalist approach—although I reject the notion that a culture
can ever be "Christianized" in any thoroughgoing sense. While I never use
terminology like *sphere sovereignty*, the idea lurks beneath the surface.
More recent writers and theologians like Timothy Keller, Lesslie Newbigin,
Michael Goheen, and N. T. Wright form the bedrock of much of my thinking on the topic of Christ and culture. Like them, I understand there is
much wisdom to be gained from nonreformed streams of Christianity. For
example, the trainer chapter draws heavily on the anabaptist vision of the
church as counterculture, and the protester chapter draws heavily on the
black church's vision of the church as a prophetic witness.

While I never use the term *subsidiarity*, by the end of part 2 it will be
clear that I believe Christians take the most responsibility in their local

culture, and that our contemporary focus on national politics is mostly a distraction. Thus, my view of government and culture is whiggish, shaped more by Burke than Rousseau. I believe that our middle institutions matter tremendously, as evidenced in the builder chapter, and thus draw on the thinking of Tocqueville, Putnam, and Levin. I am generally in favor of pluralism and liberalism, though I know they are not without weaknesses—which is to say I want the kind of robust pluralism Stout imagined in *Democracy and Tradition*.

At the end of the day, I am a citizen of heaven and understand that our current arrangements are temporary and, to the best of our abilities, *ad hoc*. Thus, while I have opinions on the current arrangement of Babylon, I choose to live loosely to the powers.

I find the theological arguments for two kingdom theology, theonomy, Christian nationalism, and integralism unconvincing. I have little to say about Oliver O'Donovan because I can't honestly claim to comprehend his dense prose. Maybe one day someone will write an introduction to O'Donovan for normal pastors, like me.

A concluding thought: Augustine's narrative formulation of the City of God and the City of Man is, in my view, the best available articulation of the church's role in culture, in part because it clearly articulates the *difference* between both cities while robustly challenging citizens of God's city to cultivate the city of man. I hope to capture the same idea with the "resist *and* cultivate tension" that I lay out later in this chapter. Augustine's writing points toward the need for a missionary encounter (as Lesslie Newbigin saw much later) between the kingdom of God and the kingdoms of this world in every era—and this is a message both the evangelical right and left desperately need to heed, though for different reasons. If you're interested to learn more you can read *The City of God* yourself, or start with Chris Watkin's *Critical Biblical Theory*, which is the finest, most approachable rearticulation of Augustine's work in print.

13. Jer. 50:2 NIV.
14. Jer. 50:4b, 5b NIV.
15. Jer. 51:6 NIV; cf. Rev. 18:4–8.
16. Jer. 28:1–9; 29:7–9, 15–23.
17. Jer. 29:4–7 NIV; cf. 1 Peter 2:9–25; 1 Tim. 2:1–2.

18. 1 Cor. 12:12–26.

19. Heb. 12:1–2 NIV.

20. Kevin Vanhoozer helpfully explores the idea of improvisation in *The Drama of Scripture*, not that our improvisation is not freewheeling, nor is different for the sake of being different. Instead, it seeks to faithfully retell and expand upon the grand narrative of Scripture: "Canonical-linguistic theology shapes Christian identity in new situations by looking to the canon as both catalyst and criterion for 'creative fidelity' and 'ruled spontaneity.' The directions drawn by Scripture's normative specification of the theo-drama enable the church to improvise, as it were, with a script. It is precisely by gaining canonical competence that one is enabled to be creative and faithful in new contexts. The best illustration of such creative fidelity comes, surprisingly enough, from the practice of biblical translation." Kevin J. Vanhoozer, *The Drama of Doctrine: A Canonical-linguistic Approach to Christian Theology* (Westminster John Knox Press, 2005), 129.

21. Lesslie Newbigin, *The Open Secret: An Introduction to the Theology of Mission* (Eerdmans, 1995), 62.

22. Phil. 2:12–13.

Chapter 6: The Trainer: Changing Babylon by Changing Habits

1. "Five Gang Members Go Free in Gang Attack - UPI Archives," UPI, April 13, 1983, https://www.upi.com/Archives/1983/04/13/Five-gang-members-go-free-in-gang-attack/9250419058000/.

2. Dallas Willard, *The Spirit of the Disciplines: Understanding How God Changes Lives* (Zondervan, 1990), 222.

3. Ibid., 225.

4. Ibid.

5. "Therefore, just as sin entered the world through one man, and death through sin, and in this way death came to all people, because all sinned—To be sure, sin was in the world before the law was given, but sin is not charged against anyone's account where there is no law. Nevertheless, death reigned from the time of Adam to the time of Moses, even over those who did not sin by breaking a command, as did Adam, who is a pattern of the one to come" (Romans 5:12–14 NIV).

6. 1 Tim. 4:7–8 NIV.

7. Willard, *The Spirit of the Disciplines*, 158–159.

8. Ezra 7:10 NIV.

9. Ezra 7:25 NIV.

10. Ezra 8:21 NIV.

11. Thomas A. Kempis, Aloysius Croft, and Harold Bolton, *The Imitation of Christ* (Dover, 2003), 37.

12. Dallas Willard writes, "Keep in mind that the practice of abstention does not imply that there is anything essentially wrong with these desires as such. But in today's distorted condition of humanity, it is these basic desires that have been allowed to run a rebellious and harmful course, ultimately serving as the primary hosts of sin in our personalities." *The Spirit of the Disciplines*, 159–60.

13. "I was ashamed to ask the king for soldiers and horsemen to protect us from enemies on the road, because we had told the king, 'The gracious hand of our God is on everyone who looks to him, but his great anger is against all who forsake him'" (Ezra 8:22 NIV).

14. Willard, *The Spirit of the Disciplines*, 174–75.

15. Ezra 7:10 NIV, emphasis added.

16. In 2011 only 50 percent of self-identified Christians reported reading the Bible at least three to four times a year outside of church. In 2022, the number dropped to 39 percent, which means about 26 million Christians have stopped reading their Bibles. Jeffery Fulks, Randy Petersen, and John Farquhar Plake, *The State of the Bible 2022* (The American Bible Society, 2022), https://1s712.americanbible.org/state-of-the-bible/stateofthebible/State_of_the_bible-2022.pdf.

17. Preston M. Sprinkle, *Exiles: The Church in the Shadow of Empire* (Cook, 2024), 135.

18. Stanley Hauerwas and William H. Willimon, *Resident Aliens: Life in the Christian Colony: A Provocative Christian Assessment of Culture and Ministry for People Who Know That Something Is Wrong* (Abingdon, 2014), 38, 41.

19. Charles Marsh, *Strange Glory: A Life of Dietrich Bonhoeffer* (Knopf, 2014), 256.

20. Ibid., 217.

21. Ibid.
22. Dietrich Bonhoeffer, *The Cost of Discipleship* (New York: Simon and Schuster, 1995), 89, emphasis added.
23. Marsh, *Strange Glory*, 257.
24. Ibid. These are the words of Major von Bremer, a main character in Bonhoeffer's unpublished novel.
25. Eberhard Bethge, *Dietrich Bonhoeffer: A Biography* (Fortress, 2000), 736.
26. Bonhoeffer, *The Cost of Discipleship*, 270.
27. Kathryn Teresa Long, *The Revival of 1857–58: Interpreting an American Religious Awakening* (New York: Oxford University Press, 1998), 140.
28. Hauerwas and Willimon, *Resident Aliens*, 47.

Chapter 7: The Advisor: Changing Babylon by Influencing Leaders

1. Rembert Browne, "Genius: A Conversation With 'Hamilton' Maestro Lin-Manuel Miranda," *Grantland*, September 29, 2015, https://grantland.com/hollywood-prospectus/genius-a-conversation-with-hamilton-maestro-lin-manuel-miranda/.
2. James Davison Hunter, *To Change the World: The Irony, Tragedy and Possibility of Christianity in the Late Modern World* (Oxford: Oxford University Press, 2010), 36–37.
3. Ibid., 41.
4. Dan. 6:3 NIV.
5. Dan. 1:8 NIV.
6. Dan. 3:16–18.
7. Dan. 2:14 NIV.
8. Dan. 4:19.
9. Dan. 6:3 NIV.
10. Dan. 6:4 NIV.
11. Steven Garber, *The Seamless Life: A Tapestry of Love and Learning, Worship and Work* (InterVarsity Press, 2023), 122.
12. The stories in this section are largely drawn from Nancy Gibbs and Michael Duffy, *The Preacher and the Presidents: Billy Graham in the White House* (Center Street, 2008).
13. John Dart, "Billy Graham Recalls Help From Hearst," *Los Angeles Times*,

June 7, 1997, https://www.latimes.com/archives/la-xpm-1997-06-07-me -1034-story.html.

14. Kenneth S. Jeffrey, "The Threat of Crisis in the Sermons of Billy Graham During the All Scotland Crusade in 1955," *Scottish Church History* 51, no. 1 (April 1, 2022): 53–69, https://doi.org/10.3366/sch.2022.0064.

15. Billy Graham, *Just as I Am* (HarperOne, 1997), kindle loc. 229 of 13720.

16. Ibid., loc 229 of 13720.

17. Gibbs and Duffy, *The Preacher and the Presidents,* Chapter 10.

18. Gibbs and Duffy, *The Preacher and the Presidents,* Kindle loc. 5147 of 8835.

19. Frank Newport, "In The News: Billy Graham on 'Most Admired' List 61 Times," *Gallup,* February 7, 2024, https://news.gallup.com/poll/228089 /news-billy-graham-admired-list-times.aspx.

20. Billy Graham in Justin Taylor, "Bob Jones Sr. to Billy Graham: A Bad Prediction, Some Good Advice," *The Gospel Coalition* (blog), May 9, 2011, https://www.thegospelcoalition.org/blogs/justin-taylor/bob-jones-sr-to -billy-graham-a-bad-prediction-some-good-advice/.

21. Graham made derogatory comments about Jews in Oval Office conversations with President Nixon in 1972. When those comments became public with the release of the Nixon tapes by the National Archives in 2002, the 83-year-old Graham apologized for speaking negatively about the perceived power Jews had in the news media and Hollywood. Even though Abraham Foxman, the national director of the Anti-Defamation League, eventually accepted Graham's apologies, irreversible damage had been done to the relationship between Jews and evangelical Christians.

22. Johnnie Moore, "Evangelical Trump Adviser: Why I Won't Bail on the White House," Religion News Service, September 5, 2017, https://religionnews.com /2017/08/24/johnnie-moore-why-i-wont-bail-on-the-white-house/.

23. 1 Kings 22:6 NIV.

24. 1 Kings 22:13 NIV.

25. 1 Kings 22:14 NIV.

26. Gibbs and Duffy, *The Preacher and the President,* Chapter 21.

27. From the song "Aaron Burr, Sir," Lin-Manuel Miranda, "Hamilton: An American Musical," in *Hamilton: The Revolution*, ed. Jeremy McCarter (Grand Central Publishing, 2016).

28. Prov. 9:19.

Chapter 8: The Artist: Changing Babylon by Making Beauty

1. "I Have a Dream" quotes from Npr, "Read Martin Luther King Jr.'s 'I Have a Dream' Speech in Its Entirety," *NPR*, January 16, 2023, https://www.npr.org /2010/01/18/122701268/i-have-a-dream-speech-in-its-entirety.

2. Makoto Fujimura, *Culture Care: Reconnecting with Beauty for Our Common Life* (InterVarsity Press, 2017), 38.

3. Ibid., 38.

4. Ibid.

5. T. S. Eliot, *Notes towards the Definition of Culture* (Houghton Mifflin Harcourt, 2014), 27.

6. Ibid.

7. C. S. Lewis, *Weight of Glory* (Zondervan, 2001), 31.

8. Walter Brueggemann, *Hopeful Imagination: Prophetic Voices in Exile* (Augsburg Fortress Publishing, 1986), 6.

9. This is likely because the British romantics shaped how the English world thinks about creativity in general. They imagined the greatest artists much like this—they connected their literary genius to some transcendental force or muse and poured forth poetry.

10. Mark 4:10–13.

11. Paul Tillich, *Dynamics of Faith* (Zondervan, 2001), 48–49.

12. Ps. 33:3 NIV.

13. Consider the most famous couplet from Zechariah's poetry:

> See, your king comes to you,
>> righteous and victorious,
> lowly and riding on a donkey,
>> on a colt, the foal of a donkey. (Zech. 9:9 NIV)

We've become so accustomed to this image that it's easy to miss its power. Zechariah imagines a victorious king in the first part of the couplet, only to *subvert* expectations in the second part: he was *lowly* and poorly mounted. Zechariah's listeners knew that victorious kings, like the royalty they'd seen in Persia and Babylon, rode only the finest Nisean mares. Their stables were full of impressive horses, purchased and bred with the wealth they gathered through conquest and the backbreaking taxation of subjugated peoples.

For the Jews, their humble donkeys were a symbolic parade of shame, poverty, and humiliation. But through his imagination and skillful use of couplets, Zechariah "evoked new realities in the community." What if the greatest kings were humble, gentle, non-violent, and self-sacrificial? What if their own humility and poverty were symbolic of God's promise to turn the world's power structures upside down? What if their crown of ashes could become a crown of beauty?

See Brueggemann, *Hopeful Imagination*, 2, for a fuller exploration of how imagination evokes new realities in communities.

14. Zech. 8:3 NIV.
15. Zech. 12:8 NIV.
16. Fujimura, *Culture Care*, 44.
17. Through Zechariah's art, they learned to "receiv[e] from God what [they] thought God would not give, namely a new way to be human." Brueggemann, *Hopeful Imagination*, 6.
18. Carol A. Berry, *Learning from Henri Nouwen and Vincent van Gogh: A Portrait of the Compassionate Life* (InterVarsity Press, 2019), 39.
19. Vincent wrote to Theo, "You surely know that one of the roots or fundamental truths, not only of the Gospel but of the entire Bible, is 'the light that dawns in the darkness.' 'Through darkness to Light.' Well then, who will most certainly need it, who will have ears to hear it? Experience has taught that those who work in darkness, in the heart of the earth like the miners in the black coal-mines, among others, are very moved by the message of the gospel and also believe it." Ibid., 34.
20. He wrote to Theo, "I should like to start making rough sketches of one or the other of the many things one meets along way, but the considering that it would actually not take me very far and that it would most likely keep me from my real work, it is better I do not begin." Ibid., 40.
21. Vincent Van Gogh, *The Letters of Vincent van Gogh* (Penguin Classics, 2003), Kindle loc. 3236 of 9491.
22. Ibid.
23. Ibid., Kindle loc. 1339 of 9491.
24. Berry, *Learning from Henri Nouwen and Vincent van Gogh*, 67.

25. Ibid., 90.

26. Ibid., 92–93.

27. Ibid., 88.

28. In his first published story Wallace wrote, "Some people say it's like having always before you and under you a huge black hole without a bottom, a black, black hole, maybe with vague teeth in it, and then your being part of the hole." D. T. Max, *Every Love Story Is a Ghost Story: A Life of David Foster Wallace* (Penguin, 2013), 311.

Chapter 9: The Ambassador: Changing Babylon by Winning Hearts

1. Ziad W. Munson, *The Making of Pro-life Activists: How Social Movement Mobilization Works* (University of Chicago Press, 2009), 20.

2. Eph. 6:20 NIV.

3. Phil. 4:22 NIV.

4. Phil. 1:15–18.

5. Eph. 1:18.

6. Col. 4:3.

7. Eph. 6:19 NIV.

8. Titus 2:10 NLT.

9. Rom. 14:13.

10. "But I feel that the greatest destroyer of peace today is abortion because it is a war against the child, a direct killing of the innocent child, murder by the mother herself. And if we accept that a mother can kill even her own child, how can we tell other people not to kill one another? How do we persuade a woman not to have an abortion? As always, we must persuade her with love and we remind ourselves that love means to be willing to give until it hurts. Jesus gave even His life to love us. So, the mother who is thinking of abortion, should be helped to love, that is, to give until it hurts her plans, or her free time, to respect the life of her child. The father of that child, whoever he is, must also give until it hurts." Patty Knap, "Mother Teresa: 'The Greatest Destroyer of Love and Peace Is Abortion,'" *National Catholic Register*, August 29, 2020, https://www.ncregister.com/blog/mother-teresa-the-greatest-destroyer-of-love-and-peace-is-abortion.

11. Among the many lives she touched were Dawson Trotman, the founder of

the Navigators; Jim Rayburn, the founder of Young Life; Richard Halverson, the U.S. Senate chaplain for fifteen years; Ronald Reagan, the fortieth president; Billy Graham; and, of course, the Brights. Not a bad legacy!

12. John G. Turner, *Bill Bright and Campus Crusade for Christ: The Renewal of Evangelicalism in Postwar America* (University of North Carolina Press, 2008), 45.

13. Ibid., 162.

14. Ibid.

15. Ibid., 201.

16. Turner, *Bill Bright and Campus Crusade for Christ*, 183.

17. Ibid.

18. Meg Sullivan, "Archivist Finds Long-lost Recording of Martin Luther King Jr. Speech at UCLA," *UCLA*, January 13, 2021, https://newsroom.ucla.edu /stories/archivist-finds-long-lost-recording-of-martin-luther-king-jr-s -speech-at-ucla.

19. Luke 4:18–19 NIV.

Chapter 10: The Protester: Changing Babylon by Challenging Injustice

1. Shawn Fain, "UAW President Shawn Fain: 'It Is Long Past Time to Stand Up for the Working Class,'" *Jacobin*, September 16, 2023, https://jacobin.com /2023/09/shawn-fain-speech-uaw-stand-up-strike-working-class-unions -uaw.

2. Ibid.

3. Erica Chenoweth, *Civil Resistance: What Everyone Needs to Know* (Oxford: Oxford University Press, 2020), 114.

4. Zeynep Tufekci, "Why Protests Work," *Atlantic*, June 24, 2020, https://www .theatlantic.com/technology/archive/2020/06/why-protests-work/613420/.

5. Luke 22:33 NIV.

6. Isa. 41:10 NIrV.

7. Dan. 3:16–18 NIV.

8. Martin Luther King, "Nonviolence and Racial Justice," The Martin Luther King, Jr. Research and Education Institute, n.d., https://kinginstitute .stanford.edu/king-papers/documents/nonviolence-and-racial-justice.

9. Omar Wasow, "The Protests Started Out Looking Like 1968. They Turned

Into 1964.," *Washington Post*, June 17, 2020, https://www.washingtonpost
.com/outlook/2020/06/11/protests-started-out-looking-like-1968-they
-turned-into-1964/.

10. Ibid.

11. Martin Luther King, "The Nobel Peace Prize 1964," NobelPrize.org, n.d.,
https://www.nobelprize.org/prizes/peace/1964/king/lecture/.

12. Matt. 5:39, 44 NIV.

13. Clarence Jordan, *The Inconvenient Gospel: A Southern Prophet Tackles War,
Wealth, Race, and Religion* (Plough Publishing House, 2022), 76.

14. Charles Marsh, *God's Long Summer: Stories of Faith and Civil Rights*
(Princeton University Press, 2008), 10.

15. Ibid., 12.

16. Ibid.

17. State of Mississippi, "SWORN WRITTEN APPLICATION FOR
REGISTRATION," 1955, https://www.crmvet.org/info/ms-littest55.pdf.

18. Bruce Hartford, "Veterans of the Civil Rights Movement—Voter
Registration in Mississippi Before the Voting Rights Act," n.d., https://www
.crmvet.org/info/ms-test.htm.

19. Kay Mills, *This Little Light of Mine: The Life of Fannie Lou Hamer* (Lexington,
KY: University Press of Kentucky, 2007), 38.

20. Marsh, *God's Long Summer*, 16.

21. Ibid., 35.

22. Ibid.,18.

23. Ibid., 22.

24. Ibid., 22.

25. Edwin King, "Go Tell It on the Mountain," *Sojourners*, December 1982,
https://sojo.net/magazine/december-1982/go-tell-it-mountain.

26. Mills, *This Little Light of Mine*, 125.

27. Fannie Lou Hamer, "Veterans of the Civil Rights Movement—I Don't Mind
My Light Shining," 1963, n.d., https://www.crmvet.org/docs/flh63.htm.

28. Kevin Draper, "A Disparaging Video Prompts Explosive Fallout Within
ESPN," *New York Times*, July 5, 2021, https://www.nytimes.com/2021/07/04
/sports/basketball/espn-rachel-nichols-maria-taylor.html

29. Alison Flood, "How to Be an Antiracist Author Ibram X Kendi Awarded
MacArthur 'Genius Grant,'" *The Guardian*, September 28, 2021, https://

www.theguardian.com/books/2021/sep/28/how-to-be-an-antiracist
-author-ibram-x-kendi-awarded-macarthur-genius-grant.

30. Stephanie Saul, "An Ambitious Antiracism Center Scales Back Amid
Allegations of Poor Managment," *New York Times,* September 9, 2023,
https://www.nytimes.com/2023/09/23/us/ibram-x-kendi-antiracism
-boston-university.html.

31. Tim Alberta, *The Kingdom, the Power, and the Glory: American Evangelicals
in an Age of Extremism* (Harper Paperbacks, 2024), 264.

32. Martin Luther King, "'Loving Your Enemies,' Sermon Delivered at Dexter
Avenue Baptist Church," The Martin Luther King, Jr. Research and
Education Institute, n.d., https://kinginstitute.stanford.edu/king-papers
/documents/loving-your-enemies-sermon-delivered-dexter-avenue-baptist
-church.

33. Nicolaus Mills, "She Scared L.B.J.," *New York Times,* February 7, 1993.

34. Eph. 2:14.

Chapter 11: The Builder: Changing Babylon by Building Institutions

1. The details and quotes in this story are drawn from Jason DeParle's
interactive feature in *New York Times Magazine* 2010 retrospective, *The
Lives They Lived.* It can be viewed online here: https://archive.nytimes.com
/www.nytimes.com/interactive/2010/12/26/magazine/2010lives.html.

2. Luke 4:18 NIV.

3. Jeffrey Stout, *Democracy and Tradition* (Princeton University Press, 2005),
28, emphasis added.

4. Brian Fikkert and Kelly M. Kapic, *Becoming Whole: Why the Opposite of
Poverty Isn't the American Dream* (Moody, 2019), 74.

5. Rachel Minkin and Juliana Menasce Horowitz, "Parenting in America
Today," Pew Research Center, April 14, 2024, https://www.pewresearch.org
/social-trends/2023/01/24/parenting-in-america-today/.

6. Ibid.

7. Just under half of Americans report a *deep* sense of loneliness. About
12 percent of the population say they have *no* friends, and 49 percent
have few close friends. Vivek H. Murthy, "Our Epidemic of Loneliness and
Isolation: The U.S. Surgeon General's Advisory on the Healing Effects of

Social Connection and Community," 2023, https://www.hhs.gov/sites /default/files/surgeon-general-social-connection-advisory.pdf.

8. Fikkert and Kapic, *Becoming Whole*, 34.

9. Ibid., 86.

10. Nehemiah 5 is a fascinating case study because it cuts across contemporary partisan interests in institution building. Poorer members of the community were selling their properties to wealthier members so that they'd have enough money to pay their taxes and eat food. The wealthy then mortgaged the land back to the poor but charged such extravagant interest that the poor needed to sell their children into slavery just to pay their debts. To solve the problem, Nehemiah cut taxes dramatically (much to the pleasure of paleoconservatives), called the landowners to cancel debts and stop collecting interest (much to the pleasure of progressives), and then personally assisted in the feeding of the poor from his own treasury. Each step required institutional overhauling.

11. Yuval Levin, *A Time to Build: From Family and Community to Congress and the Campus, How Recommitting to Our Institutions Can Revive the American Dream* (Basic Books, 2023), 19.

12. This is why builders don't expend too much energy on one-off missionary trips, short-term fundraisers, and pop-up shops that come and go. Instead, they build institutions that outlast them. They design their charities, churches, businesses, or community groups to serve long-term goals.

13. Levin, *A Time to Build*, 19.

14. Neh. 1:4; 2:4.

15. "Then I said to them, 'You see the trouble we are in: Jerusalem lies in ruins, and its gates have been burned with fire. Come, let us rebuild the wall of Jerusalem, and we will no longer be in disgrace.' I also told them about the gracious hand of my God on me and what the king had said to me. They replied, 'Let us start rebuilding.' So they began this good work" (Neh. 2:17–18 NIV). Nehemiah later tells them, "The joy of the LORD is your strength" (Neh. 8:10 NIV).

16. Jordan, *The Inconvenient Gospel*, 34.

17. Yuval Levin, "The Importance of Institutions, With Yuval Levin," Hoover Institution, n.d., https://www.hoover.org/research/importance -institutions-yuval-levin-1.

18. It also means that not every institution is morally good or healthy. Churches are institutions. So are cults. Businesses are institutions. So are brothels. Schools are institutions. So are cartels. The reality is that institutions can serve insalubrious ends, shape unsavory character, and generate intergenerational abuse.

19. The following quotes (unless otherwise noted) come from *Dealmakers*, a documentary about Pete Ochs' life and business. Gratis 7 Films, https://gratis7films.uscreen.io/programs/dealmakers.

20. From the Westminster Shorter Catechism, question 1. Westminster Assembly, The Westminster Confession of Faith: With Proof Texts (Great Commission Publications, 1992).

21. Quoted from the documentary *Dealmakers* about Pete Ochs.

22. "Episode 15 - Multiple Bottom Line Investing with Pete Ochs—Faith Driven Investor," *Faith Driven Investor* podcast, May 27, 2020, https://www.faithdriveninvestor.org/podcast-inventory/2020/2/17/pete-ochs.

23. Luke 12:15 NIV.

24. Ashley Rindsberg, *The Gray Lady Winked: How the* New York Times's *Misreporting, Distortions and Fabrications Radically Alter History* (Midnight Oil Publishers), 53.

25. "New York Times Statement About 1932 Pulitzer Prize Awarded to Walter Duranty | the New York Times Company," The New York Times Company, n.d., https://www.nytco.com/company/prizes-awards/new-york-times-statement-about-1932-pulitzer-prize-awarded-to-walter-duranty/.

26. Rindsberg, *The Gray Lady Winked*, 58–59.

27. Ibid.

28. Neh. 13:25.

29. 310revelation, "Mark Driscoll - There Is a Pile of Dead Bodies Behind the Mars Hill Bus," November 3, 2012, https://www.youtube.com/watch?v=BfTmgPhmlto.

30. The refrain has several variations but essentially amounts to, "Remember me with favor, my God, for all I have done for this people" (Neh. 5:19 NIV). Also see Neh. 13:22, 24, 30–31. Nehemiah's refrain should strike us as strange for two reasons. First, no one else in the Bible speaks this way. Of course, many others do many great things, but they rarely suggest that their approval with God is based on their works, or that God may owe

them future favor for those works. Second, it seems as though Nehemiah is taking credit for the work of God—after all, it is ultimately Yahweh who is doing much for his people *through* Nehemiah. While some commentators argue that there's nothing wrong with Nehemiah's beliefs, others suggest it's the narrator's way of subtly communicating that Babylon's vanity has infected Nehemiah. Given that the refrain becomes more frequent during Nehemiah's darkest days, I believe the latter view (Nehemiah had grown proud) makes the most sense of the text. The entire book of Ezra-Nehemiah is clouded with moral ambiguity, and it seems as though the narrator wants his audience to grow circumspect about their own efforts to create revival and reestablish God's kingdom apart from God's action. Jesus, of course, is the one who does what Ezra and Nehemiah could not: establishing a new covenant, transforming God's people, and inaugurating God's kingdom.

31. Levin argues that today many senators and representatives don't see the legislature as an institution designed to form them but instead as a platform they can leverage for their own celebrity. The introduction of cameras in the House and Senate allowed politicians to begin grandstanding for the camera rather than doing their actual job: legislating. Now that cameras are, quite literally, in every pocket, the problem has spread to churches, businesses, newspapers, and charities. Levin, *A Time to Build*, 6.

32. Ibid., 170.

33. Luke 4:18–19 NIV.

Conclusion: A Unified Witness

1. Kazuo Ishiguro, *The Remains of the Day* (Vintage, 1990), 36.

2. Ibid., 36.

3. Ibid., 42–43.

4. Garber, *The Seamless Life*, 69–70.

5. Ibid.

6. Heb. 12:1–2.

Key Practices and Suggested Reading for Joyful Outsiders

1. We see this in Nehemiah 8:2, 7–8 (NIV): "So on the first day of the seventh month Ezra the priest brought the Law before the assembly, which was

made up of men and women and all who were able to understand. . . . The Levites—Jeshua, Bani, Sherebiah, Jamin, Akkub, Shabbethai, Hodiah, Maaseiah, Kelita, Azariah, Jozabad, Hanan and Pelaiah—instructed the people in the Law while the people were standing there. They read from the Book of the Law of God, making it clear and giving the meaning so that the people understood what was being read."

2. 1 Tim. 2:2 NIV.

3. Est. 4:14 NIV.

4. Dan. 2:21 NIV.

5. Dan. 2:23 NIV.

6. Ex. 31:4 NIV.

7. Makoto Fujimura, *Art and Faith: A Theology of Making* (Yale University Press, 2021), 3, 102.

8. Mark J. Boda, *The Book of Zechariah* (Eerdmans, 2016), 39–41.

9. Jesus in Matthew 27:46, quoting from Psalm 22:1 NIV.

10. Ps. 40:3.

11. For example, Isaiah 2 and Micah 4 clearly echo one another, suggesting a collaboration. Likewise, Zechariah 8:9–13 and Haggai 1:6; 2:4. Boda, *The Book of Zechariah*, 41.

12. Matt. 4:19.

13. Matt. 28:19 NIV.

14. John 4:36 NIV.

15. Davis, Graham, and Burge, *The Great Dechurching*, 29.

16. Martin Luther King, "'Pilgrimage to Nonviolence,'" The Martin Luther King, Jr. Research and Education Institute, n.d., https://kinginstitute .stanford.edu/king-papers/documents/pilgrimage-nonviolence.

17. Ibid.

18. Martin Luther King, "Why We Can't Wait," The Martin Luther King, Jr. Research and Education Institute, n.d., https://kinginstitute.stanford.edu /why-we-cant-wait.

19. Bob Burns, Tasha D. Chapman, and Donald C. Guthrie, *Resilient Ministry: What Pastors Told Us About Surviving and Thriving* (InterVarsity Press, 2013), 199.

20. Ibid.

21. Ibid.

22. Lan Liu, *Conversations on Leadership: Wisdom from Global Management Gurus* (Wiley, 2010), 159.
23. Garber, *The Seamless Life*, 42–43.
24. Simon Sinek, *Start with Why: How Great Leaders Inspire Everyone to Take Action* (Penguin, 2009), 39.
25. Summarized by Liu in *Conversations on Leadership*, 159–60.

From the Publisher

GREAT BOOKS

ARE EVEN BETTER WHEN THEY'RE SHARED!

Help other readers find this one:

- Post a review at your favorite online bookseller

- Post a picture on a social media account and share why you enjoyed it

- Send a note to a friend who would also love it—or better yet, give them a copy

Thanks for reading!